DATE DUE			
ILL		ILL.	
7243367		SWIFT #	2523647
CQU		Four Mile C.C.	
8-24-04		7 - 6 - 06	
ILL			
SWIFT		ILL	
#2117596		2/29/08	
ACC, Comm City			
5-19-05			
DEC 0 2 2005			
GAYLORD		PRINTED IN U.S.A.	

Handbook of
Alternative Materials
in Residential
Construction

Construction Books from McGraw-Hill

BIANCHINA • *Forms and Documents for the Builder*

BOLT • *Roofing the Right Way, Third Edition*

CLARK • *Retrofitting for Energy Conservation*

DOMEL • *Basic Engineering Calculations for Contractors*

GERHART • *Everyday Math for the Building Trades*

HACKER • *Residential Steel Design and Construction*

HUTCHINGS • *National Building Codes Handbook*

HUTCHINGS • *OSHA Quick Guide*

HUTCHINGS • *Construction Claims for Residential Contractors and Builders*

JAHN, DETTENMAIER • *Offsite Construction*

JAHN • *Residential Construction Problem Solver*

KOREJWO • *Kitchen Installation, Design, and Remodeling*

MILLER, BAKER • *Carpentry and Construction, Third Edition*

PHILBIN • *Painting, Staining, and Refinishing*

POWERS • *Kitchens: Professional's Illustrated Design and Remodeling Guide*

POWERS: • *Bathrooms: Professional's Illustrated Design and Remodeling Guide*

SCHARFF AND THE STAFF OF ROOFER MAGAZINE • *Roofing Handbook*

SCHARFF AND THE STAFF OF WALLS & CEILINGS MAGAZINE • *Drywall Construction Handbook*

SHUSTER • *Structural Steel Fabrication Practices*

TRELLIS • *Documents, Contracts, and Worksheets for Home Builders*

VERNON • *Professional Surveyor's Manual*

WOODSON • *Be a Successful Building Contractor, Second Edition*

Dodge Cost Books from McGraw-Hill

MARSHALL & SWIFT • *Dodge Unit Cost Book*

MARSHALL & SWIFT • *Dodge Repair and Remodel Cost Book*

MARSHALL & SWIFT • *Dodge Electrical Cost Book*

Handbook of Alternative Materials in Residential Construction

Richard T. Bynum, Jr., AIA

Daniel L. Rubino, CSI

McGraw-Hill

New York   San Francisco   Washington, D.C.   Auckland   Bogotá
Caracas   Lisbon   London   Madrid   Mexico City   Milan
Montreal   New Delhi   San Juan   Singapore
Sydney   Tokyo   Toronto

Library of Congress Cataloging-in-Publication Data

70262

+H
4811
.B95
1999

Bynum, Richard T., Jr.
    Handbook of alternative materials in residential construction /
Richard T. Bynum, Jr., Daniel L. Rubino.
        p.   cm.
    Includes index.
    ISBN 0-07-011978-3
    1. House construction.   2. Building materials.   3. Dwellings—
Materials.   4. Appropriate technology.   I. Rubino, Daniel L.
II. Title.
TH4811.B95   1998
691—dc21
                                                98-25182
                                                    CIP

McGraw-Hill

A Division of The McGraw-Hill Companies

ISBN 0-07-011978-3

*The sponsoring editor for this book was Zoe G. Foundotos, the editing
supervisor was David E. Fogarty, and the production supervisor was
Tina Cameron.*

Printed and bound by R. R. Donnelley & Sons Company.

This book is printed on recycled, acid-free paper containing a
minimum of 50% recycled, de-inked fiber.

For Valerie and Patti.
Thank you for the support, love, and
friendship throughout this project.

Contents

Chapter 3. Floors and Floor Systems   3-1

Chapter 4. Wall and Roof Structures   4-1

Chapter 11. Electrical Systems and Accessories   11-1

Preface

The traditional building materials used throughout the twentieth century have predominantly been wood, brick, stone, steel, glass, and concrete. Although it is impossible to envision the built world without any of these today, it is logical to assume that each of these may have been considered "alternative" upon their initial introduction.

An alternative simply means that a choice can be made between at least two similar objects or actions. Taking a different route home from work or jogging on one set of streets on Monday and a different path on Tuesday are alternatives. Alternative does not necessarily imply that an artifact or product is of inferior quality or based on an abstract concept. Instead, it is simply a deviation from convention or tradition.

Convention, tradition, and norm are rarely constant given the human dynamic. For example, today's homebuyer is quite different from the homebuyer of the 1960s. Recyclable products, renewable energy sources, indoor air quality, daylighting strategies, and thermal envelope efficiency are a few topics that were not a part of the typical residential lexicon used only 40 years ago. From the first Earth Day in 1970 to Rio de Janeiro's Earth Summit in 1992, an era of increasing environmental awareness has prompted greater concern for the effects and limits of the planet's natural resources.

Another influence on today's generation of homebuyers has been the escalating price of many building materials and the ever-inflating cost of living. Each of these combines to make the financial aspects of home ownership more of a strain on the family's budget than ever before. Subsequently, the homeowner is beginning to demand, and rightly so, a constructed product that is more durable, requires less maintenance, and is aesthetically pleasing while being of superior value.

Finally, it is no secret that people are living longer but remaining healthy at an older age. The aging baby boomer, on the cusp of retirement age, not only desires to be more independent than previous generations, but is less likely to be confined to institution-like nursing homes.

Unfortunately, the home construction industry has changed very little in response to these factors. With the exception of asbestos and lead paint, the construction materials used in the 1960s are virtually unchanged. (In fact, the 2×4 has been the predominant material of choice in home construction for over 100 years.) One can only surmise that this lack of change by the majority of the homebuilding industry may be attributed to a propensity for the convenience of convention or simplicity of tradition rather than a lack of alternative construction choices.

This book acknowledges the need to think, design, and build in a new way. For example, the typical home is designed for young, healthy, and fully ambulatory adults. Stairs, door widths, and even doorknobs can become barriers to anyone with a physical impairment, is wheelchair-dependent or even has arthritis. This book will demonstrate how simple modifications and sensitive design approaches can make it possible for a home to be universally accessible to inhabitants of all ages and disabilities at a reasonable cost.

Although the residential materials discussed in this book may be considered "alternative," the origins of many of these are not new. For example, simulated masonry has been around since the 1920s, plastic laminates were first used in 1907, and glued laminated timber was invented in 1893.* The materials discussed herein have been tested, approved by various code authorities, and implemented in residential projects throughout the country (and some throughout the world).

Many of the products discussed within this text are the results of our constant desire to improve on the status quo. For example, solid dimensional lumber can now be replaced by engineered lumber products that are straighter, stronger, and dimensionally stable. Concrete masonry products can be replaced by precast autoclaved aerated concrete units that are lighter, larger, can be cut with a hand saw, and have higher insulation values. The climate control systems can be more efficient by using renewable energy sources such as geothermal heat pumps and photovoltaic panels while improving indoor air quality with the installation of an ultraviolet light filtering system.

A new sophistication toward construction means and methods provides the opportunity for the design or construction professional to approach homebuilding with a "whole-building" approach. In other words, the superior properties of these assemblies must be recognized and understood in order to guarantee the proper implementation of each. A simple component-by-component substitution of alternative

---

*Thomas C. Jester, ed., *Twentieth-Century Building Materials* (New York: McGraw-Hill, 1995), pp. 127–137.

residential materials with traditional materials (i.e., metal studs for wood studs) may not be efficient or cost effective without understanding the advantages and appropriate application.

For example, a homeowner could choose between a 75 cent, 75-W light bulb and a $20.00 compact fluorescent tube. The answer may not be as apparent as it seems. The tube will last for 10,000 hours while the bulb is estimated to last 750 hours. Given a nominal kilowatt/hour cost, the total cost for the incandescent bulb(s) over a 10,000 hour lifespan is $70.00, while the fluorescent tube life cycle cost is $35.00 for the same time period. This $35.00 savings (50 percent) is similar in concept to understanding the value of the alternative materials discussed in this text. Although many are cost competitive with traditional products, some are initially higher in cost but when implemented in a whole-building approach, value and savings are subsequently realized. Similarly, the increased spans and stability of structural components, the additional fire resistance of wall materials, the energy efficiency of a geothermal HVAC system, and fiberglass windows applied in a barrier-free design must be evaluated with respect to the aspects of increased structural strength, greater safety, environmental sensibility, and universal accessibility.

Many of these materials are interchangeable depending upon the budget or predilection of the homeowner. For example, a home could have an exterior wall structure of structural insulated panels, an interior floor structure using Wood-I-joists, and interior framing of light-gauge steel. The innovation of the architect, the experience of the builder and the comfort level of the homeowner are the only limits to the possibilities.

The text was stringently researched and is presented in a logical manner of construction sequencing; i.e., design, foundations, walls, roof, interiors, etc. Manufacturers also contributed a large portion of the information contained herein. Although accuracy of the information is expected, the homeowner, the contractor, or the architect must review all specifications for code compliance, proper construction sequencing, and material compatibility. This handbook is intended to enlighten, edify, and encourage the reader to learn more. Like studying a foreign language, the architect and builder will need to become "fluent" with the alternative materials for residential construction. This will not only enhance the homebuilding industry, but provide the homeowner with a better place to live.

Richard T. Bynum, Jr.

Daniel L. Rubino

Acknowledgments

The authors would like to thank the following individuals and companies for assisting in the preparation of this book:

Peggy Woodward

Alex Cash

Reid Hunter

Thomas W. Hinkle, AIA

Timothy F. Hullihan, AIA

James W. McGlade, AIA

Mark P. Crittenden, AIA

AFM Corporation

American Iron and Steel Institute

Cope Polysteel

Eemaxx Inc.

Energy Efficiency and Renewable Energy Clearinghouse

FCP

FischerSIPS, Inc.

Geothermal Heat Pump Consortium

James Hardie Building Products

Hebel

HEWI, Inc.

Hickson Corporation

Home Automation Systems, Inc.

Hubbel Premise Wiring, Inc.

Masonite Corporation

NetMedia, Inc.

OmniGlass, Ltd.

Simpson Strong-Tie Co., Inc.

Star Sprinkler Inc.

Steril-Aire, Inc.

Stone Products Corporation

Superior Walls of America, Ltd.

Therma-Tru Corporation

Tri-Steel Structures, Inc.

Trus Joist MacMillan

Unimast Inc.

US Gypsum Corporation

Vanguard Plastics Inc.

VT Industries

WeatherShield Windows & Doors

The WireMold Company

Wirsbo Company

Handbook of
Alternative Materials
in Residential
Construction

1

The Accessible Home

INTRODUCTION

It has been said that the only book to have more interpretations than the building code is the Bible. Interpretations of the various codes applicable to a specific design project can not only be obscure but sometimes confusing or even contradictory. For example, the 1997 Standard Building Code (SBCCI) calls for the outside diameter of a handrail to be between $1^1/4$" and 2" and located between 34" and 38" above the leading edge of the stair tread. The NFPA Life Safety Code Handbook restricts this railing size to have a range of $1^1/2$" to 2". The UFAS Guidelines (Uniform Federal Accessibility Standards) allows the handrail diameter to be $1^1/4$" to $1^1/2$" but located between 30" and 34" above the tread. The Americans with Disabilities Act Guidelines call for this same rail profile to be located between 34" and 38" above the tread. Had this been a residence, a similar requirement in the One and Two Family Dwelling Code (CABO) calls for the railing to be located between 30" and 38" above the tread.

Building codes, which are varied in their attempts to be all encompassing, are but a minimum standard with regards to the design of dwellings and buildings alike. It is the combination of common sense and design sensibility that creates an environment that is not only safe and functional but is also pleasing to the eye. Unfortunately, we able-bodied citizens all too often take for granted our freedom of mobility. Because of this lack of awareness, accessible design methods were too often an afterthought, usually due to a building code requirement rather than an actual increased sensibility by designers. This changed in 1990 due to the introduction of The Americans with Disabilities Act. This civil rights legislation, signed into law by President Bush, brought the physical barriers of our everyday world to the forefront of the collective consumer conscious. This sweeping legislation dealt with the issues of employment, public transportation and services as well as telecommunications. It is estimated that over 49 million Americans are affected with a personal disability or the disability of a family member, friend, or co-worker.[1] Although all of the aforementioned topics warrant discussion, it is the removal of physical barriers that is to be presented here. Title III: Public Accommodations (of the ADA) was the definitive guide to guarantee that persons with disabilities are to be provided accommodations and access equal to, or similar to, that available to the general public. The architectural guidelines, officially referred to as the Americans with Disabilities Act Accessibility Guidelines (ADAAG) were written by the United States Architectural and Transportation Barriers Compliance Board, also known as the Access Board (Fig. 1-1). A revised set of guidelines, intended to coordinate the ADAAG and other accessibility codes, is to be published in 1998.

Figure 1-1 Accessibility symbol. *(Delta Faucet Company)*

Although the ADA specifically targeted public facilities, the increased awareness of the existence of such architectural barriers has brought us to study the typical single-family residence. (The Fair Housing Act of 1968 focused on multifamily housing units only.) As the baby boomers move toward retirement, the forward-thinking homeowner can be best prepared for the task of caring for an ailing parent or disabled partner by making simple modifications during the design and construction of a new or renovated home. It is important to note that not all persons directed by this legislation are permanently confined to a wheelchair. Disabilities of a temporary nature, such as a broken leg in a cast, a runner with a sprained ankle, a weekend athlete on crutches, or an elderly loved one with a broken hip using a walker can have their quality of life greatly improved by following some or all of the design guidelines discussed in this chapter. Likewise, chronic health ailments like an emphysema patient strolling with an oxygen tank or an arthritic person struggling with decreased mobility can move with greater ease when living in an accessible dwelling. The important message is this: The purchase of your home is the largest single investment of your life. Why should a homeowner be forced to abandon or be restricted in his or her abode due to a disability? Why should a resident be incapable of caring for a loved one due to architectural barriers that could have easily been removed if anticipated in the design process?

Several factors may impede the logic needed when building a new home. Cost constraints, the psychological pressure of addressing the day when mobility is more of a struggle, or simple ignorance may prevent the implementation of concepts and necessary products of universal design. Nevertheless, smart design planning can prepare now for the future space allowances necessary in the event accessible modifications will be made (at a fraction of the cost of retrofitting.)

Self-sufficiency is at the core of personal well-being. This ideology, enhanced by the application of universal design standards, is essential to maintaining a suitable quality of life for the disabled and infirm as well as the able-bodied majority.

The recommendations discussed herein are not intended to be all encompassing or serve as a definitive interpretation of the ADA. It is only through increased sensibility by the general public that such standards will become commonplace. Besides, because it is a civil rights law, building code officials cannot enforce the ADA. Enforcement of the ADA is only applied when the aggrieved party shows that discrimination is about to or has occurred. The only application relative to housing is either a multifamily dwelling or when an office used by the public is contained within a private residence. In the case of the home office, the areas affected would be those subject to public accommodation such as the entrance, a meeting area, and a bathroom.

Federal accessibility guidelines, such as the 1986 edition of ANSI A117.1 (the ADA was based on the 1980 edition) or other more stringent building code requirements may apply, dependent upon your local building official. The Fair Housing Act of 1968 applies to multifamily developments. Regardless of the title, all of the codes and guidelines referenced have the same intent: to allow equal access to all individuals regardless of disability. Although some or all of the guidelines mentioned in this book could be implemented, the ultimate goal of this chapter is to demonstrate the rational and logical choices required to live in a dwelling for the rest of your life.

From a designer's viewpoint, the clearances, technical arrangements, and general ideology is sound for all users. The fully ambulatory individual will benefit from many of these recommendations as well those individuals with a physical disability.

THE SITE

The proper selection of a level but well-drained lot is the first consideration that will impact the overall accessibility of the home. Sloped lawns are usually more difficult to maintain. The location of the property should also have good proximity to shopping, bus lines, or other public transportation options. Although not discussed specifically in this chapter, the exterior materials of the home should be durable, resilient, and require minimal maintenance.

ARRIVAL

The path of travel from the vehicle or sidewalk to the front door of a home is best if flat and level and located as close to the door as possible. (A minimum slope is necessary for water runoff.) The frequent imposition of a home onto a heavily contoured landscape without regard to the existing terrain is more frequently the situation at hand. A 16' wide driveway will accommodate a typical van with side door loading access for wheelchairs. (13' is the minimum width recommended.) This configuration will allow for 8' to be dedicated to a typical van with doors in the open position as well as an additional 8' (5' is the minimum) in pavement width to allow for wheelchair maneuvering. A 24' driveway width is necessary for two cars parked side by side with an accessible route between. The driveway should be sloping toward the afternoon sun, which will help facilitate ice and snow removal in the winter.

In addition to a remote control garage door opener, additional vertical clearance may be necessary for some vans to access a carport or garage. The typical garage door used by homebuilders is 7' but an 8' vertical clearance is recommended for a conversion van. Always verify the actual dimensions necessary for your specific application.

It is good practice to use the least slope possible in the approach to the front door. This walkway should be a minimum of 36" in clear width. Sidewalks shall have a maximum running slope of 1" in 20". It is recommended to have a landing, 60" in length at the top and bottom of a ramped sidewalk (Fig. 1-2). If an extensive run is required, a flat landing, 60" in length is required every 30" of vertical rise. The cross slope on such a walkway shall not be greater than about 2% (1:48 or a little less than $3/4$" on a 3'-wide sidewalk). The walkway should drain well and be free from snow, ice, or other obstructions. Radiant heating coils, located in the concrete slab, are an additional option. If the required slope is greater than 1:20, then an accessible ramp is required. The maximum ramp slope is 1" in 12".

Houses constructed using a concrete slab on grade will be lower to the existing grade than houses constructed using a crawlspace foundation system. This is not meant to suggest one system is superior to the other, but rather to be used as a factor in a system's selection. It is important to note that the walk's layout need not suggest it be for a utilitarian purpose of accessibility only. A gentle slope or subtle curve with proper landscaping can easily address the need for access as well a sensitive response to the project site and finished floor elevation.

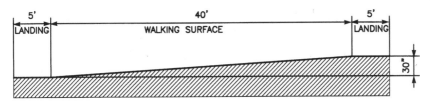

Figure 1-2 Running slope of sidewalks.

Although handrails can be added at a later time dependent upon the specific owner's needs, several characteristics are required to insure satisfactory performance. The handrail should be no lower than 34" and no taller than 38"

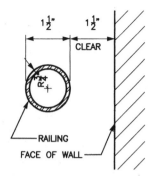

Figure 1-3 Railing or grab bar clearance.

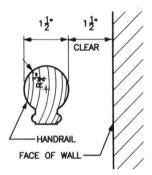

Figure 1-4 Handrail clearance.

above the sidewalk surface. If the rail is wall mounted, a clearance of $1^1/2$" is required from the wall face (Figs. 1-3 and 1-4). (Railings are required on all ramps having a rise greater than 6" and slopes greater than 1:20 but less than 1:12.) The rail should be continuous and easily grasped. Although decorative railings come in a variety of shapes and sizes, it is recommended that the cross sectional diameter be between $1^1/4$" and $1^1/2$". Strokes, which strike approximately 650,000 Americans every year, can cause paralysis on one side of the body.[2] This can be a problem if a person with left-side paralysis is confined to a home with handrails only on the left side. It is with this in mind that railings should be planned for, if not installed, on both sides of an accessible path.

Although cost prohibitive for most residential-scale projects, stair-lifts, elevators, and other mechanically operated devices are available for residential application.

GETTING IN THE FRONT DOOR

The minimum clear width for single wheelchair passage is 32". A wider opening, 36", is necessary for someone on crutches to pass through. The industry standard residential door width is 2'-8" and in many production homes, 2'-6" is more common. Subtract the $1/2$" for the doorstop on the strike-side and an additional 2" for the door thickness when in the open position and the net width is 30" or 28" respectively (Fig. 1-5). A 3'-0" door will allow for the minimum passage width to be accomplished with $1^1/2$" for additional clearance (Fig. 1-6). The associated cost difference when upscaling from 2'-8" to 3'-0" is only about $25.00 per door. This cost is offset by the deletion of wall materials. A keyed push-button lock will allow the homeowner to avoid the use of keys. As discussed in Chapter 11, home automation systems allow for a number of other options, such as remote control locks or coded doorbell operations.

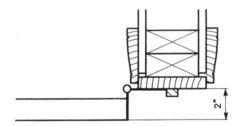

Figure 1-5 Door swing clearance.

In the event of a household renovation in which the widening of the door opening is not possible or not cost effective, offset hinges may be used to increase the clear opening width when the door is in the open position.

Although not usually an issue with the typical steel door used in residences, an oversized solid-core door can present a problem due to its weight. The homeowner should verify that the force required to open the door is within a comfortable range. 7 lb is the maximum opening pressure suggested for entrance doors but 5 lb is recommended.

Universal design is not just concerned with the implementation of physical clearances. The increased awareness of enhanced design sensitivity is also required to be successful. For example, the speed associated with an able-bodied person entering a house does not always emphasize the need for a protection from the elements. A covered entrance or canopy is an additional asset to a home that is designed to provide a comfortable experience for all users. Ambient light that sufficiently illuminates the keyhole is also recommended. Sidelights will make identification of visitors by the homeowner convenient and unobscured. The bottom of the vision panel should be located a maximum of 43" above the finished floor (a.f.f.). If possible, a light fixture on a motion sensor control will aid outdoor visibility as well as safety.

A small shelf or bench located adjacent to the door is an optional convenience element. This will allow for the temporary placement of packages in order to ease door opening.

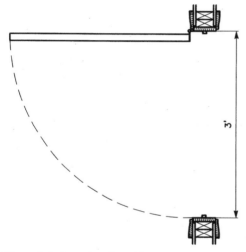

Figure 1-6 Door opening clearance.

Any change in surface elevation can serve as a potential tripping hazard. Sidewalk joints should be flush. A 1" vertical displacement in a sidewalk joint will stop a wheelchair "in its tracks," prohibiting any forward movement. The typical door threshold is another culprit; ¼" is the maximum change in level without some form of edge treatment. (¾" is allowed for exterior sliding doors or existing thresholds). A height difference of ¼" to ½" is allowed with a beveled slope no greater than 1:2 (Fig. 1-7). A number of door thresholds are now available that meet the ½" maximum total threshold height (Figs. 1-8 and 1-9). If the change in level is greater than ½", the transition must be ramped.

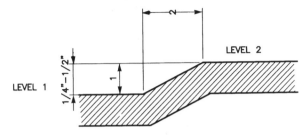

Figure 1-7 Changes in level.

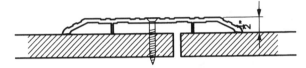

Figure 1-8 Threshold height.

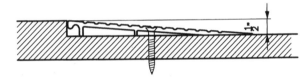

Figure 1-9   Threshold height.

The door handle is another element that deserves attention. Any operating mechanism that requires tight grasping or twisting of the wrist can be difficult for a person of limited mobility. This can be easily avoided by choosing a door-opening device that is lever-operated and easily opened with one hand. (Knobs are discouraged.) This hardware shall be mounted no higher than 48" above the floor surface. An additional clearance of 12" beyond the opening mechanism (strike) side of the door and 48" deep is necessary to allow maneuverability when approaching the push side of the door. If a storm door is also installed, and the user is approaching the pull side of this door, an additional 24" beyond the latch side of the door is necessary (Fig. 1-10). (Review Table 404.2.4.1 of the proposed ADA Guidelines Revisions for alternate applications.) A level and clear area 60" deep on the pull side is also required. Brighter colors and stronger contrasts are also recommended for users whose eyesight has begun to deteriorate.

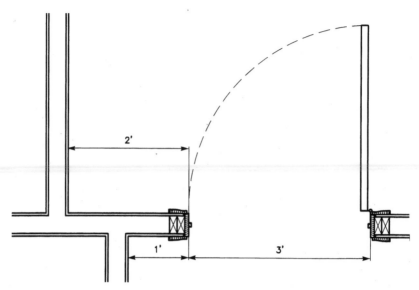

Figure 1-10   Push-pull clearance.

Pocket doors are a popular feature in homes where the encumbrances of a door swing are not desired or possible. Although more difficult to operate than a standard hinged door, a simple modification of the wall will allow for easier grasping of the recessed door handle. Notching the wall 4" on each side of the pocket door at handle level in conjunction with recessed door pulls (in lieu of the typical jamb pull) will moderately improve an already undesirable operation.

INSIDE THE HOME

Once inside the home, all necessary facilities for sleeping, eating, and going to the bathroom should be on the same level. This does not mandate that multistory homes will be a thing of the past, only that the essential activities be located on the main floor. A living room, great room, or den can easily be converted to an accessible sleeping area when required.

The interior vestibule, foyer, or hall should allow a 60" diameter circle to be inscribed in the floor plan (Fig. 1-11). A 72" diameter turnaround is preferred but may not be appropriate or cost effective due to spatial limitations. A "T-shaped" space is another method of allowing for wheelchair turning space. The space shall be a 60" square with arms and base 36" wide (Fig. 1-12). Today's residential floor plans, in the relentless pursuit of economy, allows stairs to run too close to the front door or is void of comfortable greeting areas for visitors. This space functions as an "anteroom" but even more importantly would allow maneuverability for a disabled visitor or resident upon entering the home. Minimum hallway widths are 36" per most building codes although 48" wide hallways are desired for greater accessibility.

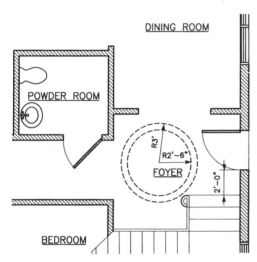

Figure 1-11   Foyer design with turning space.

Floor finishes are to be stable, firm, and slip resistant. Many ceramic floor tiles commercially available have begun adding abrasive grit to allow for enhanced slip-resistance. Likewise, a growing number of wood flooring products are now becoming commercially available that meet the necessary slip resistant requirements by laminating a vinyl sheet on top of the hardwood veneers.   Carpet is to be securely attached, installed with a firm cushion or pad or without a pad entirely. (No underlayment is preferred.) Low-density, high-pile (the infamous shag carpet, for example) is discouraged. The actual depression created in thick padded carpet is difficult for wheelchairs to turn in or even to walk through. The maximum pile thickness shall be $1/2$" and fastened to surfaces (those not against a wall) with a trim piece along the entire length of the exposed edge.

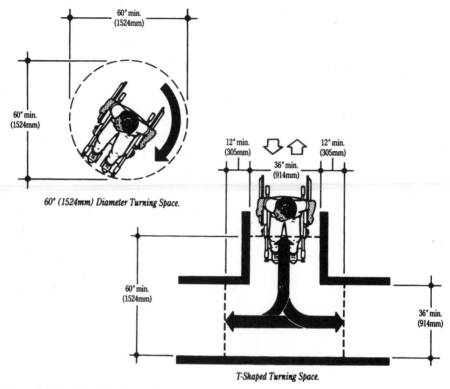

60" (1524mm) Diameter Turning Space.

T-Shaped Turning Space.

Figure 1-12   Wheelchair turning space.

Double-hung windows can be difficult to open by someone of limited upper body strength or mobility. A rollout casement window is a suitable alternative. Casement windows also allow for full ventilation of the window unit as opposed to 50 percent allowed by a double hung. The casement window unit will also allow a greater viewing angle by a seated homeowner when a 60" tall unit (taller than a typical unit) is installed at 22" a.f.f. (lower than typical).

With the onset of aging, the eyes begin to fail. Light fixtures that produce excessive amounts of glare can be especially troublesome. The American Lighting Association recommends recessed lighting fixtures, wall sconces, and cove lighting throughout the home. Adjustable halogen task lamps are most effective for reading, although the heat generated by these lamps can be a safety issue. Electrical receptacle outlets and communications jacks must be at least 15" a.f.f. but 20" is preferred.

USING THE KITCHEN

The accessible path to the kitchen needs to be a minimum of 36" clear in width. Items along this path will include a light switch, for example, that is mounted no higher than 48" above the finished floor level when reached from the forward position. Although a side reach height limit of 54" is possible, it is not recommended. In fact, if the side reach is over an obstruction, such as a bookcase or TV set, the upper limit is 44" a.f.f. Wide rocker light switches are easier to switch than the industry standard light switch and for only pennies more apiece (Fig. 1-13).

The holistic approach to a universal kitchen involves the logical and convenient placement of the work centers. Any work center that involves extensive stationary placement (standing or sitting) should not be placed near the main room circulation path. An island in the middle of a U-shaped kitchen will allow sensitive and practical placement of kitchen equipment. Although the 60" turn-a-round is ideal for wheelchair access, a 48" wide aisle is the minimum clearance recommended.

Figure 1-13 Light switch. *(Leviton Manufacturing Company)*

Implementing universal design features in a kitchen layout will also benefit the able bodied. For example, a dishwasher installed 18" a.f.f. in lieu of the typical 6" a.f.f. will make loading and unloading much easier (Fig. 1-14). The typical countertop is 36" a.f.f. however some length of countertop installed at 31" a.f.f. with open knee space below will allow access by a wheelchair user. This area could also function as a child's desk until the day that universal access is necessary. Any opportunity to install rollout shelves and bins or lazy susans with a touch latch mechanism will ease the process of base cabinet access. Although not possible with smaller kitchen plans, maximum expanses of continuous countertop will allow the sliding of heavy objects when necessary. Wall cabinets with glass doors, clear plastic shelving, and low-voltage lighting can simplify the process of making visible kitchen items that are typically concealed.

Figure 1-14 Raised dishwasher. *(Whirlpool)*

Where equipment is to be installed at a height of 31", a 42" countertop may be necessary (Fig. 1-15). These units include microwave ovens and conventional ovens. Cooktops should also be installed in a 31" counter with knee space below. Ceramic glass cooktops are easier to clean up than traditional surface units and are best if installed with front-mounted controls. The intent is to reduce stooping and bending where possible. Countertop space on each side of cooking appliances will allow convenient layoff space for cooking operations. Side-by-side refrigerators have doors that are not only lightweight but allow easy access to frozen foods. Models that include pullout shelves and baskets and even gallon door storage are even easier to use. Through-the-door ice and water dispensers are also recommended. Trash compactors are an added convenience because such a unit reduces the number of trips required for outdoor garbage disposal. Hot-water dispensers are convenient for the preparation of instant foods and reduce the burden associated with extensive use of heavy cooking utensils, pots, and pans.

A built-in lunch counter could be located adjacent to the island counter for ease of access. The countertop should be between 28" and 34" and allow a clear kneespace area beneath of 27" high, 30" wide and 19" deep (Fig. 1-16).

Figure 1-15 Countertop heights. *(Whirlpool)*

Kitchen sink placement is the most difficult. Due to the extensive standing involved with dishwashing operations, a lower sink height (31") may cause discomfort for the able-bodied. On the other hand, a lower, shallow basin sink will allow the disabled to perform normal kitchen functions without assistance.

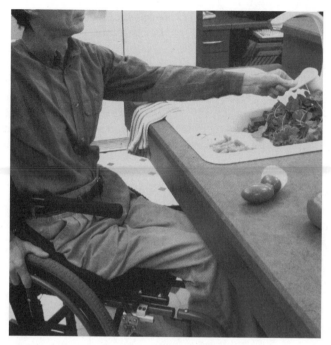

Figure 1-16 Under the counter kneespace. *(Whirlpool)*

Adjustable kitchen sink and countertops are available but are not cost effective for a residential application. These units can be raised or lowered mechanically. A 34"-high countertop with knee space below may be the most appropriate compromise for a universal design application. In this application, the kitchen flooring shall extend under the sink. The cabinet doors, if installed, will swing open and slide back into pockets. The sink and cooktop should be in close proximity to each other and at the same counter level if possible.

If the laundry area is located in the kitchen, similar considerations apply. For example, raising the clothes dryer 12" off of the floor will allow easier access into the machine (Fig. 1-17). It is important to locate some shelving within the 48" maximum and 15" minimum reach range for a forward approach or 9" minimum for a side approach.

Visual impairment can be aided by the installation of contrasting borders on the countertops, helping weaker eyes find the edges easier. A less obvious impairment is hearing loss.

Figure 1-17 Raised clothes dryer. *(Whirlpool)*

Whether it is a gradual deterioration or the user is already wearing a hearing aid, background noises make it difficult to audibly interpret or understand voices. A number of kitchen and laundry appliances are rated on the quietness of operation and can be used as a basis for selection. Sound batts can also be installed in laundry room and kitchen walls to help restrict the appliance noise to the respective rooms when doors are closed.

BATHROOM ACCESSIBILITY

As mentioned earlier, the minimum door is 3'-0" in width and has 12" clearance on the push side of the latch or 18" on the pull side. (Review Table 404.2.4.1 of the proposed ADA Guidelines Revisions for alternate applications.) The door handle should be of a lever type. The light switch mounted no higher than 48" a.f.f. and adjacent to the latch side of the door shall be a wide rocker type.

The flooring material should be a nonslip vinyl, cork, or textured surface ceramic tile. A 60" turnaround (180-degree turn by a person in a wheelchair) floor space should be located within the toilet room (Fig. 1-18). If space permits, the room should allow for this space to be beyond the arc of the door swing. If this is not possible, space for a wheelchair turnaround must be allowed immediately outside of the bathroom door. This is designed to allow the necessary maneuverability for the most difficult yet most important activity the able-bodied take for granted. The "lateral transfer" is the procedure in which a wheelchair-bound person moves to the toilet seat. The toilet should be designed such that its placement is square against a rear wall and a minimum 52" side wall is to one side.

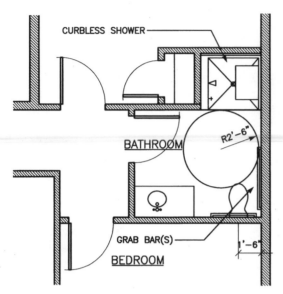

Figure 1-18   Bathroom layout.

Available in a variety of colors and finishes (polished brass, stainless steel, white, or other colors), grab bars can be integral to your scheme or added later if the need exists. The rear wall grab bar is to be centered on the toilet and 24" to 36" long. The sidewall grab bar should be 42" long and mounted a maximum of 12" from the rear wall. Grab bar mounting heights are to be between 33" and 36" a.f.f. (see Fig. 1-3). Additional blocking should be installed in the wall framing to support grab bars. The grab bar, similar to the handrail, shall be $1^1/4$" to $1^1/2$" in diameter and if wall-mounted should project $1^1/2$" from the wall face. The grab bars must be designed to support 250 lb per lineal foot. As stated in the old adage "an ounce of prevention is worth a pound of cure," installing wood blocking during construction will save countless dollars if grab bars are to be installed at a later time.

The toilet paper dispenser should be located between 7" and 9" in front of the water closet. The bottom of the toilet paper roll is located between 15" and 48" a.f.f..

The lavatory mirror must be mounted no higher than 40" a.f.f.. This still presents problems for up-close grooming, so a pullout extension mirror could also be wall-mounted. Outlets shall be located within the appropriate reach range as specified earlier. The bathroom sink must be mounted no higher than 34" a.f.f. with a minimum knee space at 29" a.f.f. The bowl should be no deeper than $6^1/_2$" deep. A 30" × 48" clear floor area in front of the sink is required (Fig. 1-19). This area may overlap or be included in the 60' turnaround area. It is encouraged to place the sink as close to the front of the counter as possible.   Any exposed plumbing under the sink must be insulated or configured to avoid incidental contact with the user. If a custom built vanity is constructed, a 30" wide, 9" high toe space that extends 25" deep (under any plumbing, etc.) is suggested. Minimum knee clearance is to be 27" high and 8" deep. Decorator quality wall mounted lavatories are readily available (Fig. 1-20).

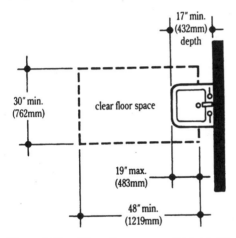

Figure 1-19   Clear floor space. *(Bobrick Washroom Equipment, Inc.)*

Lavatory fixtures shall be equipped with lever type handles. Medicine cabinets shall be mounted no higher than 44" a.f.f. Finally, raising the seat to be 17" to 19" a.f.f. easily modifies the toilet. Installing a new, standard accessible water closet is one option (Fig. 1-21). If an existing toilet is to remain, a raised toilet seat attachment can be added. Adjacent fixtures should be placed to assure 18" clearance each side of the centerline of the toilet.

Barrier-free bathing is available but only with diligent planning or fixture selection. In the simplest of post-installation modifications, grab bars should be mounted on each wall at 33" to 36" a.f.f. Adding a folding shower seat will be the most cost-effective solution. If a shower is custom-built for the home, a 3'-0" × 3'-0" stall or 2'-6" × 5'-0" curbless roll-in design are the minimum sizes (Fig. 1-22). The floor joists can be lowered to allow for the necessary depth when sloping the shower floor to a drain. The roll-in shower design with grab bars on each wall with a full depth L-shaped seat is the most preferred solution. Saddles or curbs should be avoided if possible. Wall-to-wall floor tile and integral floor drain will also allow for easy cleaning. Prefabricated molded fiberglass barrier-free shower stalls, although expensive, are also available.

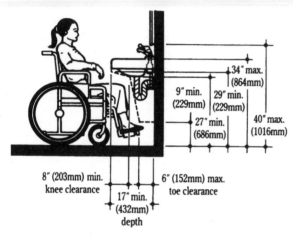

Figure 1-20 Lavatory clearance. *(Bobrick Washroom Equipment, Inc.)*

For bathtubs, two grab bars should be located on the rear wall. One is located between 33" and 36" a.f.f. and one is located 9" above the rim of the tub. A grab bar 24" long is to be installed on the front edge of the foot end of the tub (Fig. 1-23).

Shower and bath controls should be easily accessible by locating the faucet, drain, and even thermostat controls offset to the outside of the fixture. This is a minimal cost due to the short run of additional plumbing pipe necessary. The showerhead should be adjustable by sliding up or down on a vertical rod or hand-held spray head with a 5' length hose.

The installation of a pressure balance valve or a thermostatically controlled valve is an asset for convenience and safety. The pressure balance valve is not a temperature-control device but does protect against scalding. For the limited-budget

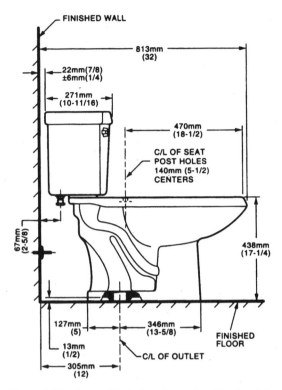

Figure 1-21   Accessible toilet. *(American Standard, Inc.)*

project, this is the best choice. Although more expensive, the thermostatic valve allows the water to flow better in multihead showers and at a personalized, preset temperature.

GETTING AROUND IN THE BEDROOM

As stated earlier, the path of travel must be considered regarding furniture placement. Although not ideal, this room, based on unforeseen changes such as an ill in-law, teenager with a fractured leg, or other sudden change in a homeowner's life, may be a converted den or living room. Sleeper sofas, cots, or even futons can easily allow a disabled resident a more self-sufficient style of living by being able to remain on the main floor of the home. A 36" clear path on each side of the bed is necessary for equal access and departure to and from the bed. The 60" clear turnaround space is to be implemented if space allows.

Figure 1-22   Accessible shower. *(Aqua Glass Corporation)*

"Doing the laundry" is another ritual that the able-bodied often take for granted. If the laundry room is not on the same floor as the bedroom, a laundry chute should be installed.

Drapery opening and closing is especially problematic when a person is confined to a bed. Mechanically operated systems (motorized roller shades, vertical blinds, or drapery tracks) may be the more technologically advanced option but not very practical due to their expense. Although new to the residential market in this country, light-omitting diode (LED) charged window units might be an affordable option of the immediate future. A conveniently located switch would allow the resident to "open" or "close" the shade by activating or canceling a light-prohibiting charge through the window unit.

The opening and closing of double-hung windows is problematic for someone possessing limited upper body strength or mobility. Crank-operated casement windows are a suitable option.

ADA-compliant intercom systems are also available.

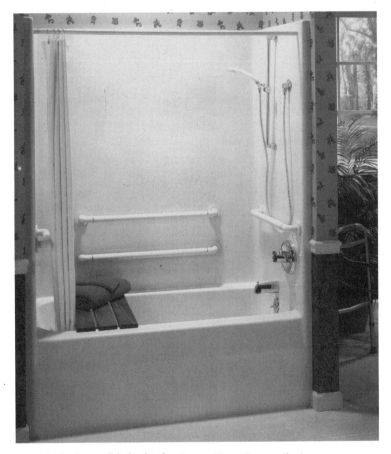

Figure 1-23   Accessible bathtub. *(Aqua Glass Corporation)*

CLIMBING THE STAIRS

The Consumer Product Safety Commission has shown that one in seven people will be injured and require hospitalization due to a stairway accident.[3] Depending upon the specific disability, this activity may or may not be practical. Several simple stair design concepts should be implemented for easier climbing. A report by the National Electronic Injury Surveillance System in 1990 estimated that 998,871 people were treated at hospitals for injuries sustained in stair-related accidents. It may be easy to conclude that the stair may be the most dangerous element in the home. With this in mind, improvements in stair design could benefit everyone.

All steps on a flight of stairs shall have tread widths of 11", measured from riser to riser (exclusive of nosings), and uniform, closed riser heights. Nosings shall project a maximum of $1^1/_2$" and have a maximum radius of curvature of $^1/_2$". The underside of the nosing should not be abrupt. A piece of trim, not exceeding a 60 degree angle, can be placed below the nosing to prevent a tripping hazard (Fig. 1-24). Once again, handrails shall be continuous, $1^1/_4$" to $1^1/_2$" in diameter or have a noncircular cross section with a perimeter dimension between 4" and $6^1/_2$" and a maximum cross-section dimension of $2^1/_4$". The top of gripping surfaces should be mounted between 34" and 38" above the tread and have a clearance from the wall of $1^1/_2$". The handrails should extend horizontally above the landing at the top of the stairs for an additional 12" if possible. If space permits, the handrails should also extend the slope one tread depth beyond the last riser nosing and an additional 12" parallel to the floor.

Adequate lighting is also a wise precaution where safety is concerned. Overhead lighting at the top and bottom of the stairway is essential. Low-voltage lighting at each riser is ideal.

Residential elevators and light-duty platform lifts are available but may be cost prohibitive for most applications.

CONSIDERATIONS FOR CHILDREN

It is important to note that not all physically impaired individuals are full grown or mature adults. Anthropometrics of children vary a great deal and need to be considered in a long-term care situation. In response to this reality, the U.S. Department of Justice and the Access Board published the proposed rule modification of the Americans with Disabilities Act and Children's Facilities in 1996. Although the final rule had not been adopted at the time this book went to print, the proposed rule included technical recommendations for a variety of circumstances regarding children with disabilities. The amendment to the ADA presents clearances and fixture mounting in facilities where usability by children is of primary importance such as daycare centers, elementary schools, and

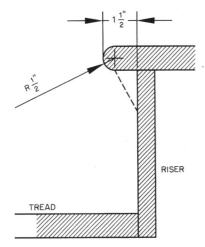

Figure 1-24   Stair nosing.

nursery schools. An additional proposed rule would include regulations regarding recreation facilities, playground equipment, etc. The recommendations discussed herein are not intended to be all-encompassing or serve as a definitive interpretation of the ADA.

Although the number of children that have to deal with a permanent disability such as muscular dystrophy or paralysis are fortunately small relative to the larger population, few children get through life without a temporary disability such as a broken leg or arm. Some designers have designed rooms to a child's scale. These include lower height doors and windows and even a lowered ceiling. Korners Folly in Kernersville, NC, is one of a historical significance, built in the late 1800s.

Children using a cane take shorter strides and have a narrower and lower cane sweep than adults. Children can typically detect protruding objects up to 12" from the ground as opposed to 27" for adults. An object mounted on a wall, projecting more than 4" from the wall (such as a wall-mounted bookcase) may have a leading edge no more than 12" above the floor.

Handrails at stairs should be lowered to a range of 20" to 28" above the stair nosing. The gripping surface of the handrail should also be reduced to a diameter of $1^1/4$" to $1^1/2$".

Lavatories shall be mounted with a rim no higher than 30" a.f.f. and a clearance of 27" to the bottom of the apron. Clear toe space shall be 12" high. Mirrors shall be mounted a maximum of 34" a.f.f.

Additional research is recommended when designing closets, storage shelves, water closet selection, etc., due to the varying reach ranges of children. The proposed rule designates children to be in one of three age groups with different requirements for each. Copies of the proposed rule can be obtained by contacting the Architectural and Transportation Barriers Compliance Board or the Department of Justice.

THE FUTURE

"Smart house" technologies, discussed later in the book, present opportunities to remove even more barriers to the disabled as well as removing a lot of the nuisances of everyday living. For example, preset water thermostat controls at each bathtub, intellectual comfort systems that dim lights or balance individual room temperatures, or voice-activated mechanisms could be standard features once the technologies become more affordable.

Growing awareness by the public of the need for accessible options will continue to drive the need for new product development. Products designed to comply with accessibility design standards are designated by the universal accessibility symbol in order to simplify the selection process. Sweets Catalogs, Arcat, First Source, or other manufacturer catalogs are excellent resources. These are even available on CD-ROM.

CONCLUSION

Few people have the opportunity to plan for sudden disability. If a homeowner accepts the possibility that he or she could one day be physically disabled or anticipates the need to care for an elderly parent or loved one, money and distress can be avoided or lessened by incorporating some or all of the universal design recommendations previously mentioned. In any event, it makes good design sense to allow for convenience and accessibility. To learn more about compliance with the ADA, ANSI A117.1 or

UFAS standards, contact your local building official or refer to the universal design sources referenced in Appendix B.

REFERENCES

1. "Understanding the Americans with Disabilities Act" *Sweet's Accessible Building Product Catalog File*, 1997, p. 17.
2. "Accessibility...as seen from the inside looking out....." *Southern Building,* March/April 1997, p. 4.
3. Gary D. Branson, The Complete Guide to Barrier Free Housing (Crozet, VA.: Betterway Publications, 1991), p. 25.

Chapter

2

Foundations and Basements

INTRODUCTION

Dr. Jacob Field, one of the first engineers to publicly lecture about construction failures, once assembled 10 rules toward the successful design and construction of buildings. Rule #1 states "Gravity always works, so if you don't provide permanent support, something will fail."[1] Like feet that support the human skeleton above, a building's foundation is the very essence of its structural stability. The purpose of a foundation is to convey the weight of a building to the soil without being subjected to excessive settlement, differential settlement (causing cracks in the structure), or the total failure of the soil leading to a complete collapse of the building. It must also anchor a building's superstructure against the unpredictable forces of uplift caused by wind, racking caused by earthquakes, and the covert yet devastating effects of groundwater.

Although this chapter is not a discussion on foundation design, an understanding of the basic principles are an educational tool. The analysis in theory is very simple: A stationary object exerts force by its sheer weight on the ground. Force cannot be applied to any material without causing deformation. The ground provides a resisting force, or reaction. When these forces are in equilibrium, a structure is said to be stable.

SUBSTRUCTURE TYPES

There are three types of substructures (foundations) using simple wall footings:

- Slab-on-grade
- Crawlspace
- Basement

Concrete slab-on-grade is typically the least expensive foundation system and is suitable to most homes, provided a relatively level grade is established. The main drawback to slab construction is the inability to work, repair, or relocate utilities and plumbing once the concrete is poured. Moisture, groundwater, or settlement problems can make repairs impractical, impossible, or economically unfeasible.

Crawlspaces, usually constructed with concrete masonry units, brick masonry units, or a combination of both are more suitable for sloping grades. Although more expensive than slab-on-grade construction, plumbing is easily accessible should repairs be necessary or a renovation take place. Depending on the site, the crawlspace may serve as a low storage area but is usually too small to be practical. If not constructed or maintained properly, the crawlspace can be a major culprit in insect infestation as well as long-term moisture damage.

Basements are usually constructed of concrete masonry units but can be constructed using wood frame construction or poured-in-place concrete. Basement walls are in essence retaining walls, not only resisting soil pressure but also providing an impervious barrier to both groundwater and hydrostatic pressure. This is accomplished typically with a variety of waterproofing methods (membranes, bituminous coatings, or modified portland cement plaster) on the exterior of the wall and a drainage system. (Typically a perforated pipe set in gravel.)

Typical concrete masonry unit basements will leak in time, even if the exterior face is waterproofed correctly. Due to the many joints in the wall, the slightest settlement of the foundation will result in cracking at the joints or wall corners. Concrete masonry units are also an inferior insulator. Concrete poured in place creates a solidly built wall, but it is very labor intensive.

Given this brief overview of the basic residential foundation systems, many drawbacks to conventional construction methodology are obvious. One obvious culprit is the basic building unit of which these are constructed. Whether it be concrete block or brick, these masonry units are generic building blocks that over time have served a multitude of purposes. Their shortcoming is that neither was designed specifically for one application. One must re-examine what the foundation/ basement wall is doing in order to improve upon traditional methodology. In response, there are a number of products which have been designed for one purpose and one purpose only: to provide a structurally sound, well-insulated, waterproof residential basement. This chapter will discuss the following two different technologies:

- ICF (Insulating concrete formwork)
- Preinsulated, precast concrete panels.

INSULATING CONCRETE FORMWORK

Insulating concrete formwork (ICF) is a cost-effective, flexible, modular, permanent concrete form system. The basic unit of this system are expanded polystyrene (EPS) forms that are filled with concrete and steel reinforcement (Fig. 2-1). The departure from typical poured-in-place concrete construction is that the EPS formwork is left in place after the concrete cures for permanent insulating value. There are two types of forms: planks and blocks.

EPS is foamed polystyrene, a common plastic. (Close visual inspection reveals thousands of tiny white beads.) Its closed-cell, air-filled cellular structure possesses a high resistance to heat flow as well as high mechanical strength relative to its weight. EPS gives the added advantage of being lightweight. In combination with concrete, the system has high insulation values for both thermal and acoustical applications. The flexibility as a wall system makes it unique in that almost any type of wall or foundation system can be built cost-effectively, whether or not thermal and acoustical qualities are required. The EPS is flame-retardant and is designed to withstand the rigors of wet-poured concrete. Finally, no chlorofluorocarbons (CFCs) or hydrogenated chlorofluorocarbons (HCFCs) are used or produced during the creation of EPS. (Many extruded polystyrene products do create these environmentally harmful gases. Extruded polystyrene is a closed-cell thermal material and is usually pink or blue in color. It is commonly used as rigid insulation.)

Figure 2-1 Insulating concrete formwork. *(AFM Corporation)*

Product Description

Although the specific cross section and modular relationships may vary from product to product, the basic concept does not. The foundation or basement wall is assembled by placing interlocking EPS forms one on top of the other (as well as side by side) in a running or stack bond fashion (depending on the system) (Fig. 2-2). The forms are held together (or apart, actually) by integral plastic web ties, teeth, or other interlock design mechanisms. Steel reinforcing is then placed within the forms and the concrete is poured. It is important to note that although discussed primarily as a foundation system in this chapter, most ICF systems can also be used for full-height walls, including door and window openings. One manufacturer's portfolio includes bridge abutments, swimming pools, and even grade beams.

Product Properties

The basic ICF concept of a stay-in-place, easy-to-assemble formwork is the same among manufacturers; however, proprietary dimensions and physical properties vary slightly. This book does not pass judgment on the superiority of one product over another. The contractor or homeowner can review the advantages and disadvantages of each. For example,

Diamond Snap-Form® by AFM Corporation, Polysteel®, SmartBlock®, and AAB Blue Maxx® were reviewed for this text. (See Appendix at end of chapter for manufacturer data.) Polysteel® has been manufacturing ICF since 1978; AFM has been making EPS products for over 30 years.

Figure 2-2 Insulating concrete formwork assembly. *(AAB Building System)*

As mentioned earlier, the ICF system(s) are either assembled on site or are prefabricated. Two examples of the site-assembled ICF systems are the Diamond Snap-Form® and the SmartBlock® by ConForm (Fig. 2-3). Diamond Snap-Form® uses 1' × 8' EPS panels connected by a Diamond Snap Tie every 12" horizontally and vertically. These panels are factory-notched for tie placement, field assembled, and can be custom-configured for the appropriate condition. The wall thickness, determined by the wall tie, is available in 4", 6", 8" and 10". Diamond Snap's EPS panel has an insect-resistant additive (Fig. 2-4). ConForm's SmartBlock® is 10"w, 10"h and 40"l which creates a $6^{1}/_{2}$" thick, 87 percent solid concrete wall. Each block weighs approximately 2 lb. (The variable form is 12"h and creates nominal wall widths of 4", 6" and 8".)

In contrast to the site-assembled plank-type systems, Polysteel® is a prefabricated block unit, commonly referred to as an "oversized Lego block". The basic unit measures 48"l, 16"h and $9^{1}/_{4}$" or 11"w. Each block weighs approximately 5 lb, has interlocking tongue and grooves, and has integral furring strips. AAB Blue Maxx®'s standard unit measures 48"l, $11^{1}/_{2}$"w and $16^{3}/_{4}$"h and weighs approximately 6.2 lb (Fig. 2-5).

Figure 2-3 ICF block types. *(ConForm)*

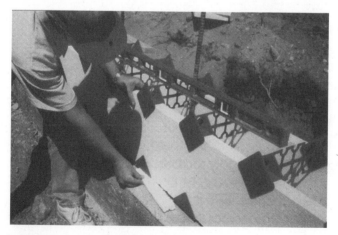

Figure 2-4 ICF block types. *(AFM Corporation)*

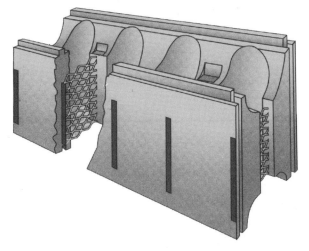

Figure 2-5 ICF block types. *(Polysteel)*

Engineering Standards

The EPS formwork is nonstructural since the structural integrity of the assembly comes from the concrete poured within. The strength of the assembly permits it to be used in almost any civil or structural application to replace concrete block, poured-in-place, or low-rise tilt-up concrete construction. Concrete, when placed inside a formed wall, cures under almost ideal conditions. This temperature control during curing provides a 50 percent increase in compressive strength than with conventional formed concrete according to the Portland Cement Association.

Cost Savings

Cost advantages when using ICF can be seen in a variety of ways. According to the ConForm literature, comparative costs range from 30 to 50 percent lower than conventional walls. Stay in place formwork eliminate the need for, and cost of, buying, stripping, cleaning, transporting and storing reusable forms. The improved fire rating frequently reduces insurance costs and results in higher appraisal values than stick built homes. Polysteel Forms® reports lower life cycle costs, such as cost savings from utility bills. For example, a home that costs $820 per year to heat and cool with stick built construction is reduced to $240 per year for a home built entirely of poured in place concrete. Construction time and manpower is also reduced. The

AAB Blue Maxx® system states that a three man team can erect the formwork, place the steel and pour the concrete for a 2000 SF house in one day.

Insulation and Thermal Value

The moisture resistant, closed cell configuration of EPS gives superb insulating qualities that will not deteriorate with age. The typical R values are as follows: Diamond Snap-Form® is R-20, Polysteel® is R-22, SmartBlock® is R-22 and AAB Blue Maxx® is R-26. The principle of permanent insulated form work containing a high heat-capacity material such as concrete creates the optimum thermal construction assembly since the structure (concrete) is the thermal mass and the form work is the insulation. Thus, the costly application of additional insulating material is eliminated. The result is an ideal combination of materials that significantly reduces energy consumption in moderate and extreme climates. Polysteel Forms® create a super-insulated concrete wall which reduces heating and cooling costs by 50 to 80 percent.

American Polysteel, manufacturer of Polysteel® Forms, performed an ASHRAE computer simulation on their 6" Polysteel® Form R wall filled with concrete as compared with a low mass, high R-value wall. A Polysteel® wall of R-17 was used for the test. Although the test simulation was run for all climates and regions, the illustration results were quite astounding. An exterior wood frame wall of a home in Miami, Phoenix or Seattle would need to be insulated to more than R-50 while a home in New York City, St. Louis or Washington D.C. would have to equal R-37 in order to equal the thermal properties of the test wall.

An air barrier is not necessary because of the inherit solid mass properties value of the concrete. One common culprit is also eliminated in that outlets do not allow air infiltration. A vapor barrier is also not needed due to the high insulation of the wall assembly. Dampproofing and waterproofing are required in wall assemblies when used below grade. As stated earlier, verify construction assemblies with the manufacturer's details and instructions.

Acoustic Value

The STC (Sound Transmission Class) ratings of concrete and gypsum-board, along with the ideal separation that EPS creates between the two materials provides sound insulation qualities, both airborne and impact, that meet the separation standards of the major building codes and FHA without the application of other acoustic material.

Polysteel® walls provide an STC of 48 as compared to 32 with a 2 × 6 wood frame wall. AAB provides an STC of 53 while ConForm (including 2 layers of $^1/_2$"GWB) provides an STC of 52.

Finishes

Interior finishes of wood paneling or GWB and exterior finishes of board and batten siding, wood, vinyl or aluminum siding, brick stone or even stucco can be applied to any of the products. The method of attachment varies with each product. For example, screws are set only at each tie with the Diamond Snap-Form® system, whereas Polysteel® has integral furring strips, and GWB is typically adhered to ConForm's SmartBlock® (Figs. 2-6 and 2-7).

Figure 2-6 Residence during construction. *(Polysteel)*

Figure 2-7 Residence after construction. *(Polysteel)*

Lightweight

Because each modular unit is so lightweight, pallets can be easily lifted manually from delivery trucks, moved around and placed anywhere on the building site. The need for fork-lifts or other heavy equipment is usually eliminated, resulting in more cost savings for the contractor and the consumer. For example, one 6 lb Polysteel Form creates the same amount of wall area as would 140 lb of concrete block. Similarly, a 40 lb ConForm pallet produces the equivalent of 500 lb of concrete block for the same area.

Building Codes

EPS forms are designed to meet or exceed the minimum material requirements of all major building codes in the United States, Uniform Building Codes (UBC), Southern Building Code Congress International (SBCCI), International Conference of Building Officials (ICBO), and Building Officials Code Administration (BOCA). It is important to note, however, that not all of the "newer" manufacturers have been approved by the proper code authorities. Specifiers and homeowners need to verify that the product to be used has been code approved.

Polysteel® walls, with an insulation value of R-22, (filled with reinforced concrete) are bullet resistant. Proper detailing, caulking and waterproofing will minimize outside air infiltration, leaks, and drafts. Although some manufacturers claim the formwork will not be eaten by wood-eating termites or ants it is still prudent, and recommended to sufficiently treat the soil and ICF for these vermin.

Miscellaneous Installation Tips

These products are described as "builder friendly" and do not require a special skilled labor force. Most manufacturers indicate that the "learning curve" is minimal. Since each system reviewed in this text varies to some degree, specific installation instructions must be followed relative to the specific manufacturer. No two systems are alike so the following are generalized application directions that were not covered elsewhere in this text (Figs. 2-8 and 2-9).

Figure 2-8 ICF installation. *(Polysteel)*

Footings are required and should include rebar dowels for tying the walls to the footing. If stepped footings are required, it is preferred to step in vertical increments consistent with the modular form unit height.

Nail a 2 × 4 to the footing to guide placement of the first course. Brace corners and angle cuts on both sides; and apply vertical bracing with "kickers" and ladder bracing per manufacturer's recommendations.

In the case of a prefabricated modular block, such as Polysteel®, the first block is set at the corner. Each ICF block is set upon another in a running bond after each course is completed.

In the case of Diamond Snap Form, preformed corner pieces are set against the outside toe-plate (used as a guide) (Figs. 2-10 and 2-11). The first pair of 8' planks are assembled upside down with half ties and then flipped. The remaining pre-built sections are set continuously around the perimeter and the second and subsequent courses are set in a stack bond.

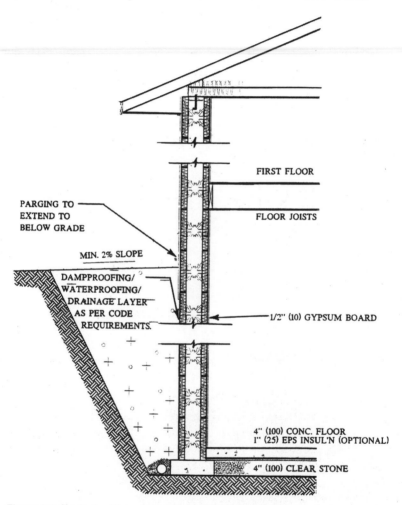

Figure 2-9 Typical wall section. *(The AAB Building System)*

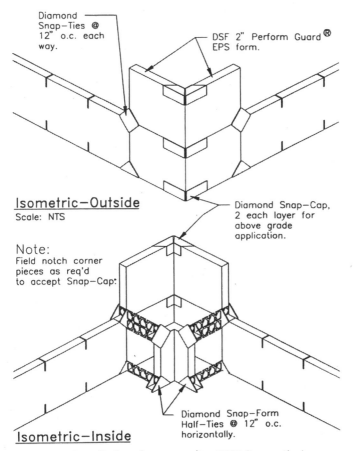

Diamond
Snap—Ties @
12" o.c. each
way.

DSF 2" Perform Guard ®
EPS form.

Isometric—Outside
Scale: NTS

Diamond Snap—Cap,
2 each layer for
above grade
application.

Note:
Field notch corner
pieces as req'd
to accept Snap—Cap.

Diamond Snap—Form
Half—Ties @ 12" o.c.
horizontally.

Isometric—Inside

Figure 2-10   Installation of corner units. *(AFM Corporation)*

Figure 2-11   Installation of corner units. *(AFM Corporation)*

Concrete should have a slump no greater than 6" with a recommended aggregate size of $3/8$". Always check slump yourself before pouring. On hot days, or if concrete stays in the truck too long, recheck slump. Stiff concrete is a problem. If high-strength concrete is used, or if significant rebar is placed, extra care must be taken to assure proper filling and elimination of air pockets. Using a rebar to spread the concrete will help, and vibrating by pounding with a mallet (use a section of plywood to protect the foam) will help consolidation. Concrete admixtures can be used for special applications (Fig. 2-12).

Figure 2-12   Concrete preparation. *(AFM Corporation)*

At the top of the wall, the concrete is screeded, troweled smooth, and anchor bolts are set.

In general, hot- and cold-water pipes, electrical conduit, and wiring can be placed in chases routed with a hot knife or cut into the wall after the concrete has cured sufficiently (Fig. 2-13).

INSULATED PRECAST CONCRETE FOUNDATION SYSTEM

Although the intent of this book is to discuss the means, methods, and materials in a multiproprietary manner, this is not always possible given the nature of innovation and the reality of patents. This text is not to be construed as an advertising medium for one specific manufacturer, the Superior Wall System. (The evaluation is based upon information provided by Superior Walls of America and has not been independently verified.)

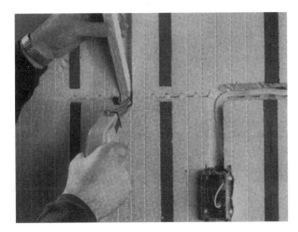

Figure 2-13   Electrical installation. *(The AAB Building System)*

Superior Walls of America, Ltd., was founded in 1981 in an effort to establish an innovative residential and light commercial foundation system. The company is presently installing 190 units a month with over 20,000 installations completed and reportedly no documented structural failure. The company has 18 independently licensed manufacturing and installation facilities throughout the United States, and plans for several operations in Europe and Russia are in the works.

Product Description

Superior Walls are custom-made, precast with concrete studs, insulated foundation wall panels (Fig. 2-14). The ready-to-finish wall panels feature 1'-diameter prebored plumbing and electrical access holes and are manufactured to accommodate door and window openings. Panels are formed in average lengths up to 16', and standard heights of 4', 4'-8", 8'-2", 9' and 10'. The panels can be cast to virtually any shape for unlimited design flexibility (Fig. 2-15).

Product Properties

The Superior Walls System, which is also engineered for above-ground applications, consists of steel-reinforced concrete studs, reinforced top and bottom footer beams, preattached wood nailers for a ready-to-finish interior, 1" continuous rigid DOW® Styrofoam insulation for an R-5 rating, precast access for wiring, plumbing, and sill plates; and 5000-psi concrete (a $1^3/4$" thick concrete facing) (Fig. 2-16). This proprietary system eliminates the need for additional waterproofing or tarring. (The American Concrete Institute states that a 4000-psi design is watertight.) Superior Walls are completely custom made to accommodate door and window openings. Openings are framed with pressure-treated lumber. The top bond beam is perforated to allow the bolting on of pressure-treated sill plates; $1/2$" diameter holes are precast at 24" o/c (see Figs. 2-3 and 2-4). Panels are normally formed in lengths up to 16' and standard heights of 4', 4'8", 8'2", 9' and 10' can be cast to virtually any shape for unlimited design flexibility. Overall wall thickness is $10^{1}/4$" with concrete stud spacing at 24' o/c. Wall systems are guaranteed to be free of structural defects and water filtration. A 15-year limited warranty is available in most areas.

Engineering Standards

Panels are manufactured with 5000-psi concrete, combined with a top and bottom bond beam and solid concrete studs reinforced with rebar. The bond beams and concrete facing are cast in one continuous pour. They connect to the studs by encapsulating vertical rebars, and are lifted by galvanized hooks and pins which protrude from the top and back of each stud (Fig. 2-17). The vertical rebar is located near the inner edge of each stud. According to analyses performed by ATEC Associates of Baltimore, Md., the tensile strength is higher than a poured concrete foundation and 10 times that of a concrete block foundation.

One interesting element that is missing from a Superior Walls basement/foundation is the traditional footing (Fig. 2-18). According to the Superior Walls literature, the gravel footer system allows water to drain away from the wall and eliminates hydrostatic pressure on the walls and floors. Brick and support ledges as well as beam pockets are easily manufactured. Beam pockets are engineered for a weight of 10,000 lb. Double and triple studs can be manufactured allowing point loads of up to 15,000 lb to be displaced.

Cost Savings

Builders realize substantial time and labor savings because experienced Superior Walls installation crews can install an

Figure 2-14   Insulated precast concrete foundation. *(Superior Walls)*

Figure 2-15   Insulated precast concrete foundation. *(Superior Walls)*

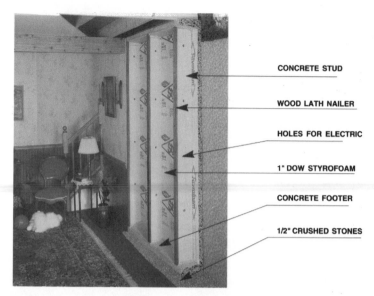

CONCRETE STUD

WOOD LATH NAILER

HOLES FOR ELECTRIC

1" DOW STYROFOAM

CONCRETE FOOTER

1/2" CRUSHED STONES

Figure 2-16   Section through foundation. *(Superior Walls)*

Figure 2-17   Panel hoisting. *(Superior Walls)*

average system, above or below grade, in about 5 hours in most weather conditions. The panels are precast, so curing delays associated with conventional poured-in-place foundations are eliminated. Backfilling can begin as soon as the floor slab is poured and the subfloor is properly attached to the top of the wall system. The actual initial cost according to one estimate is 10 percent higher than a masonry block wall.[2]

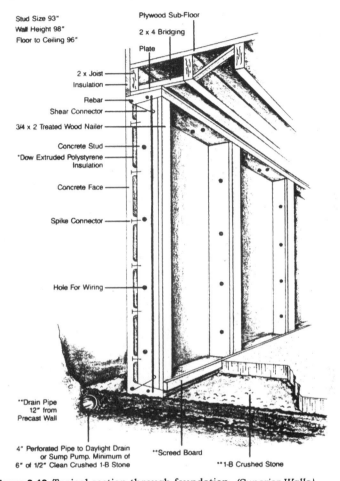

Stud Size 93"
Wall Height 98"
Floor to Ceiling 96"

Plywood Sub-Floor
2 x 4 Bridging
Plate

2 x Joist
Insulation
Rebar
Shear Connector
3/4 x 2 Treated Wood Nailer

Concrete Stud
*Dow Extruded Polystyrene Insulation

Concrete Face

Spike Connector

Hole For Wiring

**Drain Pipe 12" from Precast Wall

4" Perforated Pipe to Daylight Drain or Sump Pump. Minimum of 6" of 1/2" Clean Crushed 1-B Stone

**Screed Board

**1-B Crushed Stone

Figure 2-18 Typical section through foundation. *(Superior Walls)*

Insulation and Thermal Value

Superior Walls panels are preinsulated with DOW® Styrofoam with an R-5 rating. This gives the wall an overall R-value of 7.46 An additional 6" of insulation may be added within the $7^1/2$"-deep wall cavity to increase the total R-value up to 26. The system is guaranteed to protect basements from water and moisture damage, mold and mildew, and to prevent serious structural damage.

Finishes

A treated wood nailer is factory installed to the inside of the reinforced concrete studs, allowing for the application of wallboard or paneling. The exterior is finished concrete, which will serve as a substrate for most waterproofing, dampproofing, or parging materials. If a finish material is preferred, a ledger is available to support a brick veneer. If exterior siding is desired, wood nailers can be precast into the panel exterior.

For interior finishes, pressure-treated furring strips are pre-attached to the inner face of each stud to provide a base to accommodate a variety of wall finishes. In addition, holes are cast into each stud, allowing for the installation of wiring and plumbing.

Building Codes

According to the manufacturer's literature, Superior Walls meets or exceeds BOCA, ICBO, and SBCCI building codes. Superior Precast Walls have been reviewed by BOCA Research Report #89-53 and are presently installed throughout the United States (SBCCI in the South, ICBO in the West). All three major codes and CABO do not discourage new products, but accept alternate materials and systems. Superior Walls of America has made available an *Inspection Procedure Support Data* booklet for the building inspector since new materials and systems must be reviewed by the local building inspector for his or her acceptance. This booklet will guide the inspector and enable him or her to properly inspect the foundation according to the standards established by the code. Superior Walls of America has designed and tested its precast foundation wall system in accordance with the requirements of American Concrete Institute Standard No. 318. ACI, which contains the recognized national standards for concrete, concrete products, and structures and is recognized by all national codes as an authority on all types of concrete construction. Sealed engineering approvals are available if required.

Radon Ventilation

Superior Walls can easily accommodate a simple and economical ventilation system to remove contaminated air and radon gas from the basement. Supplied and installed by the builder, a small in-line fan and piping system can be very effective. Special built-in features of Superior Walls add to the effectiveness of this air exchange system. The cast concrete panels offer a very low permeability rate, which is even further enhanced by the factory-installed DOW® Styrofoam insulation. Additionally, the crushed stone foundation allows for the free flow of air from all points of the excavation into the exhaust system beneath the floor (Fig. 2-9).

Miscellaneous Installation Tips

The builder must be sure that the site is accessible for the delivery truck and crane. Check for mud, sharp turns, hills, bumps, trenches, trees and overhead wires. A 35' × 35' level area clear of overhead obstructions must be provided for the crane.

The drainage system must be in place and functional. Crushed stone must cover the entire floor area and be level to within 1". Corner pins of the foundation must be clearly indicated (Fig. 2-19). The basement must have an over dig of 24" at the bottom of the excavation (Fig. 2-20).

Foundation walls shall extend below the frost line of the specific locality. Site soil conditions shall be adequate for the calculated bearing pressure. The height of the backfill shall not exceed 10' without additional engineering (Fig. 2-21).

The system is to be used for one- and two-family residences $2^1/2$ stories or less in height unless engineered to meet the necessary code requirements.

Other recommendations are specified for colder climates. See manufacturer's literature.

CONCLUSION

Leon Battist Alberti once wrote, "We must never trust too hastily to any ground...I have seen a tower at Mestre, a place belonging to the Ventians, which, in a few years after it was built, made its way through the ground it stood upon...and buried itself in earth up to the very battlements."[3] The layperson may not be aware of the tower at Mestre, but had engineers not intervened several years ago, a similar fate would have awaited the famous, or infamous, Leaning Tower of Pisa. Although the typical residential foundation will never take on the prestige or notoriety of the aforementioned examples, it is nevertheless just as essential to

Figure 2-19   Crushed stone base. *(Superior Walls)*

the stability and structural integrity of its assigned purpose. Insulated concrete formwork systems and precast insulated wall panels are but two examples of new residential construction systems that attempt to improve upon the traditional methodology of poured-in-place and precast concrete used so prevalently throughout this century.

APPENDIX

AFM Corporation
P.O. Box 246
Excelsior, MN 55331
1-800-255-0176
Diamond Snap-Form

Figure 2-20 Foundation preparation. *(Superior Walls)*

American Polysteel Forms
5150-F Edith NE
Albuquerque, NM 87101
1-800-9PS-FORM
Fax: (505) 345-8154

Superior Walls of America, Ltd.
P.O. Box 427
Ephrata, PA 17522-0427
1-800-452-9255

CASE STUDY 2-1[4]

Back in 1994, the Oosterwyks of Fond du Lac, Wisconsin built a walkout rambler with AFM's R-Control Structural Building

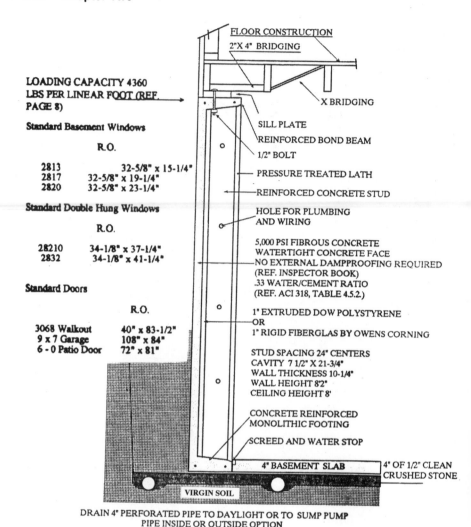

Figure 2-21   Wall section. *(Superior Walls)*

Panels. The panels were manufactured by AFM Partner Plant, Wisconsin EPS of Fond du Lac, Wisconsin. The home also used Perform Perimeter Insulation around the foundation of the structure to provide insulation and comfort to the lower level of the home.

The particular structure was approximately 3300 ft² and used AFM's R-Control Structural Building Panels for the walls of the structure. The family began heating the home with liquid propane gas in August of 1994. The family also used a gas water heater and a gas log fireplace. They spent $400.03 from August of 1994 through the end of March 1995. For the next complete year, gas was purchased three times, for a total gas bill of $446.05. For the year of 1996-1997 the gas bill was $494.33. During this year, the price of liquid propane did increase slightly.

The average cost of gas for the year of 1995-1996 was $37.17 a month and this is for heat, hot water, and their gas fireplace. The Oosterwyk's home was built by Gruenwald Construction of Fond de Lac, Wisconsin, and designed by Marla Janes of the Stock Lumber Company.

CASE STUDY 2-2[5]

R-Control Structural Building Panels were compared to that of stick framing costs in labor and time. Data were compiled from a single-family, two-story home with a two-car attached garage (1357 ft^2 on main floor, 1300 ft^2 in basement) built in Missoula, Montana.

The exterior walls were erected in 22 worker hours. This includes prep work on panels and the cutting in of doors and windows, for a total cost of $6543.

Traditionally, exterior walls framed with 2 × 6 studs, shear paneled with OSB, headers built for doors and windows, and insulated would have taken 47 worker hours and have a total cost of $11,684.

Building this house using R-Control Structural Building Panels generated a cost savings of $5141. This does not include savings incurred by the case in which subcontractors, i.e., electricians, plumbers, etc., can work within the structure.

Substantial savings are also passed on to homeowners in the form of owning an energy-efficient home.

REFERENCES

1. Dov Kaminetzky, *Design and construction Failures, Lessons From Forensic Investigations* (New York: McGraw-Hill, 1991), P. 53.
2. Gary Kunkle, a partner with Kunkle Brothers in East Earl, PA during an interview for Builder magazine in 1985. Reprinted from Superior Walls literature.
3. Edward Allen, *Fundamentals of Building and Construction.* (New York: John Wiley & Sons, 1990), p. 39.
4. Text provided by AFM Corporation.
5. Text provided by AFM Corporation.

3

Floors and Floor Systems

INTRODUCTION

Wood light frame construction has been referred to as the first uniquely American structural system.[1] Many architectural historians point to the great Chicago Fire of 1871 as the most important event to impact residential wood light frame construction but they are not quite right. It was invented in the 1830s by George Washington Snow, an engineer in Chicago. The wake of the fire cleared the way for not only new commercial construction projects by Louis Sullivan, Daniel Burnham, Henry Hobson Richardson and Frank Lloyd Wright but for residential projects as well. This devastating event provided the proper place and time required for an enormous stick built building boom. The platform and balloon framing construction methods were essential in restoring Chicago to a thriving city. According to Siegfried Giedion, "The balloon frame is closely connected with the level of industrialization which had been reached in America (in the early nineteenth century). Its invention practically converted building in wood from a complicated craft, practiced by skilled labor, into an industry..."[2] But that is just the problem. In the past 100 years, floor framing methods have continued on their course virtually unchanged. Refinements and technological improvements have been made over the years, but the practice of cutting boards from trees, (leaving 40 percent of the tree unusable) is still the same. It has been said that it takes one acre of trees to frame the average house. Even as a renewable resource, the strategy is flawed. In addition to the great amount of waste, there are other inherent problems with 2× solid sawn lumber:

1. Warpage or bowing (Fig. 3-1)
2. Cupping (Fig. 3-2)
3. Twisting (Fig. 3-3)
4. Crooking
5. Knots (Fig. 3-4)
6. Variance in moisture content
7. Additional cross bridging to avoid overturning.
8. Decay by organisms that inhabit the wood

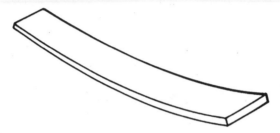

Figure 3-1 Warpage.

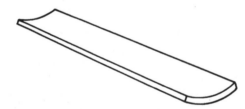

Figure 3-2 Cupping.

Figure 3-3 Twisting.

In addition to these "behavioral" problems, squeaky and out-of-level floors can also be a nuisance. On the business end of the lumber industry, a number of events over the previous years have contributed detrimentally to the industry as well. Timber harvest in the Pacific Northwest plunged from 10.4 billion board feet in 1990 to 3.1 billion board feet in 1995 due to federally mandated cutbacks on public lands. However, lumber producers were able to compensate slightly by looking elsewhere in the United States.. The Canadian export market, standing to reap the benefits of such a cutback on U.S. production was curtailed by a Clinton administration imposed tariff on Canadian lumber imports. In a nutshell, the big loser in all of this political manipulation of fair trade practices is the homebuilder and subsequently, homeowner. A homeowner in 1997 is paying an additional $2000 for a 2000 ft^2 home and lumber prices are twice as high they were in the peak home-building years of the 1980s.[3]

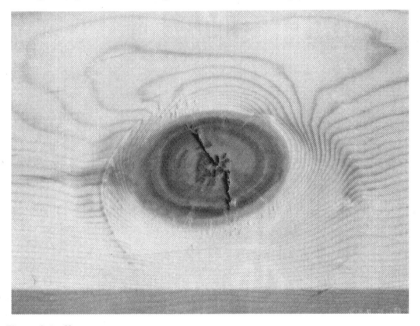

Figure 3-4   Knots.

Culls are becoming more of a problem with homebuilders for a variety of reasons. Lumber mills are using immature trees for lumber, and improper handling and storage results in moisture content and drying problems. Builders are then forced to purchase a higher grade or species of wood in order to attain a minimum level of quality that was previously possible in a lower (and less expensive) grade. Hence, the price increase is passed along to the consumer.

So why does a structural system with so many flaws continue to be used so prevalently? The reasons are varied, but the most obvious is "tradition." We as humans, or building professionals, are creatures of habit, especially when risk is involved. If something has worked before, why change the program? This makes sense systematically until it crosses the threshold into the world of ignorance. To ignore new systems, practices, technologies, and methods is to not take full advantage of our abilities to exploration, inquiry, and adaptation (Fig. 3-5).

Figure 3-5   Engineered wood products. *(Georgia Pacific)*

The introduction of engineered wood products has the ability to revolutionize framing methods and materials. Engineered wood products are made from wood strands, veneers, or other forms of wood fiber of trees that have been peeled, chipped, sliced, or cut. Defects in the wood pieces are removed or randomly dispersed and the remaining pieces are then glued together under heat and pressure. According to the Canadian Wood Council, the result is that 95 percent of the tree is used for consumer products rather than the 60 percent for solid lumber products. Furthermore, these composite products are superior in strength to solid lumber, carrying up to twice the load of an equivalent sawn piece of wood.[4] The main difference is that unlike the visual grading systems used for solid lumber, these composite elements possess design values that are "engineered."

The advances in this technology are considerable. We will review several types of structural components in this chapter as well as structural attachment methods and subfloor systems.

STRUCTURAL COMPONENTS

The three structural components available in engineered wood systems are:

* Wood-I-Joists (Wood-I-beams)
* Laminated beams
* Open-web joist
* Subfloor sheathing

WOOD-I-JOISTS

Wood-I-Joists (Fig. 3-6), as the name implies, are I-shaped. The upper and lower flanges are made of solid high-quality lumber or bonded veneers with an exterior adhesive for more load-carrying capacity. The webs are made from either strong oriented-strand board or plywood. (Oriented-strand board, or OSB, are panels made from strands of wood. Two-way strength is achieved by orienting the direction of the strands in different layers. Plywood is a panel product composed of thin veneers glued in layers with the grain placed at right angles to each subsequent layer.) In principle, the Wood-I-Joists performs as a truss, albeit flat. The top chord is in compression, the bottom chord is in tension. Unlike the triangular components of the truss, which are in pure compression or pure tension, the OSB or plywood web of a Wood-I-Joist is subjected to shear stresses. These elements can be used for floor joists or roof rafters. (See Chapter 4.)

Wood-I-Joists are implemented in a floor system the same way traditional dimensional lumber has been: to span between substructure below. But that is where the comparison ends. The spanning capabilities of Wood-I-Joists are superior to dimensional lumber. For example, the maximum span of a 2 ×

12, as listed in southern pine span tables, for a 40 psf live load, 10 psf dead load and a stiffness ratio of L/360 is 23'-3" when the joists are spaced 16" o/c. A Wood-I-Joist, with identical loads and stiffness ratio, can span 29'-8" when a standard 16" joist is used. (It is beyond the scope of this book to provide a one-to-one analysis of all members. The stiffness ratio is an expression of the maximum deflection allowed in a given span. L is the length in inches and the denominator is determined by building codes. For example, a ratio of L/360 indicates span of 30' would allow for a deflection of 1". L/240 would be $1^1/_2$" while L/180 would be 2".)

Figure 3-6 Wood-I-Joists. *(Alpine Structures)*

The Wood-I-Joists are prefabricated with deeper cross sections to make not only greater clear spans possible but economical. Deeper dimensional lumber is available but is cost prohibitive in a typical residential project. Wood-I-Joists are also manufactured with a stiffness ratio of L/480 (a deflection of $^1/_2$" over a 30' span), thereby providing a sturdier and stiffer floor that is less prone to squeaking and "bouncing." These stiffness ratios can be substantially improved by other factors. Reducing joist spacing, increasing subfloor thickness, gluing the subfloor prior to mechanical attachment, and gluing of the tongue-and-groove joint all contribute to a superior and stiffer floor system.

Although the actual stiffness ratio specified will be decided by the architect or builder, one rule of thumb is to use L/360 for spans up to 15' and L/480 for spans between 15' and 30'.[5]

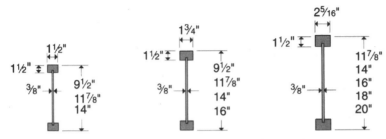

Figure 3-7 Wood-I-Joist depths. *(Boise Cascade)*

Their greater load carrying capacity allows for greater spacing between the joist. Various depths are available from $9^1/4$" to 24" and may vary depending on the manufacturer. One manufacturer's joist sizes are shown below (Fig. 3-7). Typical joist spacing for floors can vary from 12" o/c to 24" o/c for standard layouts. Although typical joist spans may run to 36" in length (16" joist, 40-psf live load, 10-psf dead load, L/360, 12" o/c) lengths are available by all manufacturers to 60'-0", and some manufacturers offer lengths up to 80'-0".

Wood-I-Joists are segregated into "series," which designate the structural properties of each joist. The dimensional difference is the width of the top and bottom flange or in some products, a different material composition altogether.

Most manufacturers provide engineering services and software at no charge. This is usually available to a builder when he or she is converting a dimensional lumber framing plan to one using Wood-I-Joists. It is far more prudent to design the residence with the early involvement of the engineer in order to fully realize the product's superior spanning capabilities and design advantages. One contractor has pointed out another advantage of Wood-I-Joists. "We've found that the more complicated the house, the easier it is to frame with engineered lumber."[6] Most building professionals, architects, engineers, and contractors alike are able to size members by using the simplified span tables and product literature available from the manufacturer. It is important to note that presently each manufacturer has its own proprietary nomenclature. One should not assume joists from different manufacturers are interchangeable. This is a temporary inconvenience, since The Engineered Wood Association is formulating a universal system of member nomenclature that will make interchangeability and product verification by building code officials easier.

It is easy to see that this creates a building element which is strong, more uniform than solid sawn joints, structurally consistent, and straighter.   Wood-I-Joists are manufactured with no camber (bow at the top), so there is no chance of crown down or upside-down installation. This also means the builder does not have to inspect each piece of lumber prior to installation.

Wood-I-Joists are designed to allow ductwork, piping, and wiring to penetrate the web of the joist (Figs. 3-8 and 3-9). Generally speaking, holes that remove the web completely must be located in the center third of the span. Holes this large are impossible with a solid sawn-wood joist.

Up to a 1-1/2" diameter hole allowed anywhere in the web. Closest spacing 1'-0" o.c.

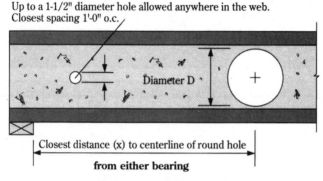

Closest distance (x) to centerline of round hole
from either bearing

Figure 3-8   Web cutouts.   *(Louisiana Pacific)*

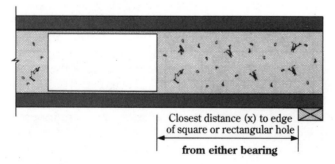

Closest distance (x) to edge of square or rectangular hole
from either bearing

Figure 3-9   Web cutouts.   *(Louisiana Pacific)*

Wood-I-Joists weigh less than solid sawn joists, even up to half the weight of a comparable-sized kiln-dried lumber member. This means Wood-I-Joists are easier to install, which saves construction cost and time. For example, a 40' Wood-I-Joist can be easily lifted by one person. (It is important to note that Wood-I-Joists over 24' should be carried by two people.)   It is also important to note that care needs to exhibited when handling Wood-I-Joists. They are more prone to damage than solid lumber. Especially vulnerable are the flanges, which can be damaged if dropped during delivery on a rocky surface. According to one contractor, "a $1/2$" chip out of a 2 × 12 will not affect its performance but a similar chip could be disastrous for a Wood-I-Joist...We've seen flanges pop off the webs when they're dumped by a delivery truck."[7] Upon delivery, joists should be laid flat in order to avoid twisting. The apparent fragility of Wood-I-Joists is inherent in an efficient construction product that is specifically designed for a particular purpose. The "lightness" of the product is due to the fact that all redundant structural properties are removed, making the product an efficient design intended for a specific application. The only requirement of the builder, in order to "reap the benefits" of such a product, is to be conscious of the handling requirements.

Wood-I-Joists may be hung by nailing (when supported on a continuous top plate) or supported by joist hangers (Figs. 3-10 through 3-15).   Specific nailing requirements must be followed, so always consult the manufacturer's literature and details.

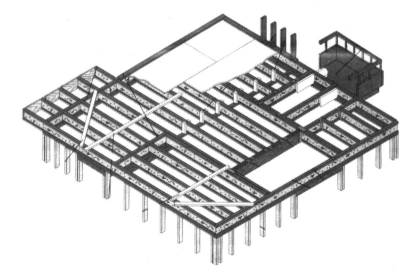

Figure 3-10 Typical floor layout. *(Louisiana Pacific)*

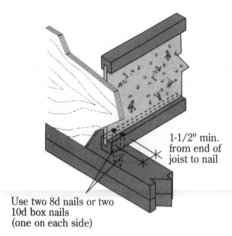

1-1/2" min. from end of joist to nail

Use two 8d nails or two
10d box nails
(one on each side)

Figure 3-11   Joist nailing.   *(Louisiana Pacific)*

One manufacturer's alternative to solid lumber is the "engineered header." The standard $3^{1}/_{2}$" wide member is designed to sit flush in a 2 × 4 wall without additional plywood spacers or blocking (as necessary in a typical 2x header). The design is a typical Wood-I-Joist with OSB sheathing attached for the full length from top chord to bottom chord (Fig. 3-16).

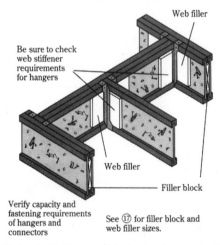

Web filler

Be sure to check
web stiffener
requirements
for hangers

Web filler

Filler block

Verify capacity and
fastening requirements
of hangers and
connectors

See ⑰ for filler block and
web filler sizes.

Figure 3-12   Hanger detail.   *(Louisiana Pacific)*

The disadvantages of a Wood-I-Joist system appear to be relatively minor. Wood-I-Joists are made of wood and are therefore combustible. Having less mass than traditional sawn lumber, they will be consumed by fire more rapidly. One- and two-hour fire ratings are available when implemented as a system of components involving gypsum board, mineral wool, and furring channels. (This should be verified with Underwriters' Laboratories (UL) or other accepted testing agencies.) This property of having less mass may also decrease sound attenuation when compared to solid sawn lumber. This is not always an issue with homeowners but should be taken into consideration when the building type involves multiple floored tenants. The necessary sound attenuation can be achieved by the addition of furring channels and sound attenuation blankets. The glue used in fabrication may also be dangerous when ignited. It is not known if all glues used by various manufacturers do not produce significant outgassing.

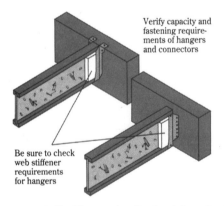

Figure 3-13   Hanger detail. *(Louisiana Pacific)*

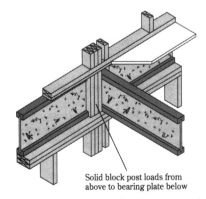

Figure 3-14   Post loads. *(Louisiana Pacific)*

Other disadvantages would be better classified as "inconveniences," including the hand nailing required of joist hangers (in lieu of power nailers), and the skill required in accurately and cleanly cutting an "I" profile to its correct length. Framers may complain initially, but with a little practice and skill, these complaints quickly subside.

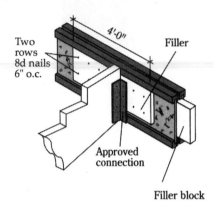

Two rows 8d nails 6" o.c.

4'-0"

Filler

Approved connection

Filler block

Figure 3-15   Stair hanger.   *(Louisiana Pacific)*

Rim Board

The perimeter of the Wood-I-Joists are closed off with a rim board (Figs. 3-17 and 3-18). The rim board ties together all floor joists, acting as an integral component for lateral bracing and wall support in the Wood-I-Joist system. Also referred to as a band joist or edge banding, the rim board has traditionally been of solid lumber but can also be made of plywood, glued laminated timber, or laminated veneer lumber. Engineered rim boards made of OSB are typically $3/4$" to 1" thick (depending upon the manufacturer), have less vertical shrinkage than green lumber and have a flat surface for easy nailing. OSB rim boards, when provided by the Wood-I-Joist manufacturer, are precision cut to match the joist height, eliminating time involved to rip plywood rim boards.[8] Manufactured in lengths up to 24', less joints generally means faster erection time of the Wood-I-Joist system. (Verify the allowable rim board thickness with the local building official or applicable agency.)

The flat surface also allows for easy fastening for siding or other exterior materials. As a strong, cost-effective complement to the engineered floor system, OSB rim boards are manufactured using fast-growing trees, a renewable resource that leaves our old-growth forests for future generations to enjoy.

Figure 3-16   Engineered header. *(Alpine Structures)*

Application

Although manufacturer's literature and instructions must be adhered to when installing Wood-I-Joists, the following recommendations will provide general guidelines for the product's handling and installation:

As stated previously, the Wood-I-Joist is an engineered product for the specific task of serving as a floor or roof structure. Care must be taken upon its delivery to the project site. Keep joists dry, and store on a hard, level surface. Don't use joists for unintended purposes such as ramp or planks.

Wood-I-Joist flanges must not be cut, drilled, or notched. Concentrated loads should be applied to the upper surface of the top flange only, not suspended from the bottom flange.

The high load capacity of OSB rim boards means squash blocks are unnecessary on most multi-story applications. (It is still prudent to install squash blocks or at least verify the specific application with an engineer even though the manufacturers do not require it (Figs. 3-19 and 3-20). Squash blocks are made from 2× lumber. Mounted flat against the top and bottom chords, the squash blocks are cut $1/16$" higher than the top chord in order to transfer most of the load imposed on the joist. Typical squash block locations include, but are not limited to, exterior walls, load-bearing walls at mudsills, and beneath beam-carrying posts.

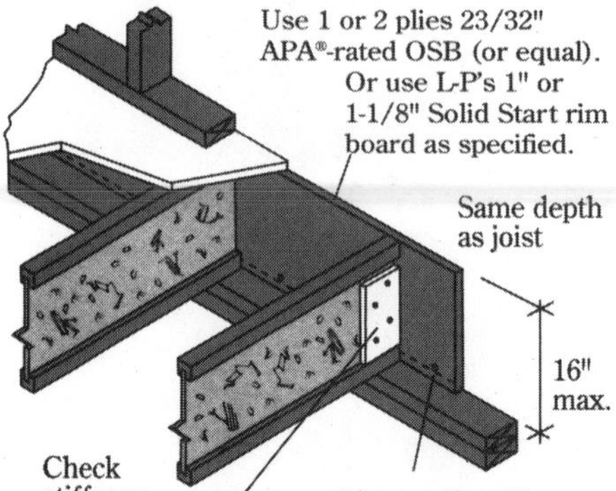

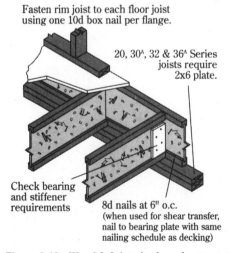

Fasten rim joist to each floor joist using one 8d nail per flange.

Use 1 or 2 plies 23/32" APA®-rated OSB (or equal). Or use L-P's 1" or 1-1/8" Solid Start rim board as specified.

Same depth as joist

16" max.

Check stiffener requirements

8d toe nail at 6" o.c. nailed from outside of building

Figure 3-17 OSB rim board. *(Louisiana Pacific)*

Fasten rim joist to each floor joist using one 10d box nail per flange.

20, 30ᴬ, 32 & 36ᴬ Series joists require 2x6 plate.

Check bearing and stiffener requirements

8d nails at 6" o.c. (when used for shear transfer, nail to bearing plate with same nailing schedule as decking)

Figure 3-18 Wood-I-Joist rim board. *(Louisiana Pacific)*

Web stiffeners are also necessary in certain applications. Typically cut $^1/_8$" shorter than the web height (so as not to separate the flange from the web) web stiffeners are placed in areas where concentrated loads are applied, especially with taller Wood-I-Joists.

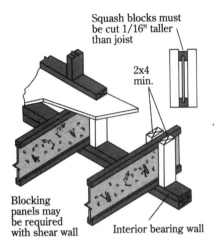

Squash blocks must be cut 1/16" taller than joist

2x4 min.

Blocking panels may be required with shear wall

Interior bearing wall

Load bearing walls must be aligned or stacked

Figure 3-19 Squash blocks. *(Louisiana Pacific)*

The proper sequencing required after joist placement (until the sheathing is attached to the joists) may require temporary bracing to prevent the joists from twisting. Use at least 1 × 4 bracing members nailed to each joist with two 8d nails, keeping the bracing parallel and approximately 8'-0" apart. Long pieces, not short blocks, should be used, lapping the ends to keep a continuous line of bracing. To prevent endwise movement of the continuous 1 × 4 lines of bracing, anchor them into a stable end wall or area braced by sheathing or diagonal bracing.

Use particular care removing temporary bracing when applying sheathing. Remove the bracing as the sheathing is attached. All rim joist, blocking panels, connections, and temporary bracing must be installed before erectors are allowed on the structure. No loads other than the weight of the erectors are to be imposed on the structure before it is permanently sheathed. After sheathing, do not overload joists with construction materials exceeding design loads.

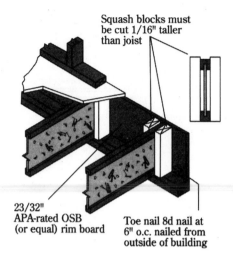

Squash blocks must
be cut 1/16" taller
than joist

23/32"
APA-rated OSB
(or equal) rim board

Toe nail 8d nail at
6" o.c. nailed from
outside of building

Figure 3-20 Squash blocks. *(Louisiana Pacific)*

LAMINATED BEAMS

Engineered wood is not relegated to smaller joist members. Beams, whether glulam (glued laminated timber), PSL (parallel-strand lumber), LSL (laminated-strand lumber) or LVL (laminated veneer lumber) are used where solid dimensional lumber beams would normally be placed. Engineered wood beams make residential framing faster and less costly. The beams are consistent dimensionally, possess exceptional workability, and exhibit strength far exceeding that of conventional lumber.

Glued laminated timber beams (Fig. 3-21) are made by gluing together horizontal pieces of solid dimensional lumber, typically $1^1/_2$" thick. Glulams can be manufactured to meet a range of design stresses with the strongest laminated lumber on the bottom and top of the beam where the greatest tensile and compressive stresses occur. The lumber is used more efficiently by placing the highest-grade lumber in zones that have the maximum stress and lesser-quality lumber in lower-stressed zones.

Glulams are available in custom and stock sizes. Stock beams are manufactured in commonly specified depths and cut to length when the specific beam is ordered. These depths range from $3^1/_8$" to $6^3/_4$" but are available in virtually any size.

Glulams can be manufactured in straight or curved sections. Many applications leave the Glulam beam exposed for aesthetic purposes. PSL beams are made from strands of wood glued together into long, wide members. LVL is a layered composite of wood veneers and adhesive, not unlike plywood. The grain of each ply, however, runs in the long direction and is commonly used as beams, headers, and flanges for Wood-I-Joists. The LVL is the most common and will be referenced in this text.

Figure 3-21 Glued laminated timber. *(APA/EWS)*

LVL (Fig. 3-22) is manufactured to be thicker, wider, and longer than solid sawn lumber beams. Using ultrasonic veneer grading and selection, most of the flaws common in solid sawn lumber (twisting, splitting and checking) have been removed or dispersed. Job site performance is increased since the previously unaccountable time of sorting out the bad members is eliminated. LVLs will not shrink or distort because any tendencies of the veneers to distort will be counteracted by the opposing tendencies of the adjacent veneers.

Figure 3-22 Laminated veneer lumber. *(Louisiana Pacific)*

Sizes vary from manufacturer to manufacturer, but sizes up to 7" thick by 66' long are readily available (Fig. 3-23). Joist hangers are used to connect these beams to other beams and columns (Figs. 3-24 through 3-29).

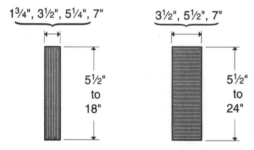

Figure 3-23 LVL sizes. *(Boise Cascade)*

Laminated beams can be used in an exposed application. Since laminated beams are very attractive, they can be stained or painted. Although LVLs are typically constructed of a series of vertical plies, one manufacturer provides an LVL beam constructed of horizontal plies, priced competitively with other LVL products. The unique horizontal grain is an aesthetic alternative while relying on the structural advantage of LVL construction. (LVL is also available as an exterior wood trim product. The exterior face is a phenolic-based MDO (medium density overlay)).

OPEN-WEB TRUSSES

Open-web trusses are an alternative form of floor structure to the Wood-I-Joist system. Also called flat trusses, the most common design consists of 2 × 4 chords and webs with steel plate connectors. These prefabricated trusses are engineered for specific applications and are delivered to the site ready for installation. Although often set in place with a crane, these

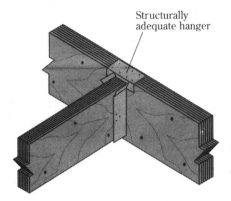

Structurally
adequate hanger

Hanger must apply load equally to
each ply or special design required.

Figure 3-24 LVL-to-beam connection. *(Louisiana Pacific)*

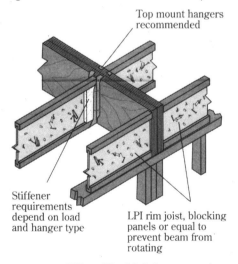

Top mount hangers
recommended

Stiffener
requirements
depend on load
and hanger type

LPI rim joist, blocking
panels or equal to
prevent beam from
rotating

Figure 3-25 LVL to Wood-I-Joist connection. *(Louisiana Pacific)*

Simpson GLB
Kant-Sag LBS or
equal seat.

NOTE: Protect wood from contact
with concrete as required by code.

Figure 3-26 LVL-to-concrete connection. *(Louisiana Pacific)*

Framing details such as joists and sheathing
must be provided to prevent beam from
twisting or rotating at support.

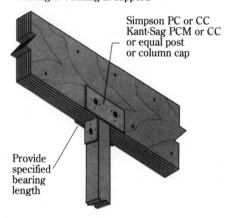

Simpson PC or CC
Kant-Sag PCM or CC
or equal post
or column cap

Provide
specified
bearing
length

Figure 3-27 LVL on wood column. *(Louisiana Pacific)*

lightweight structural members can be easily lifted in place
without mechanical assistance. The wood truss has dominated
the residential market during the previous decades since the
invention of the first metal truss connector plate in Florida in
1952.[9] A new hybrid truss is quickly gaining in popularity in
multi-family residential and commercial applications and could
serve as a structural alternative in larger residential projects.

Trus-Joist MacMillan invented the composite wood and
steel open-web truss in 1960. This capitalized on the

combination of the two materials' lightweight and efficient resources. They combined the workability of wood with the strength of tubular steel (Fig. 3-30). That credo continues today with an entire series of open-web trusses to meet the needs of light commercial construction. The web of the truss can take on variety of configurations and profiles based on the specific application.   The increased flexibility allowed by open web trusses allows for pipes, ductwork, sprinkler systems or other

Framing details such as joists and sheathing must be provided to prevent beam from twisting or rotating at support.

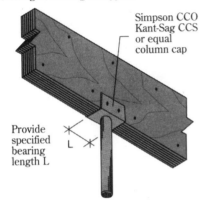

Simpson CCO
Kant-Sag CCS
or equal
column cap

Provide
specified
bearing
length L

Figure 3-28 LVL on steel post. *(Louisiana Pacific)*

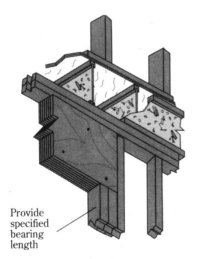

Provide
specified
bearing
length

Figure 3-29 LVL header. *(Louisiana Pacific)*

Figure 3-30 Open-web trusses. *(Trus-Joist MacMillan)*

Figure 3-31 Mechanical run in open-web trusses. *(Trus-Joist MacMillan)*

services to be hung or run within the webbing of the truss (Fig. 31). The most common design for residential applications has top and bottom chords of $1^{1}/_{2}$" × $3^{1}/_{2}$" machine stress-rated lumber or LVL. The webs are 1" or $1^{1}/_{8}$" diameter tubular steel members. The minimum depth at the wall bearing is 14" and increases to a maximum depth of 50", depending upon the span (Fig. 3-32).

Figure 3-32 Open-web truss bearing. *(Trus-Joist MacMillan)*

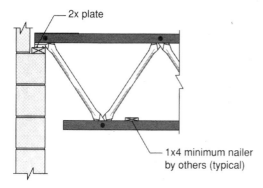

Figure 3-33 Open-web truss bearing. *(Trus-Joist MacMillan)*

Sound reverberation is a minor concern over the heavier mass properties of solid lumber but can easily be neutralized by using sound-absorptive materials, such as loose-fill insulation, placed in the floor space. Carpeting and underlayment can also contribute to the sound-dampening properties of the floor system.

Pound for pound, these open-web trusses are among the strongest structural members produced. They are strong, lightweight, stable, nailable, and easy to install. They cover a range of spans, from medium to exceptionally long. Every open-web truss is custom manufactured precisely to the specifications of the individual job[10].

JOIST HANGERS AND CONNECTORS

Joist hangers and connectors are engineered metal fabrications used to connect and support joists, trusses, rafters, and beams to the appropriate structural components in creating an integrated floor, roof and wall system.

Joist hangers are designed for support of solid dimensional lumber or engineered wood products (Wood-I-Joists, LVLs, Glulams, etc.). Many different joist hangers are available to allow for the most cost-effective solution.

There basically two types of hangers, face mount and top flange. Face mount hangers transfer the load from the joist into the support (i.e., beam, etc.) through shear in the nails driven through the face of the hanger. Face mount hangers typically accommodate lighter allowable loads than top flange hangers but can be more adaptable in their application. Top flange hangers support the joist through bearing of a top flange or tabs on the top of the supporting member. Top flange hangers can have higher allowable loads while using fewer fasteners than face mount hangers. Top flange hangers must be correctly chosen since the hanger must be the same exact height as the supported member.

Most hangers and other connectors are made from galvanized steel. Due to the corrosive environments in which many projects are located, alternative finishes are usually available. Some products can be hot-dip galvanized after fabrication to provide additional environmental protection, but hot-dip galvanized fasteners must also be used. One manufacturer provides a triple zinc coating as a superior alternative to normal galvanizing. Many connectors are also available in stainless steel. For the best protection against harsh enviroments, stainless steel connectors and stainless steel fasteners should be used.

Hangers are available for almost any application. Joists to wood, joists to masonry, beam to beam, wood or steel post to beam, even sloped joist connectors are all standard applications. Column bases, bridging, plywood clips, metal strapping and multiple rafter hip connectors are also available (Figs. 3-34 through 3-37). Providing a better connection between like and

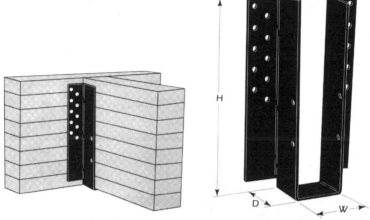

Figure 3-34   Glulam face mount hangers. *(United Steel Products)*

unlike members, these connectors protect the integrity of the nailed member as well as guarantee proper engineering minimums for connections have been implemented.

A real concern to all is how to prevent damage to wood construction when high wind loads exist. In examination of hangers and connectors used for roof applications, the most important factor is uplift and its influence on the structure. If an engineered truss system is used for the roof, the uplift can be determined from the truss design certificates. The most common uplift design load can be obtained from the Truss Industry's

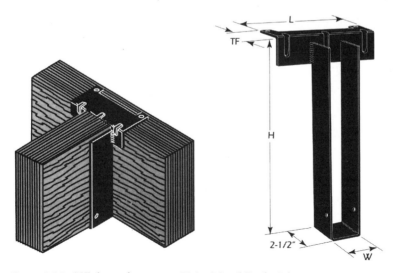

Figure 3-35   LVL beam hangers. *(United Steel Products)*

tables, which calculate the uplift values for the engineering products. Another source of design criteria is from engineers and architects who calculate and design the structures for a variety of applications. One document that can be used to determine the load specifications, which uses the design windspeed of a specific area or region, is the SBCCI "Standard for Hurricane Resistant Residential Construction, SSTD-1096."

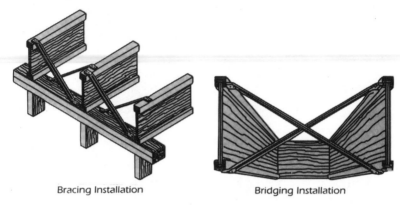

Bracing Installation   Bridging Installation

Figure 3-36 Bracing and bridging. *(United Steel Products)*

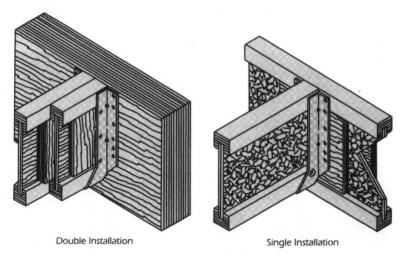

Double Installation   Single Installation

Figure 3-37 Wood-I-Joist hangers. *(United Steel Products)*

The basic principle when analyzing the load requirements is that all loads must be transferred from the top of the structure down to the foundation to properly protect against the forces of wind. Each joint and connection along the way will require a connector or fastener to resist the loads created by wind action.

Strict adherence to manufacturers' instruction is mandatory when using connectors. Incorrect fastener quantity, size, type, material, or finish may cause the connection to fail. As mentioned earlier, nail guns can be used for attaching connectors but are a little more difficult to use than hammers. Pneumatic or powder-actuated fasteners may deflect and injure the operator.[11] Common nailing errors can severely compromise the strength of Wood-I-Joists. When a nail is driven through the hanger into the bottom flange parallel to the glue lines, separation of veneers can occur. If the nails used are too long, splitting of the bottom flange can occur or even raise the Wood-I-Joist off the seat. This can result in uneven surfaces and squeaky floors, along with reduced allowable loads.[12]

Squeaky floors can also point to joist hangers as the culprit. Proper nailing is essential but one contractor adds extra insurance by squirting a bead of construction adhesive in the seat of the joist hanger prior to setting of the joist.[13] Some manufacturers even provide a hole in the bottom of the joist hanger so that a screw can be used to pull the joist tight into the hanger.

SUBFLOOR SHEATHING

For years, when someone spoke of floor sheathing, the first product that came to mind was plywood, a cross-laminated veneer. Portland Manufacturing Company made the first structural plywood from western woods in 1905. This plywood, like all structural plywood made until the mid 1930s, was bonded with nonwaterproof blood and soybean glue. Delaminations were routine until waterproof synthetic resins were developed during World War II. The technical fix for delamination was inspired by the housing boom of the 1950s. In the late 1960s, advances in adhesive technology brought southern pine plywood to residential builders. Today, southern pine plywood accounts for about half of all structural plywood sold. [14]

Moving into the 21st century, a number of "new" products have come and gone, but one product in particular appears to have found its place in construction, oriented-strand board (or OSB). MacMillan Bloedel opened the first viable waferboard facility at Hudson Bay, Saskatchewan, in 1963.

Aspenite, the first generation waferboard (called chipboard by many builders), was manufactured from the abundant supply of aspen found in the region. Technology involving the random alignment and homogeneous composition of wood-fiber in waferboard soon gave way to the development of structurally superior oriented strandboard. Elmendorf Manufacturing Company made the first OSB in Clairmont, New Hampshire, just 14 years ago.[15]

Although often confused with inferior, nonstructural products such as particleboard (made from wood particles and bonded with resins, used for furniture and shelving), fiberboard (made from wood fibers and bonded with a steam-heated press, used for doors, moldings and cabinets), pressed board, flakeboard, and other composition-type products, OSB is an engineered product designed for structural applications in residential and nonresidential buildings. Panels manufactured under American Plywood Association (APA) performance standards are rated for three end uses: single-layer flooring (APA-rated Sturd-I-Floor), exterior siding (APA-rated siding), and sheathing for floors, walls and roofs (APA-rated sheathing). Although wall and roof sheathing applications will be discussed elsewhere in this book, subflooring will be addressed here.

Unlike plywood, which is made of thin veneers glued in layers with the grain of adjacent layers at right angles, OSB panels are made from compressed strands of wood bonded by a waterproof phenolic resin (Fig. 3-38). Two way strength is obtained by orienting the direction of the strands in alternating layers running perpendicular to each other. The panels are stronger lengthwise due to the long axis orientation of the outer

Figure 3-38 Oriented-strand board. *(APA/EWA)*

face strands. OSB panels are dimensionally stable and possess no core voids like regular plywood.

Performance is similar in many other ways, but there are also differences in the service provided by OSB and plywood. OSB is perhaps 50 strands thick, so its characteristics are averaged out over many more "layers" than plywood. OSB is consistently stiff. Plywood has a broader range of variability. During the manufacturing process, plywood veneers are randomly selected and stacked up into panels. You may get four veneers of earlywood stacked above one veneer of latewood. All wood products expand when they get wet. When OSB is exposed to wet conditions, it expands faster around the perimeter of the panel than it does in the middle. Swollen edges of OSB panels can telegraph through thin coverings like asphalt roof shingles. Dry storage, proper installation, coating panel edges, adequate roof ventilation, and application of a warm-side vapor barrier will help prevent this problem.[16]

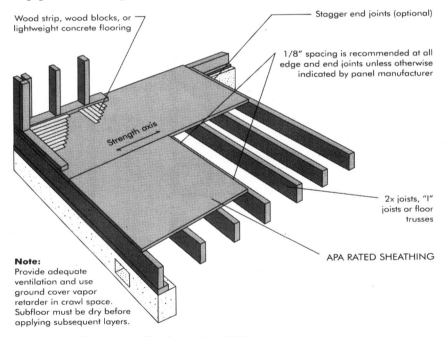

Figure 3-39 APA panel subflooring. *(APA/EWA)*

OSB responds more slowly to changes in relative humidity and exposure to liquid water. It takes longer for water to soak OSB, but conversely, once water gets into OSB, it is very slow to leave. Plywood actually gets saturated much faster than

OSB, but it is not prone to edge swelling and it dries out much more quickly.[17]

OSB is stronger than plywood in shear. Shear values, through its thickness, are about 2 times greater than plywood. (This is one of the reasons OSB is used for webs of Wood-I-Joists.[18]

APA panel subflooring (APA-rated sheathing) is a popular choice for residential flooring applications (Fig. 3-39). APA plywood underlayment is applied over the subfloor, providing a dimensionally stable system which will eliminate excessive swelling and buckling or humps around nails. Although a two-part floor assembly is sufficient, a superior product, designed especially for subflooring, is now available.

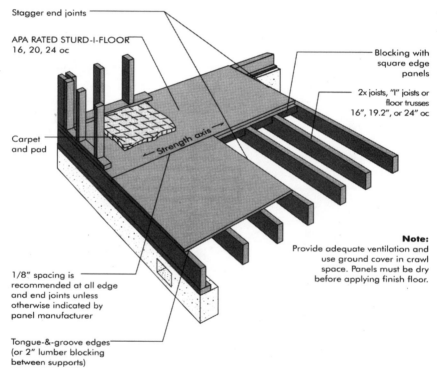

Stagger end joints

APA RATED STURD-I-FLOOR
16, 20, 24 oc

Blocking with square edge panels

2x joists, "I" joists or floor trusses
16", 19.2", or 24" oc

Carpet and pad

Strength axis

Note:
Provide adequate ventilation and use ground cover in crawl space. Panels must be dry before applying finish floor.

1/8" spacing is recommended at all edge and end joints unless otherwise indicated by panel manufacturer

Tongue-&-groove edges (or 2" lumber blocking between supports)

Figure 3-40 APA-rated Sturd-I-Floor. *(APA/EWA)*

The third type of panel, referred to as a composite panel, is one in which veneer faces are bonded to wood strand cores. This panel type combines subflooring and underlayment in a single sheet. APA-rated Sturd-I-Floor is a span-rated APA proprietary product designed specifically for use in single-layer floor construction beneath carpet and pad (Fig. 3-40). An additional thin layer of underlayment is recommended under tile, sheet flooring, or fully adhered carpet, so that finished floor levels are flush throughout. This added layer also restores a smooth surface over panels that may have been scuffed or roughened during construction, or over panels that may not have received a sufficiently sanded surface.

The product reportedly provides all of the proven cost-saving and performance benefits of combined subfloor-underlayment construction. It is relatively easy to use and specify because the maximum recommended spacing of floor joists is stamped on each panel (Fig. 3-41). These panels are designed to span floor joist spacings of 16", 20", 24", 32" and 48". (The panel application must be continuous over two or more spans with the long dimension or strength axis across supports.)

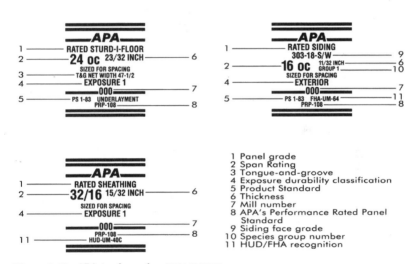

Figure 3-41 APA trademark. *(APA/EWA)*

STURD-I-FLOOR INSTALLATION

Glue nailing is highly recommended for Sturd-I-Floor panels (although panels may be nailed only.) The added strength of the glue bond creates a composite floor system between the joists and floor panels. Gluing not only increases floor stiffness, but also helps eliminate squeaks, bounce, nail-popping, and floor vibration.

The smooth panel faces and tongue-and-groove (T&G) edges should always be protected from damage prior to and during application. Install with smooth side up. If permanent exposure to the weather is required, exterior panels should be specified.

Veneer-faced Sturd-I-Floor with a "sanded face" is suitable for the direct application of resilient floor covering. All fasteners should be flush with or below surface of Sturd-I-Floor with "sanded face" just prior to installation of thin floor coverings (when floor members are dry). Glued T&G edges are recommended under thin floor coverings to assure snug joints.

Do not fill nail holes but fill any other damaged or open areas, such as splits, and sand all surface roughness. Some applications may require filling and sanding edge joints. (This may not be necessary under some carpet and structural flooring products. It is recommended to check with the flooring manufacturer.)

It is important to note that if the floor has become wet during construction, it should be allowed to dry before the application of the finish floor, including carpet, underlayment, hardwood flooring, ceramic tile, etc. After it is dry, the floor should be checked for flatness, especially at joints.

As mentioned in Chapter 1, building codes are but minimum standards for construction methods and materials. This reality is addressed by the development of the Code Plus Floor. The Code Plus Floor, constructed with APA-rated Sturd-I-Floor, provides extra strength and stability for the walls and roof.

Although very similar in application, the Code Plus Floor requirements are as follows. First of all, the floor span rating (as stamped on the panels) must be at least 24 for floor joist spacing up to 20" o/c, and 32 for joists spaced 24" o/c The floor panels must be installed with the APA Glued Floor System. Panels shall be fastened with 8d nails or other code-approved fasteners spaced 12 inches on all supports. (Nail size and spacing may vary depending on span and sheathing thickness.) Leave a $1/8$" space at all panel end and edge joints to allow for panel expansion. Panels shall be installed continuously over two or more spans with the long dimension or strength axis across supports.

In the event certain construction applications require a joist spacing greater than the typical 16" or 24", alternative Sturd-I-Floor assemblies are possible. For the 48" method, supports may also be 4× Glulams, lightweight steel beams, or floor trusses.

FIRE-RETARDANT-TREATED LUMBER

Most fire experts will agree that the first 10 minutes of a fire are the most critical for human safety. The materials that are initially ignited can either contribute to the growth of the fire or prevent it from spreading to other areas. Fire-retardant-treated lumber and plywood products, although mainly used in multifamily construction projects, are growing in popularity among single-family homeowners.

Fire-retardant treatments have little effect on the rate of heat transfer through the material. Instead, they significantly reduce any fuel contributing to a fire. How does this work? One manufacturer's explanation of the how a combustible material such as wood can be made virtually noncombustible is as follows: "When (the plywood or lumber) is exposed to fire, (it) reacts with the combustible gases and tars normally generated by wood and converts them to carbon char and harmless carbon dioxide and water. The build-up of carbon char acts as heat insulation, thus slowing down the rate at which the exposed piece of wood is reduced by fire."[19]

The National Fire Protection Association (NFPA) has published an extensive number of codes and standards that define installation, design, and composition standards for many products and materials. NFPA 703-Standard for Fire Retardant Impregnated Wood states: "Fire retardant treated wood shall be defined as any wood product which, when impregnated with chemicals by a pressure process...when tested in accordance with ASTM E84...show no evidence of significant progressive combustion when the test is continued for an additional 20 minute period."

These fire-retardant-treated lumber and plywood products are available for exterior or interior use and come with warranties of up to 40 years for roof applications. It is important to note that these are not fire-retardant coatings that are sprayed on but are actually chemicals impregnated into the product. One manufacturer states that use of their product generally results in a lowering of insurance premiums.[20]

Fire-retardant-treated lumber and plywood must have a flame spread rating of 25 or less. This constitutes a Class A rating. (Flame spread is a measure of how quickly fire will spread and develop. This is known as the ASTM (American Society for Testing and Materials) E84-Standard Test Method for Surface Burning Characteristics of Building Materials. For the testing comparison, untreated red oak lumber has a rating of 100, whereas a noncombustible asbestos cement board has a rating of 0. The higher the index rating, the greater the hazard. A Class I or Class A rating is any rating between 0 and 25.) Fire-retardant-treated lumber and plywood must also have a smoke development rating of not more than 450. (The smoke development index is a numerical quantity based on the standardized optical density of the smoke developed as a material burns.) Standards for fire retardants and fire-retardant-treated (FRT) wood are established by the American Wood-Preservers' Association (P17 for formulations, C20 for FRT lumber and C27 for FRT plywood.)

There are some limitations with regard to FRT lumber. First of all, the product's increased moisture absorption may cause some coatings, stains, and sealers to fail. Acrylic latex coatings and varnishes typically give the best results.[21] Grain raising, yellowing, or darkening of the wood may be an inherent disadvantage of FRT lumber, but since most applications are concealed by finish materials, this may not be an issue. FRT lumber should not be installed where it is in contact with the ground, exposed to precipitation, direct wetting, or regular condensation. Cutting, drilling, and light surface sanding are allowed; however, ripping and milling are not recommended.[22]

Fire-retardant treatment results in some reduction of the strength properties of the wood as compared to nontreated products. Reduction factors for mechanical properties should be obtained from the company providing the treating and redrying service.[23]

CONCLUSION

Although people's basic daily rituals have existed virtually unchanged since time began, technology remains the variable that improves and grounds those rituals in a particular time. Creating shelter is one such ritual and also the focus of this book. Our quest to improve our shelter, whether driven by economy or necessity, is largely determined by the technology available. To ignore new technologies is to deny ourselves the ability to create and improve the world we live in.

Engineered products and assemblies are now readily available, with engineered lumber becoming the recommended floor framing material of choice. Large solid sawn lumber will not only be expensive in the future, but availability is also in question. The advantages of engineered products are so numerous, the thought of using solid sawn lumber would be like using a horse and carriage in lieu of today's fuel-powered vehicles. Glued engineered wood products have less impact on the environment during the course of their manufacture and service life and come from a renewable natural resource. Engineered products are made from wood, but are able to use smaller trees which save our large older trees. New innovations continue to improve our safety, span greater distances, and enhance the value of our construction efforts. To ignore or fail to consider these ideas or products simply because they are new or unconventional will only be a step backward in time.

APPENDIX

Boise Cascade
PO Box 2400
White City, Oregon 97503-0400
1-800-232-0788

APA/The Engineered Wood Association
PO Box 11700
Tacoma, WA 98411-0700
(206) 565-6600
Fax: (206) 565-7265

Louisiana Pacific
111 SW Fifth Avenue
Portland, Oregon 97204-3601
1-800-999-9105

REFERENCES

1. *Fundamentals of Building Construction, Materials and Methods.* Edward Allen, John Wiley & Sons, NY, 1990, p. 129.
2. Ibid., p. 157
3. "Renegotiating the Lumber Agreement Should Be a Priority," Kent Colton, National Association of Home Builders, NAHB Website, 29 August, 1997.

4. "When Is a Log Stronger Than a Log?", Don Griffith, Canadian Wood Council, CWC Website, 29 August, 1997.
5. "A Proposed Rule of Thumb for Controlling Annoying Vibrations in Residential Floors," Wood Design Focus, Spring 1996, Frank E. Woeste, p. 23.
6. "Framing Floors with I-Joists," Rick Arnold and Mike Guertin, Fine Homebuilding, April/May, 1997, No. 108, p. 52.
7. Ibid., p. 53
8. "The Engineered Wood Association Design/Construction Guide," 1996, p. 23.
9. Metal Plate Connected Wood Truss Handbook, Wood Truss Council of America, Edward E. Callahan, P.E., Madison, WI, 1994, p. xi.
10. Trus-Joist MacMillan Manufacturer's literature, 1997.
11. Composite Wood Products Connectors, Simpson Strong Tie, 1996, p. 5.
12. Hardware for LPI Joists & Gang-Lam LVL Series Composite Wood, U.S. Steel Products Company, 1996, p. 8.
13. "Framing Floors with I-Joists," Rick Arnold and Mike Guertin, Fine Homebuilding, April/May, 1997, No. 108, p. 55.
14. "Choosing Between Oriented Strandboard and Plywood," University of Massachusetts at Amherst, Paul Fisette, 1997, 9/4/97.
15. Ibid.
16. Ibid.
17. Ibid.
18. Ibid.
19. DRICON Fire Retardant Treated Wood Reference Guide, Hickson Corporation, 1995, p. i.
20. HOOVER Treated Wood Products Catalog, p. 7.
21. DRICON, op. cit., p. 5.
22. Ibid., p. 14
23. Ibid., p. 3

4

Wall and Roof Structures

INTRODUCTION

"And since they were an imitative and teachable nature, they would daily point out to each other the results of their building, boasting of the novelties in it; and thus, with their natural gifts sharpened by emulation, their standards improved daily. At first they set up forked stakes connected by twigs and covered these walls with mud. Others made walls of lumps of dried mud, covering them with reeds and leaves to keep out the rain and the heat. Finding that such roofs could not stand the rain during the storms of winter, they built them with peaks daubed with mud, the roofs sloping and projecting so as to carry off the rain water."[1] So wrote Marcus Vitruvius Pollio, the Roman architect and engineer in his *Ten Books on Architecture* in the first century B.C. Like the origins of dwelling that he described, humans continue to experiment, experience, and modify structures to better suit their needs while governed or enhanced by the technologies available.

As demonstrated in Chapter 3, wood light frame construction has been the predominant structural system for residential applications over the past 100 years. Although the traditional systems may be adequate, newer, more efficient, stronger, and innovative systems and materials are available. Many of the "new" technologies and systems available for use in residential designs had previously been inspired by or used only for commercial projects. This may be analogous to the phenomenon of "high-brow" or "elite" art, music, and thought being reappropriated for the popular culture. In the course of this text, we discover the "high-brow" methods of panelized wall systems, structural steel, and precast concrete panels are now available in modified forms for residential applications. The three-wall construction systems to be discussed in this chapter are structural insulated panels, steel framing, and autoclaved aerated concrete.

STRUCTURAL INSULATED PANELS

Structural insulated panels, also known as SIPs, are emerging as a unique alternative building technology for residential building envelope construction. The basic building unit of this system is a sandwich-type panel typically made of two "skins" of wood structural sheathing with a foam core that combines the structural, wall, and roof sheathing with the insulation in a single construction step. (Other materials can be used as "skins" as discussed later in this chapter.) The system provides efficient solutions to such concerns as energy efficiency and dwindling natural resources while saving construction time and labor that results in cost savings to not only the contractor but the consumer as well.

SIP technology was first used in residential construction as early as 1952, when Alden B. Dow, architect and son of the founder of the Dow Chemical Company, began designing homes to be constructed of SIP. The first of these was built in Midland, Michigan, that year, using foam-core SIP for exterior walls, interior partitions, and roofs. They are still occupied today.

The energy crunch of the 1970s provided the opportunity for SIP manufacturers to gain additional market share, but it was not until the 1990s that the panelized system gained acceptance by forward-thinking builders and architects.

A study prepared for the Structural Insulated Panel Association (SIPA) revealed that SIP production in the United States in 1991 was 15 million ft^2, equivalent to all the walls and roofs in about 4000 homes. This rate is expected to grow to levels ranging from 50 to 112 million ft^2 by the year 2000, depending on the aggressiveness with which the industry markets its products.[2]

International markets also demonstrate the growing popularity of the use of SIP. "Opportunities overseas are enormous...All in all it appears that American-style materials are in. Builder John Kowalczyk (an Eastern Block developer) estimated potential demand in Eastern Europe at 10 million units. According to Aire Nesher, an Israeli architect and city planner, Israel will need 500,000 homes within the next five years."

Although product types vary in the industry, the common characteristic of all SIPs is two exterior skins adhered to a rigid plastic foam core (Fig. 4-1). The skin provides the tensile and compressive strength while the foam core provides the rigidity. This is analogous to the I-beam, in which the skins perform not unlike the flanges while the foam core corresponds with the web.

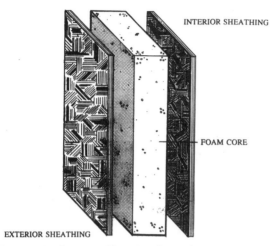

INTERIOR SHEATHING

FOAM CORE

EXTERIOR SHEATHING

Figure 4-1   Structural insulated panel. *(SIPA)*

Figure 4-2   Structural insulated wall panel. *(AFM Corporation)*

Panels are available in a variety of sizes and thickness depending on application requirements, from 2" to 12" thick, and in sizes from the standard 4' by 8' to 8' by 24'. This is ideal for their primary application: the exterior walls and roofs of low-rise residential and commercial buildings (Figs. 4-2 through Fig. 4-4).

The skins of a panel can be of the same or differing materials. The faces most commonly used are oriented-strand board (OSB), waferboard, plywood, sheet metal, cementitious fiberboard, and gypsum board. The rigid foam cores are composed of a variety of foam products depending on the proprietary product's manufacturer. These include the following:

- Expanded polystyrene (EPS) also known as beadboard
- Extruded polystyrene (XPS), commonly referred to as Green Board by Amoco or Styrofoam or Blue Board by Dow
- Polyurethane
- Polyisocyanurates, characterized by their yellowish color in foil-faced applications

Figure 4-3 Structural insulated panel. *(APA/EWA)*

EPS is most commonly used because of its low cost and simple manufacturing process, but EPS cores, with a lower R-value, must be made thicker to be equivalent to the higher insulation properties of other foam products. Nevertheless, foam products have better insulation per inch of thickness than fiberglass and better insulation at lower temperatures and higher humidity than fiberglass for decreased energy usage for heating. As a result, the U.S. Department of Energy and Environmental Protection Agency (see EPA/DOE Energy Star program) are both proponents of the use of SIP in construction.[3]

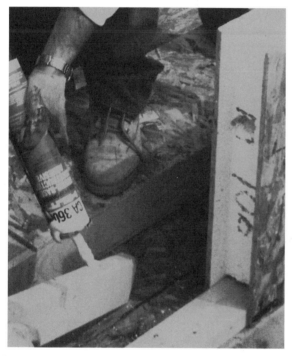

Figure 4-4   Structural insulated panel. *(APA/EWA)*

With the high insulation value and low infiltration, a SIP home can be cooled or heated with much smaller HVAC equipment and much less electrical energy. Consequently, the homeowner's electricity bill each month will be much less. The SIP home costs about 5 to 10 percent more initially, but this extra cost is quickly offset by savings in energy bills.[4] Studies have shown that building with SIP can result in homes that are up to 60 percent more efficient than site-built homes of comparable size. Wall panels can deliver R-values of 14 to 24, and roof R-values of up to 41 or more, depending on the thickness of the foam core and the manufacturer's system of fabrication.[5]

Panel shipping is economical within a 300- to 500-mile radius, although due to limited manufacturing production availability, most manufacturers indicate that 30 percent or more of their business is shipped 1000 or more miles away.

SIPs are also recognized for their added security benefits by providing a solid barrier to intruders and vandals. The design of this panel, with its two "skins" over a foam core, is far more resistant to punching or cutting through the all-too-popular thin foam wall.

Panel Manufacturing Process

SIPs are factory-fabricated under controlled conditions, usually subject to a continuous program for quality control and supervision.   Although manufacturing techniques vary among companies, two assembly processes are most prevalent: adhesive-bonding and foam-in-place.

The manufacturing process may vary slightly among manufacturers, but typically begins with an 8' × 24' OSB panel on a trolley. Six foam sheets, each measuring 4' × 8', are then placed on the OSB skin. After the structural-grade adhesive is applied, the rigid foam core is placed on top of a clean sheet of facing material and the second panel (or skin) is positioned on the opposite side of the insulation core, completing the sandwich. Pressure is applied to the newly formed panel for some duration. This is done with either an ingenous press (a vacuum on the bottom side and atmospheric pressure on the top) or a hydraulic press.   Panels are then set aside until the adhesive has completely cured, about 24 hours.

With the foam-in-place method, the facing boards are held apart by panel framing or specially made spacers. The chemical components of the foam core, together with a blowing agent, are combined and forced between the braced skins. The expanded insulation material forms a bond with the facing material without the use of any adhesives.

Material Properties

SIPs are capable of sustaining loads typically imposed on walls, floors, roofs, and other load-bearing elements.   They are essentially stressed skin panels; the cores of rigid plastic foam provide shear strength, and the exterior skins of structural materials provide tensile and compressive strength. A panel's structural composition can be compared to that of an I-beam. The panel skins are analogous to the flanges of an I-beam, while the foam core is comparable to its web. The complete assembly, with exterior and interior faces properly laminated to the foam core, allows for a system that is structurally superior to conventional stud frame structures (Fig. 4-5).

Figure 4-5   Panel strength. *(FischerSIPS)*

Axial Loading

Panels used for exterior walls are load-bearing and can be used to form the entire wall. They can also be applied to framing as non-structural exterior insulated cladding or as a curtain wall. A load-bearing wall panel has superior axial load-bearing capacity; i.e., the strength to support vertical loads from the roof or floor above (Fig. 4-6). A conventional framed wall is designed to support these vertical loads only through its studs. The exterior sheathing, if plywood, provides no contribution because it must have gaps between sheets and is not continuous. Other forms of sheathing are also discounted for the same reason. On the other hand, the sheathing on SIPs can use all of its capacity to support vertical loads because buckling is prevented by the continuous reinforcement action of the foam core.

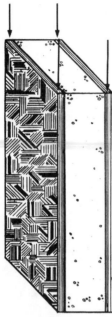

Figure 4-6 Vertical loading of SIPs. *(SIPA)*

Racking Resistance

The uniform, consistent composition of a SIP, with supportive sheathing on both sides of the core, is superior to a frame wall in racking resistance. The SIP sheathing is adhered to the foam core over the entirety of the panel and edges are fixed to splines, which results in the development of excellent racking resistance. This characteristic is an important attribute for resisting earthquake and hurricane forces.

Local Loads

SIPs exhibit other superior structural and strength characteristics. They are highly resistant to local loading. This is evident when one "thumps" a wall panel. The SIP will exhibit a uniform solid sound as opposed to a hollow sound between studs. This means that fasteners with proper anchors for railings, cabinets, fixtures, wall-mounted brackets, etc., can occur anywhere in a SIP wall, but only at studs or other reinforced locations in frame walls.

Buckling

A SIP wall has great resistance against buckling and bending when compared to equivalent conventional stud construction. This means that a taller wall can be built without increasing wall thickness, or that a wall can resist greater perpendicular loads from such forces as hurricanes.

Dimensional Stability

SIPs are virtually impervious to warping and shrinking, giving each panel excellent dimensional stability.

Fire Protection

The flammability of SIPs depends on the composition of the panel and the type of insulation used in the panel core. For example, EPS has a fire-retardant bead that is used in the manufacturing process which makes it self-extinguishing once the flame source has been removed. Building codes require installation of a thermal barrier, typically $1/2''$ gypsum wallboard, over the panels on the interior side for fire resistance.

Earthquake Resistance

SIPs have demonstrated resistance to seismic activity. One manufacturer has documentation of six homes which used its proprietary SIP that withstood the 7.2 magnitude earthquake in Kobe, Japan, in January 1995.[6]

Energy Efficiency

The foam plastic core of a SIP provides its insulation properties. Depending on the type of foam used (e.g., EPS, XPS, polyurethane, or isocyanurate), R-values are in the range of approximately 4 to 7 per inch of foam thickness. This results in superior energy performance characteristics in walls and roofs. For example, a $4^1/2''$-thick SIP wall is often used as a substitute for a 2 × 4 stud wall. (A SIP wall with $1/2''$ of drywall is 5" thick as opposed to the $4^1/2''$ overall thickness of a wood stud wall.) Although both have $3^1/2''$ of insulation, the SIP wall has insulation R-values in the range of 14 to 25, where as the stud wall with fiberglass or mineral wool only has R-value of 11 to 15.

The overall R-value of the stud wall must be downgraded to take into account the part of its area that is occupied by wood framing. This is anywhere between 15 to 18 percent of the wall which is uninsulated. The core of a SIP, which usually has no stiffeners between splines, is filled entirely with rigid foam. This means there is no thermal bridging. Moreover, when compared to stick-built structures, SIPs have fewer gaps, less settling or compression, less moisture absorption or dust saturation, and fewer cavities that permit convection or air circulation. All of these characteristics would reduce insulation performance if present in a wall system.

The results are evident in both quantified and empirical data. For example, the overall R-value of a conventional wall with 2×4 studs and $3^1/2$" of R-13 fiberglass, as indicated in the Thermal Envelope Compliance Guide to the Model Energy Code, is R-13.1. An equivalent SIP wall with $3^1/2$" of EPS foam (R-value = 17.5) is R-20.

As mentioned earlier, EPS is the most common panel core. A $4^1/2$" panel provides an R-value of R-14 to R-17, $6^1/2$" is R-22 to R-25, $8^1/4$"-thick panels are R-29 to R-36, $10^1/4$" are R-37 to R-45, and $12^1/4$" panels provide an R-value of 44. (The range of R-values is contingent on the specific manufacturer.) Needless to say, these panels also offer superior acoustical properties since noise transmission is diminished due to the wall's thickness.

Other nonspecific factors seem to influence the superior performance of SIPs when compared to stick-built wall assemblies with the same R-value. This may be due to the differences between foams and fibers in the degradation items that are not included in R-value calculations, like gaps, moisture, dust, and settling.

This was clearly illustrated in a recent field test conducted by the Florida Solar Energy Center (FSEC) under sponsorship of the U.S. Department of Energy. Two identical houses were built side by side in Louisville, Kentucky. They were built simultaneously by the same builder. One had conventional framing, the other was built with SIPs. However, wall and roof thicknesses were adjusted so that both had the same calculated R-values. Both houses were monitored for heat loss performance, and the SIP house dramatically outperformed the frame house. More importantly, efforts to forecast seasonal heating energy savings showed a 14 to 20 percent savings for the SIP house in Kentucky's climate. In the published report, the researchers stated that "there seem to be other factors, which remain unaccounted for, which cause the panel house to use less heat energy." Homeowners through out the United States are experiencing benefits though lower heating cost, reduced drafts and greater comfort.

Numerous SIPA members, for example, have cited testimonials from owners of SIP homes whose fuel bills have been as much as 40 to 60 percent below those of owners of conventional homes.

Foam Core Performance

It is widely recognized by energy performance specialists that urethane foam and XPS are subject to "thermal drift," or outgassing of blowing agents from foam cells over time. As a result, the R-value of these cores falls gradually until the thermal drift ceases to have an impact, and there is no further degradation. EPS cores are not subject to thermal drift and their R-value remains constant. Other foams, although higher in R-value that EPS, do drift over time. XPS cores have R-values of 5 per inch, listed widely for design values, indicating that this is the long-term constant after all thermal drift adjustments. Producers of other foams also quote R-values at the fully aged rate, but exact values need to be confirmed by designers.[7]

Unlike fiberglass batts, SIPs are resistant to moisture absorption. Although every attempt should be made to ensure that the panels are kept dry, SIPs will retain their R-value even if some moisture absorption does occur.

Wood frame walls are required to have vapor barriers installed "on the warm side" of fiberglass or mineral wool to prevent water vapor penetration, which may condense and degrade insulation performance. SIPs do not need vapor barriers at all because moisture does not materially affect performance.

In reality, except in such extreme climates as those in Florida and Alaska, it is difficult to identify "the warm side" of fibrous insulation. In Virginia, for example, the warm side is on the inside of the wall in the winter and on the outside in the summer. In Colorado, it can be on the inside at night and the outside by day. Whenever the vapor barrier is on the incorrect side, water vapor can penetrate and degrade the insulation. Because of nail holes, minute cracks, holes in framing for wiring, cutouts for receptacles, and other penetrations, it may be virtually impossible to prevent water vapor penetration of fibrous insulation; a concern nonexistent with SIPs.

This is also a critical issue with typical stick-built roofs. An airspace is required by code to protect the roof system. Due to the presence of water vapor, moisture can condense in the roof system. An airspace is not necessary in SIP roof construction since air vapor cannot enter the system. Another concern would be heat buildup in the roofing mass when asphalt shingles are used. This is a critical issue during the summer months, since heat can prematurely age some roofing products. Several major roof shingle manufacturers have approved the use of SIPs and are upholding their shingle warranties.

The foam core in a SIP extends uninterrupted in all directions throughout the entire panel, which can be as large as 8' by 24' in area. Breaks in the foam insulation occur less frequently, usually only at panel connections, which are few, or at openings. A frame wall has connections wherever the sheathing or drywall joints occur — every 4' or so. And, because of the nature of panel assembly, the foam is tightly packed against both sheathing faces and perimeter joints.

Air Infiltration

SIP form structural envelopes that are extremely tight against infiltration of air, a major source of energy loss. This is primarily due to the large uninterrupted areas of insulation in panels. In frame walls there are not only frequent joints between sheathing at studs (a weak link in envelope continuity), but there are nail or screw penetrations at every stud and on both sides of the wall. Moreover, common points of leakage such as electrical outlet vents and other envelope penetrations often are more difficult to seal in frame structures. Even if these penetrations are poorly sealed in a SIP structure, the insulation performance is not compromised by air circulation into the insulation cavity. This results in exceptionally tight SIP houses, when compared to framed structures, that exhibit very low levels of air infiltration with resultant increases in building energy efficiency and interior comfort.[8]

In the FSEC test in Kentucky, the SIP house proved to have a natural infiltration rate of 0.21 air changes per hour. This compares remarkably well with the average for new houses, in the range of 0.5 to 0.7. But more importantly, it is even lower than the recommended minimum of 0.35 (according to ASHRAE Standard 62-1989). Further, it may require a freshair ventilation system to provide make-up air, according to FSEC researchers. Large differences in air infiltration rates can have dramatic impacts on energy consumption. For example, a difference in air infiltration rates of 0.4 air changes per hour (0.21 versus 0.61) between a SIP house and a conventional house can represent fuel consumption savings in the range of $95.08 per year (in Texas) to $180.66 per year (in Minnesota) for a 1540-ft^2 house.[9]

Some people may question why one would build a very tight house and then install a fan to ventilate it. It is important to understand that relying on random leaks in the building and unknown pressure forces due to wind and temperature does not assure adequate ventilation. Thus it often leads to overventilation and high energy bills or underventilation with possible moisture and health concerns. Further, with leaky duct systems, there can be pressure imbalances which can cause heating systems to malfunction, resulting in health and safety problems.[10]

Environmental Attributes

SIP construction can be considered an engineered system. Innovation in the plastics and wood products industry is largely responsible for the rapid growth of new products now used in SIP: first plywood, and since 1980, oriented-strand board (OSB). The development of these products has a common goal — the need for conserving scarce resources and providing for the optimum use of the forest. SIP technology allows society to utilize forest products which are fast-growing and thus renewable. Panel manufacturers are able to remove the strength-reducing characteristics of wood (i.e., knots, splits) and produce superior engineered products. This turns moderate-cost, low-quality hardwoods and plantation thinnings into superior structural building components. As a result, a greater amount of the tree is utilized, and fewer wood fibers are used to produce a more consistent product than that used in conventional framing.

It is also important to note that the skins of SIP are made of OSB. This OSB is made with new-growth "junk" wood (aspen, jack pine, etc.) which can be regenerated in 5 to 10 years, rather than old-growth lumber such as redwood, ponderosa pine, or yellow pine, which are necessary in stick-frame construction. The panels use one-fourth as much wood as stick-framing methods. The EPS is manufactured without the use or production of CFCs or HCFCs. Since the insulation is bonded to the sheathing, there is no shrinkage of materials, saving time and money.

Quality-monitored manufacturing systems allow SIP producers to enhance the environment through the efficient use of valuable resources. Systematic design and production techniques significantly reduce process and construction site waste, requiring less landfill disposal, contributing to our country's resource and solid waste management goals. Designers can optimize the building design using SIP, resulting in more efficient utilization of construction materials.

SIP openings for windows and doors are often precut at the factory, reducing the expense of debris disposal from a jobsite. During panel manufacture, the foam-core materials are optimized for the particular application. Waste materials are limited through creative design and resource management. Sometimes leftover panel pieces and scraps are used for do-it-yourself retrofit applications or even dog houses. Often, unused foam which may be generated in the manufacturing process can be returned to the foam manufacturer who can reprocess it into appropriate applications or send it to a re-cycler for further reprocessing. Recycling is one method for handling waste. However, if recycling is not a satisfactory option given a site's geographical location, foam plastic can be safely landfilled. SIP foams are stable and will not biodegrade or create leachate or methane gas, the two major problems with all landfills. Construction materials are often used in "stable landfills" where the ground is later reclaimed for parks, stadiums, and other similar applications.[11]

In addition, SIP foams can be safely incinerated at regulated waste-to-energy facilities. Its energy value (greater than some soft coals) can provide a secondary fuel source for greater savings to the local utility company. EPS burns cleanly and produces almost no toxic ash. It does not require hazardous landfill disposal.

Noise pollution, the introduction into buildings of unwanted sound, is another form of environmental pollution that concerns many people. SIPs are excellent barriers to airborne sound penetration. This is due to the combination of their closed construction (no air movement in the panel wall) and extremely tight joint connections.

The issue of air quality is a concern to the public, regulating agencies, SIP producers, and foam manufacturers. EPS foam cores are produced using materials which have never had any adverse effect on the protective stratospheric ozone layer. All U.S. extruders of polystyrene foam switched to HCFC-142b by 1991, two years ahead of EPA deadlines for CFC phase-out. HCFC-142b is 90 percent less harmful to the ozone layer than its predecessor, CFC-12. Plastic industry members are working to exceed current and future air-quality standards though improvements in materials, processing, and control equipment.[12]

Roof Panels

The structural properties of SIPs are as beneficial in their roof applications as when they are used for walls. Flat or sloping roof panels can be standalone structures like wall panels, or can span between framing members like rafters. When they form a sloping roof, they naturally create a cathedral ceiling on the interior. In bending, the thickness of the foam core dictates and limits the spanning distance by virtue of its shear strength and bond to the sheathing. Similarly, the depth of rafters limits conventional roof spans.

Bending Strength

The horizontal loads imposed on buildings by earthquakes or extreme winds can be effectively resisted by the roof acting as a diaphragm. This two-dimensional structural continuity provides rigidity and stability to the building as well as creating an uninterrupted layer over supporting beams or bearing members. Because SIPs provide the bending strength necessary to withstand live (snow) and dead (roofing and equipment) loads, they usually can span freely from the ridge beam to exterior walls or between widely spaced beams or purlins. If greater rigidity is required, SIPs may be manufactured with increased bending strengths and reduced deflection.

In addition to wall and roof panels, SIPs can be used for floors and foundation walls when designed for these specialized applications.

Construction Techniques

Panels are used in construction either as "generic panels" or as parts of a "package unit." Generic panels are produced in varying thicknesses and different material combinations, but in standard sizes such as 4' × 8'. Each panel has explicit physical properties and strength characteristics and is typically sold to builders and others without the knowledge of the end application. This is similar to the sale of plywood panels to builders, who are informed of their strength and properties by the manufacturer's load tables and other standards. It is the builder's responsibility to cut the plywood panels and install them properly in buildings. (One manufacturer actually verifies the panel's engineering and application prior to delivery.)

A packaged unit is quite different. The plans of the entire building are analyzed and panels are specifically designed for each wall, roof, or other application. The manufacturer, often with CAD-generated shop drawings, can precut each panel to precise dimensions, with cutouts for window or door openings. Edges, angles, and all other complex configurations can be cut in the factory.

Then, all the panels required for an entire building are

packaged and shipped to the construction site. This could easily be a great distance, although it is likely that sources of panel production or distribution are locally available to most builders.

Panels are light in weight, generally under 4 lb/ft² of panel (4¹/₂" thick), and most walls are installed by hand (Fig. 4-7). Panels also may be lifted into position by crane, hoist or other equipment (Fig.4-8). Cranes are particularly useful in setting roof panels or lifting bundles of panels to upper floors. SIP walls and roofs are erected quickly and made weathertight very early in the construction sequence.

Construction time savings is evidenced when interior gypsum board or other finish is installed. The continuous nailing surface of the OSB skin allows the framer, drywall crew, etc., to be unconcerned with locating studs for screw or nailing.

The exterior finishes of walls applied to OSB or other sheathing can include the entire array of available materials (e.g., siding, brick, stucco). Sloping roof panels can be finished with shingles, tile, metal, or other materials.

The SIPs made by many if not all manufacturers are typically listed by independent testing agencies and are recognized by ICBO, SBCCI and BOCA. National and local building codes readily accept SIPs for their strength and energy performance properties, provided manufacturers can produce documentation to verify that panels meet structural and quality control requirements for their intended application. Builders and

Figure 4-7   SIP installation. *(AFM Corporation)*

Figure 4-8   SIP installation. *(AFM Corporation)*

designers should check with the manufacturer for specific compliance with applicable building codes.

Connections and Joints

One of the SIP's strength characteristics is the ability to provide superior building performance, partly because of tight connections at the joints between panels. Another strength is the connection between panels and such other adjacent structural elements such as beams, purlins, and columns.

There are several common wall panel connection methods used by SIP manufacturers today. A conventional approach involves fitting a 2 × 4, 2 × 6, or larger "two-by" (2×) spline, having the same depth as the foam core, between panels and securing it to the facing material (Fig. 4-9). Each panel edge is pre-routed to fit half of the width of each spline. The 2× splines use readily available lumber and provide stability. With the double 2× connection approach, the splines themselves bear the building loads (Fig. 4-10). This makes the system, with appropriate headers installed, a cohesive post-and-beam structure.

Panels are fastened together with wood or OSB splines and zinc galvanized screws or ring shank spikes. Dimensional lumber (2×) is used for top and bottom plates and for headers and sills. Panels are typically rated as header material up to 4'. Once a foundation is completed, a panelized shell structure can be completed in a matter of days. One erection contractor quotes 3

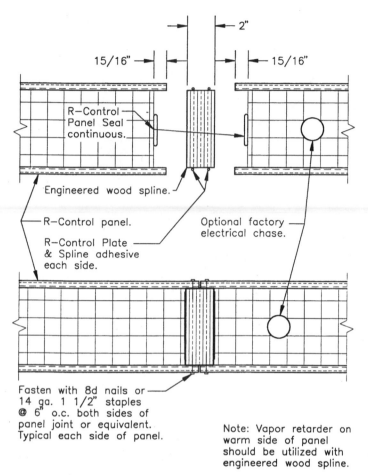

Figure 4-9 Section detail of engineered wood spline connection. *(AFM Corporation)*

days of erection time per 1000 ft^2 of building. A typical 1600-ft^2 home takes three to five days to assemble, including floor, walls, and roof.

The thin spline approach involves fitting two thin splines, (approximately $1/2$" to $3/4$" thick by 3" to 4" wide) laterally into prerouted grooves in each panel edge. Each spline is usually double-glued, stapled or nailed, and caulked at the seam between panels.

No single connection method has proven itself superior over others. Other approaches include using:

- A premanufactured, laminated, thermally broken spline.
- A premanufactured locking arm built into each panel.
- A roll-formed steel joint.

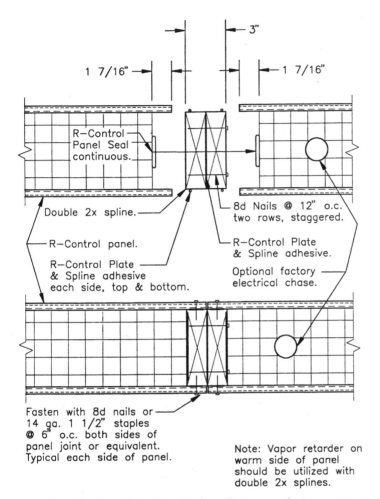

Figure 4-10 Section detail of double 2x spline connection. *(AFM Corporation)*

Individual panel manufacturers recommend the method that is most suitable for their system. For purposes of this discussion, 2x splines will be used.

SIPs are not damaged by rain, but long-term exposure to water could cause the panel edges to swell. After erection of the panels, the edges should be sanded down with a belt or disk sander.

Openings

Rough openings for doors and windows can be precut at the factory, easily cut on site, or accomplished by inserting a filler panel as required. Headers must be installed for window or door openings of more than 4' to 6' and can usually be eliminated for smaller openings. Since solid plating is installed around doors and windows, the normal technique consists of routing out approximately $1^1/_2$" of foam around the perimeter of all rough openings for a 2x framing installation. The framing works effectively as a nailing surface. When nailed to panels above rough openings, the framing let into the panel adds to the box beam effect (Fig. 4-11).

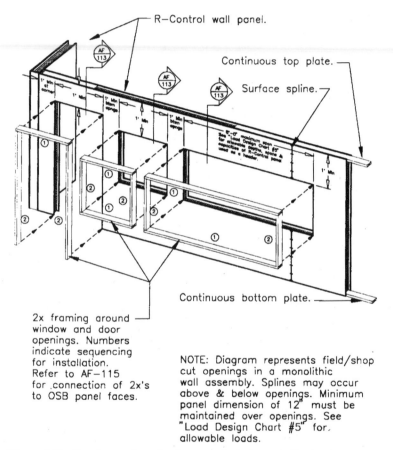

2x framing around window and door openings. Numbers indicate sequencing for installation. Refer to AF—115 for .connection of 2x's to OSB panel faces.

NOTE: Diagram represents field/shop cut openings in a monolithic wall assembly. Splines may occur above & below openings. Minimum panel dimension of 12" must be maintained over openings. See "Load Design Chart #5" for. allowable loads.

Figure 4-11   Rough openings for doors and windows. *(AFM Corporation)*

Electrical and Plumbing

Wiring the home is not difficult but may require some nonstandard techniques. Since interior partitions are typically stick built, it is best to make use of the interior walls whenever possible. Most SIP panels come equipped with prerouted electrical wiring chases. These chases create a network of cored-out space through which wiring can be run from the building exterior or basement up through walls and floors to the attic. Wiring chases are predrilled vertically at panel edges or horizontally at predetermined locations above the finished floor. Some manufacturers typically core at 12" and 44" above finished floor (a.f.f.) (Figs. 4-12 and 4-13). Many contractors prefer (or if recommended by a specific panel manufacturer) to take horizontal wiring runs through the basement or ceiling joist cavity when horizontal coring is not possible or provided. A raceway behind the wood baseboard or other type of surface-mounted wiremould is also a common design feature. This arrangement also allows for flexibility in the field as well as after construction is complete (Fig. 4-14).

Receptacle outlets and switch boxes are usually attached to panel splines or hung on brackets attached to the interior facing material. Wiring for these fixtures as well as thermostats can also be easily installed vertically in the panel edge before the rough door openings are closed in with 2 × 4s.

The chases drilled though the roof panels are ideal for running sprinkler piping throughout the roof of the house. It is

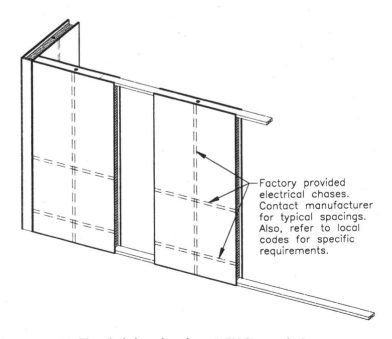

Factory provided electrical chases. Contact manufacturer for typical spacings. Also, refer to local codes for specific requirements.

Figure 4-12 Electrical chase locations. *(AFM Corporation)*

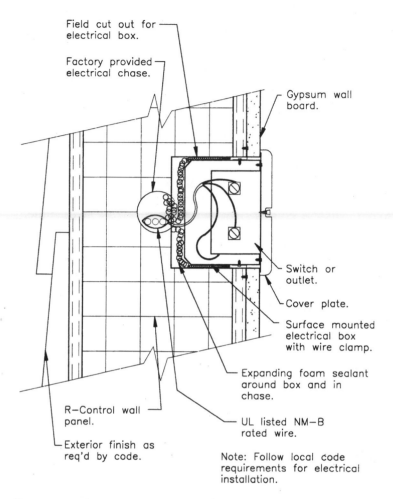

Field cut out for electrical box.

Factory provided electrical chase.

Gypsum wall board.

Switch or outlet.

Cover plate.

Surface mounted electrical box with wire clamp.

Expanding foam sealant around box and in chase.

R—Control wall panel.

UL listed NM—B rated wire.

Exterior finish as req'd by code.

Note: Follow local code requirements for electrical installation.

Figure 4-13   Field cutout for electrical box. *(AFM Corporation)*

also recommended that if plumbing fixtures are to be located along an outside wall, a furred wall is recommended. It is necessary to predrill 2× splines to allow the horizontal chases to continue unobstructed.

Cost

The material and labor cost of a SIP home is typically between $.50 and $2.00 more per square foot of finished space.[13] The added value and energy cost savings would offset the additional initial expense in a relatively short amount of time.

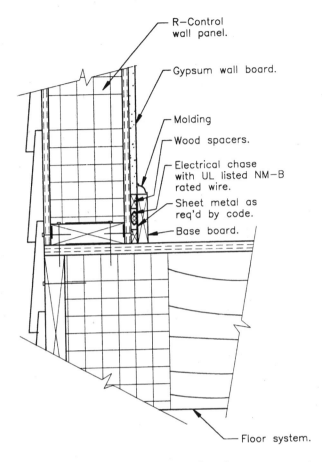

R—Control wall panel.

Gypsum wall board.

Molding

Wood spacers.

Electrical chase with UL listed NM—B rated wire.

Sheet metal as req'd by code.

Base board.

Floor system.

Figure 4-14   Electrical chase in baseboard. *(AFM Corporation)*

Warranties

Although warranties will vary per the manufacturer, many SIPs are guaranteed not to delaminate or to lose R-value for 20 years.

Summary

SIP market growth is expected to continue in the foreseeable future. Despite recent recessionary times in the construction industry, significant market growth was experienced by SIPA members since the late 1980s. This growth is being reinforced by lumber shortages, concerns about energy costs, and environmental sustainability, demand for construction quality, and other factors. Increased SIP use is also due to greater understanding and acceptance of this technology by builders, designers, homeowners, and other decision makers.

The following details for the construction system are provided to allow the reader a general visual understanding of how the system works (Figs. 4-15 through 4-23).

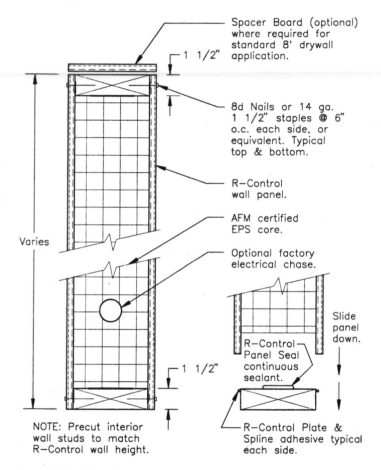

Figure 4-15 SIP wall section. *(AFM Corporation)*

To alert builders to the advantages of SIP in construction, a 2,800-ft² demonstration home was erected at the 1997 NAHB Builders' Show in Houston. Called "Engineering the American Dream," the home illustrated the latest in SIP and engineered wood products—two systems technologies that are often interwoven. The project was cosponsored by the APA—The Engineered Wood Association and SIPA.

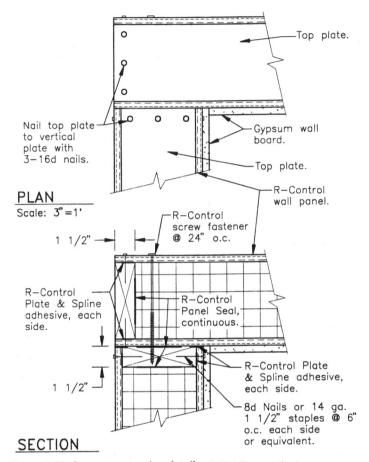

Top plate.

Nail top plate to vertical plate with 3−16d nails.

Gypsum wall board.

Top plate.

R−Control wall panel.

PLAN
Scale: 3"=1'

1 1/2"

R−Control screw fastener @ 24" o.c.

R−Control Plate & Spline adhesive, each side.

R−Control Panel Seal, continuous.

1 1/2"

R−Control Plate & Spline adhesive, each side.

8d Nails or 14 ga. 1 1/2" staples @ 6" o.c. each side or equivalent.

SECTION

Figure 4-16 Corner connection details. *(AFM Corporation)*

RESIDENTIAL STEEL FRAMING

"The Prescriptive Methods for Light Gauge Steel Framing" was formulated by the American Iron and Steel Institute, HUD, and the NAHB in May 1996. In October of that same year, the Council of American Building Officials (CABO) approved these standards for inclusion in the 1998 CABO One and Two Family Dwelling Code. Although the typical consumer may not realize the significance of such an action, this introduction into CABO is validation that residential steel framing is here to stay.

Steel has been around a long time, so why did it take so

long to arrive in home construction? "Fact is, fluctuating lumber prices and sagging quality have sent many contractors looking for alternative building materials. While most have simply incorporated more engineered-wood products, such as manufactured beams and trusses, a growing number are forsaking wood entirely and moving to steel."[14]

It is price and quality that can devastate a builder's production efficiency as well as his or her reputation. "In 1993, lumber prices jumped 100 percent, then settled down a bit, then rose again. Precut-stud prices catapulted from $1.25 to $3.20 in some areas. At the same time, lumber quality deteriorated, especially in the case of studs, many of which arrive twisted and continue to warp even when nailed in place. Unstable lumber can add to building costs and create drywall stress cracks and nail pops that drive homeowners up the wall. In fact, lumber will never be as cheap, as straight, as dry or as strong as it was when trees were 200 years old and a yard wide."[15]

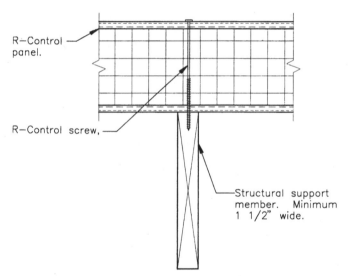

Figure 4-17 Screw connection detail. *(AFM Corporation)*

It takes about 10 mature trees to frame an average-sized home. These days, mature trees are scarce. Tropical forests are being destroyed at a rate of nearly 50 acres per minute. Deforestation in the United States is even worse than in Brazil, with 90 percent of the native American old-growth forests already logged in the Northwest. According to the National Forest Products Association, 90 percent of old-growth forest (over 200 years old) have already been harvested and second-growth forest are still 15 to 20 years away from harvestable use.[16]

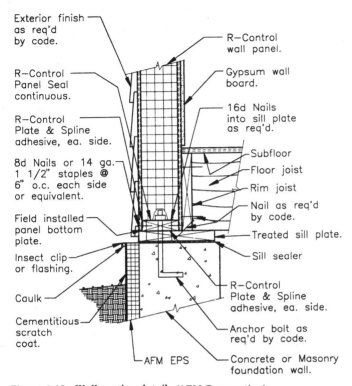

Exterior finish as req'd by code.

R—Control Panel Seal continuous.

R—Control Plate & Spline adhesive, ea. side.

8d Nails or 14 ga. 1 1/2" staples @ 6" o.c. each side or equivalent.

Field installed panel bottom plate.

Insect clip or flashing.

Caulk

Cementitious scratch coat.

R—Control wall panel.

Gypsum wall board.

16d Nails into sill plate as req'd.

Subfloor

Floor joist

Rim joist

Nail as req'd by code.

Treated sill plate.

Sill sealer

R—Control Plate & Spline adhesive, ea. side.

Anchor bolt as req'd by code.

AFM EPS

Concrete or Masonry foundation wall.

Figure 4-18 Wall section detail. *(AFM Corporation)*

There is little debate as to the fact that the quantity and quality of wood resources are diminishing. However, that factor alone is not enough to alter the all-too-comfortable framing techniques that have been in use for over 100 years. One industry source presented additional insight. "The biggest drawback of steel, is that it's not wood."[17] Wood is the primary material for exterior walls in 85 percent of the single-family homes being built, concrete masonry units are approximately 13 percent, and steel framing is used in only 1 percent. Similarly, framing lumber is the primary material for 92 percent of all interior partitions, while steel is used 8 percent of the time.[18] Of all commercial buildings, 80 percent are constructed with steel as their primary structural component. Several steel manufacturers have acknowledged that one reason for the relatively slow market share growth is due to a "fear of the unknown" by homebuilders. Contractors cite the technical inexperience of subcontractors and laborers as the real reason for their slow acceptance of residential steel framing. Education and maturity of the industry should eventually dispel these obstacles to acceptance of steel framing. Other barriers include consumer acceptance, thermal conductivity, and availability of material.[19] Nevertheless, whether these barriers are perceived to be real or not, a number of industry professionals believe it is only a matter of time before steel framing achieves the market share it deserves.

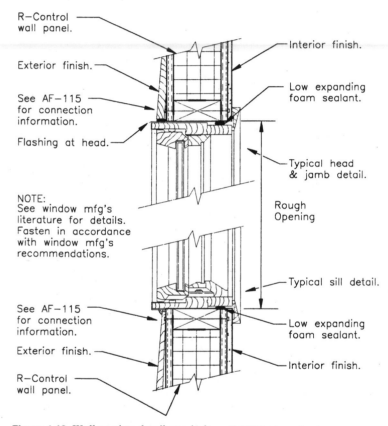

Figure 4-19 Wall section detail at window. *(AFM Corporation)*

Steel Framing Systems

Steel framing systems assume a number of construction assemblies dependent upon the contractor's or distributor's predilection. Two types are most common:

- Heavy-gauge steel frames with light-gauge infill

- Load-bearing and non-load-bearing light-gauge steel framing

Although each system has its merits, the heavy-gauge steel frame system is more suited for a production builder capable of mass-producing repetitive steel columns, beams, and girts as specified from predetermined standard home designs. Also called "post and beam," this system uses heavy-gauge steel beams and columns that are bolted together and light-gauge steel framing is used for wall infill only (Fig. 4-24).

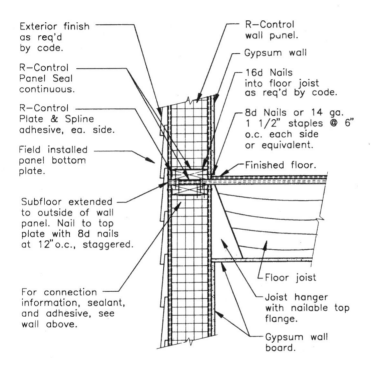

Figure 4-20 Wall section detail at joist hanger. *(AFM Corporation)*

Load-bearing and non-load-bearing light-gauge steel framing systems are also marketed by steel homebuilders capable of providing a number of predesigned home designs to choose from. This system is typically referred to as "stick frame" (Fig. 4-25). The use of light-gauge steel framing also allows any home, typically built of wood framing, to be modified for steel framing. (Although some builders are simply substituting "stick for stick" steel for wood, this method is not utilizing, or benefitting from, the true efficient potential of steel. Any builder should be familiar with the material properties and construction methods suited for steel specifically.) This application of steel framing is more economical for a nonspecific residential design and more versatile and flexible, and will be discussed in this chapter. For more information on heavy-gauge steel framing methods, an architect, structural engineer, or specialized homebuilder will be able to provide assistance.

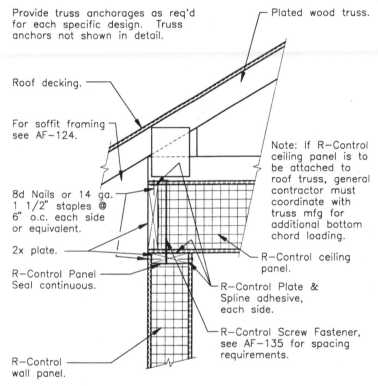

Provide truss anchorages as req'd for each specific design. Truss anchors not shown in detail.

Plated wood truss.

Roof decking.

For soffit framing see AF-124.

Note: If R-Control ceiling panel is to be attached to roof truss, general contractor must coordinate with truss mfg for additional bottom chord loading.

8d Nails or 14 ga. 1 1/2" staples @ 6" o.c. each side or equivalent.

2x plate.

R-Control Panel Seal continuous.

R-Control ceiling panel.

R-Control Plate & Spline adhesive, each side.

R-Control Screw Fastener, see AF-135 for spacing requirements.

R-Control wall panel.

Figure 4-21 Wall section detail at roof truss. *(AFM Corporation)*

Material Properties

Generally speaking, light-gauge steel framing members have always been similar in form and dimensions to wood frame members. Steel studs are channel-type components, roll-formed from corrosion-resistant zinc-coated steel. Although the exact dimensions may vary dependent upon the manufacturer, the typical sizes used in commercial construction are as follows:

- Load-bearing steel studs (or joists), referred to as C-sections, can be 14, 16, 18, or 20 gauge. The sizes available include $3^5/_8$", 4", 6", $7^1/_4$", 8", $9^1/_4$", $11^1/_2$" and $13^1/_2$" (Fig. 4-26).

- Non-load-bearing steel studs, commonly referred to as drywall studs, are available in 20, 22, and 25 gauge. The sizes include $1^5/_8$", $2^1/_2$", $3^5/_8$", 4" and 6" (Fig. 4-27).

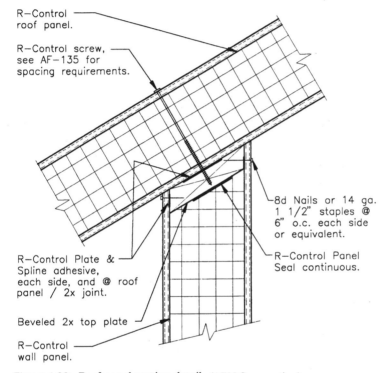

R–Control roof panel.

R–Control screw, see AF–135 for spacing requirements.

8d Nails or 14 ga. 1 1/2" staples @ 6" o.c. each side or equivalent.

R–Control Plate & Spline adhesive, each side, and @ roof panel / 2x joint.

R–Control Panel Seal continuous.

Beveled 2x top plate

R–Control wall panel.

Figure 4-22   Roof panel section detail. *(AFM Corporation)*

$1^1/_2$" × 4" slotted holes, referred to as "knockouts" or "cutouts" are typically located at 24" on center (o/c) along the length of the steel member. Knockouts are especially convenient when accommodating electrical runs or horizontal bracing channels.

Many steel roll formers are making changes to their products which will make the transition from wood framing to steel framing simpler. Steel studs are now being produced to accurately reflect the actual dimensions of wood framing members. Studs are available in widths of $3^1/_2$", $5^1/_2$" as well as 8", 10" and 12". The flange is still $1^5/_8$". Nomenclature is also being revised to avoid the confusion associated with gauge thickness. Studs can now be specified using mils (1/1000 of an inch). For example, 33 mils is 20 ga, 43 mils is 18 ga and 54 mils is 16 ga.

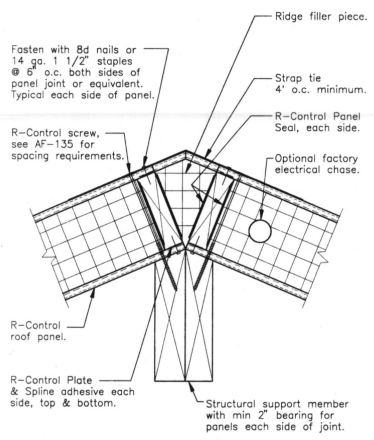

Ridge filler piece.

Fasten with 8d nails or 14 ga. 1 1/2" staples @ 6" o.c. both sides of panel joint or equivalent. Typical each side of panel.

Strap tie 4' o.c. minimum.

R-Control Panel Seal, each side.

R-Control screw, see AF-135 for spacing requirements.

Optional factory electrical chase.

R-Control roof panel.

R-Control Plate & Spline adhesive each side, top & bottom.

Structural support member with min 2" bearing for panels each side of joint.

Figure 4-23   Roof ridge detail. *(AFM Corporation)*

Variability is another advantage to using steel framing. When an increased load is to be carried by a wood stud, the framer can either increase the number of studs for support or increase the physical size of the member. This is not always possible or desired given the consistent width of a wall. Steel framing allows the framer to use the same-width stud, but can increase the mils (lower the gauge) to provide additional support.

Dimensional Stability

Steel framing members will not warp, crack, swell, shrink, split, or bow and are free of weakness caused by knots. The absence of moisture, often the culprit in wood dimensional variations, helps prevent squeaks and allows a smooth surface for attachment of surface materials.

Figure 4-24 Heavy-gauge frame with light-gauge infill. *(Classic Steel Frame Homes)*

Figure 4-25 Light-gauge steel framing. *(American Iron and Steel Institute)*

The zinc coating on these materials provides a galvanized coating that inhibits rust. (Zinc is nontoxic and is actually the second most common trace metal naturally found in the body.)[20] The potential for rotting as well as intrusion by termites and vermin is also eliminated.

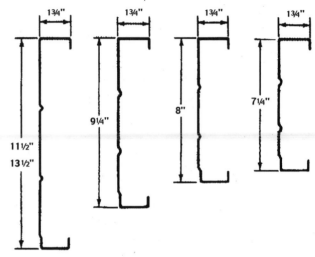

Figure 4-26 Light-gauge steel joists.

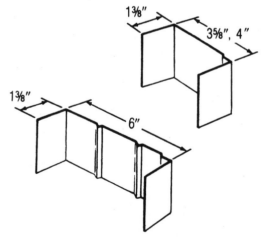

Figure 4-27 Light-gauge steel studs.

Fire Protection

Structural members and framing in wood stick-built homes are the third most commonly first-ignited material in U.S. home fires. Fires started in framing materials annually account for 347 deaths, 843 injuries, and $649 million in property damage.[21] Steel homes offer much greater protection from fire than conventional construction. Steel is noncombustible; however, it will melt and collapse when exposed to the high temperatures of a house fire. Proper encapsulation is required for a fire-resistant structure. Various testing-laboratory-approved assemblies using drywall on each side of a steel stud wall can attain up to a 2-hr fire rating. Many underwriters are providing lower house insurance premiums to reflect the fire-resistive properties of steel.

A number of house fires start while still under construction. The use of steel framing will greatly reduce the potential ignition points typically vulnerable in wood-framed homes during the unprotected framing stage of construction.

Earthquake and Hurricane Resistance

Steel homes are approved for Seismic Zone 4, the highest earthquake rating required in the United States. Steel-framed homes have also withstood hurricanes and tornadoes with little or no damage.

Environmental Attributes

Much has been discussed about the air pollution and other environmental hazards created by yesterday's steel mills. "The steel industry, for its part, has greatly reduced smokestack emissions. A typical steel mill today emits 95% less sulfur and 28% less carbon dioxide than it did a decade ago. Steel also boasts a 65% recycling rate, but this figure is a bit distorted, as it includes scrap produced in manufacturing. A rate of 50% is probably more realistic. Moreover, most recycled scrap goes into heavy steel products, with cold-formed steel claiming only 24%."[22] The American Iron and Steel Institute reports that 95 percent of the water used for steelmaking is recycled and the average North American steel mill has reduced its energy consumption by 45 percent over the past 20 years.[23] Since steel is recyclable, less waste is deposited into landfills.

Steel framing is also advantageous to use when a particular homeowner is allergic or sensitive to pine or other species of trees, as well as any preservatives used in wood for special applications. Being an inert and stable material, steel will not compromise indoor air quality. The use of termite-killing chemicals can also be eliminated since steel is unsusceptible to damage by insects or other pests.

Required Tools

Electric metal shears, aviation snips, a hand break, electric screw guns and a first aid kit are but a few of the essential tools needed for framing with light-gauge steel. A circular saw outfitted with steel blades is also necessary for trimming any nonstandard studs or angles. Screws, ties, straps, and anchors are the common fasteners used.

Construction Techniques

Framing methods, sequences, and even nomenclature (i.e., joists, studs, headers, etc.) are not dissimilar to those of wood-framing construction. Loads are transferred by a myriad of redundant members just like any other construction system. The individual components of steel framing are physically and dimensionally similar to those in wood-frame construction. In actuality, there are very little differences between the two systems.

As mentioned earlier, steel studs closely correspond with wood studs. The typical load bearing steel stud is $3^1/_2$" or $5^1/_2$" wide, has a flange width between $1^5/_8$" and 2" and has a lip of $^1/_2$". The gauge refers to the thickness of the steel coil used to roll form the individual member; 20 ga, or 33 mils, is the minimum thickness for load-bearing steel studs; 18 ga (43 mils), 16 ga (54 mils) or 14 ga (68 mils) are also used. Non-load-bearing studs, or "drywall studs," are typically 25 ga, 22 ga or 20 ga and used for interior partitions only.

Generally speaking, U-shaped channels, or tracks, are used for wall plates and are shot- or anchor-bolted into the floor slab or subfloor. The tracks, also called "runners," are analogous to the bottom and top plates of wood frame construction. Tracks are the same width as the wall studs to be used, typically have $1^1/_4$" legs, and are made from the same gauge as the wall stud. The vertical studs fit inside the tracks and the flanges are fastened together. One limitation of the bottom track is that it is not structural and will not span floor undulations. Not only is a flatter floor framed with steel possible, it is essential. Since top tracks are not structural, it is important to align the framing members, especially roof rafters over wall studs. This method is referred to as "in-line framing."

Stud spacing, as in wood-frame construction, is typically 16" or 24" o/c. Steel studs come in standard lengths between 8' and 12', although lengths up to 40' are available. The studs can be precut to any length specified by the contractor. For example, if a $9'-2^1/_2$" stud is required, the dimensional stability of steel guarantees that the length will not change relative to moisture content. The ability to precut all material translates to cost savings and less waste. (Cut-to-length is typically performed with no additional charge provided a minimum order is placed, usually around 30 pieces.)

Load-bearing steel C-sections will be galvanized and usually be color coded. (This is a form of identification indicating the stud's gauge (steel thickness), the manufacturer and yield strength.) Typical color coatings, indicating gauge are as follows: 25 ga NA, 22 ga blue, 20 ga white, 18 ga yellow, 16 ga green and 14 ga orange.

Steel-to-steel and sheathing-to-steel fasteners shall be self-drilling tapping screws. Although the size required varies per the building code or manufacturer's recommendations, a good rule of thumb is that the screw should extend through the steel for a minimum of three threads. No. 8 screws are typical for most attachments. Structural sheathing ($7/16$" OSB or $15/32$" plywood) should be installed on all exterior walls per local building codes.

Wall corners are typically framed with three studs and the tracks overlapping. When extra strength is needed, studs are paired or assembled with tracks to create support posts and jack-stud assemblies. Deeper studs (or joists) are joined back to back, or flange to flange where heavier beams and headers are required. In some cases, members are nested—joined, with flanges lapping, one inside the other, and with the web of each stud facing outward. In horizontal applications, nested beams can also be doubled or tripled for added support. Headers are typically paired C-sections with a top and bottom track, equal in width to the wall, providing additional stability. One jack stud and two king studs are typically required at each end of an opening for openings up to 8'. Two jacks and three kings are typically required at openings up to 14'. (These assemblies could vary depending upon the actual load conditions and bearing capacities of the members. Refer to "The Prescriptive Methods for Light Gauge Steel Framing," CABO, or the manufacturer's literature and table for correct assemblies.)

Bracing

The flanges of all load bearing and/or exterior wall studs are to be laterally braced by gypsum board, structural sheathing, or horizontal steel strapping. Without proper bracing, construction loads may cause studs to fail from the weight of the roof structure or the weight of framing on upper floor(s).

Lateral bracing is horizontal members designed to resist stud rotation and minor axis bending under wind and axial loads. A variety of methods can be used such as strap bracing, OSB, GWB, or hat channels. Strap bracing of $1^1/_2$" wide 20-ga steel is placed horizontally on the flanges of each stud. An alternative method requires $1^1/_2$" cold rolled channels inserted through the knockouts and attached with clip angles.

Diagonal bracing is necessary to resist racking under wind and seismic loads. Bracing straps are placed diagonally over the framing members and resist the forces in tension. Straps are typically 16 ga and are between 3" and 5". Ends of the straps are screwed or welded in order to transfer the load to the floor assembly and wall framing.

Lateral support to keep joists from twisting is called joist bridging. A cut joist section or other accessory is screwed or welded at midspans 8' o/c for spans exceeding 15'.

Span tables, stud thickness, and fastening requirements are available in the 1997 amendments to the CABO One and Two Family Dwelling Code. Guidelines are also readily available from a number of steel framing manufacturers. The following details are examples of connections and design possibilities. Although not specifically covered in this text, steel framing members are also used for floor, roof and roof truss systems (Figs. 4-28 through 4-38).

Cost

The bottom line of cost comparison is that steel framing is still slightly more expensive than wood framing. "The NAHB estimates that steel becomes competitive when lumber prices reach $350 and $400 per 1000 board feet. Today's prices run close to $360 (and moving higher), which helps explain the recent builder interest. Still, material costs are only part of the equation. Labor costs will be substantially higher on the front end of the learning curve. Mechanical and electrical contractors may also charge more in the beginning. Once a builder has a few of these houses under his or her belt, however, labor costs should level off."[24] Unlike the ever increasing, and fluctuating, cost of lumber, the price of steel has held fairly steady for the past two decades A dwindling supply of steel framing is not possible either. With recycling, the nation's iron reserves are projected to last 300 to 400 years.[25] An unwritten cost saver is that steel offers structural and material advantages that may mean fewer punchlist items or call-backs such as nail pops.

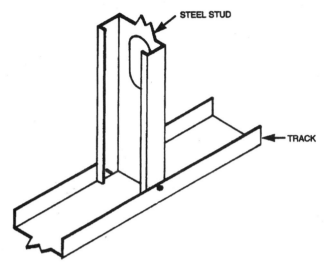

Figure 4-28   Light-gauge steel stud and track. *(Clark Steel Framing Systems)*

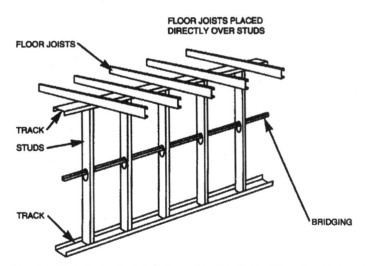

Figure 4-29   Interior load-bearing wall. *(Clark Steel Framing Systems)*

Limitations

Thermal conductivity may be the only real disadvantage to using steel framing. Steel studs conduct close to 10 times more heat than wood, thereby creating thermal bridges at studs that are attached directly to the exterior facing material. Since the lateral migration of energy through the steel stud more or less "bypasses" the insulation in the wall, adding more cavity insulation is not an effective solution. A thermal buffer is necessary and can be accomplished by sheathing the exterior walls with a high-density foam board, such as extruded polystyrene (XPS) in lieu of wood structural sheathing or other exterior sheathing material. R-5 (1" of XPS) will increase a wall with R-11 batts up to the R-13 to R-18 range. It is important to note that horizontal steel strapping may be necessary if foam is used, since structural bracing typically provided by the structural sheathing is not present[26] (consult the applicable building code for necessary requirements).

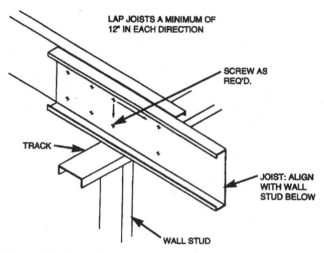

Figure 4-30   Lapped Joists. *(Clark Steel Framing Systems)*

Other methods being implemented include increasing stud spacing from 16" o/c to 24" o/c as well as taking extra care in packing corners with additional batt insulation. One contractor in the northwest United States is using thermographic analysis to assess which wall assemblies are most effective. R-6 foam board placed on the interior wall face is apparently more effective than foam on the exterior.[27] Researchers are also experimenting with nonconducting tape that can be applied to the interior surfaces of exterior members and a special insulation with plastic facing that wraps around studs. Some manufacturers are even designing structural members with raised nubs that reduce surface contact with sheathing and wallboard.[28]   Hat channels used for the furring out of exterior and interior sheathing is another common method. The need to develop superior buffers to counteract thermal bridging will guarantee that new systems and technologies will continue to be explored.

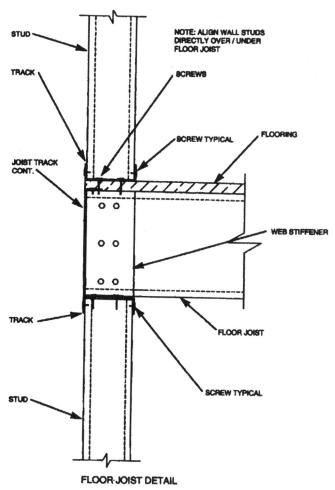

Figure 4-31 Wall section at floor joist. *(Clark Steel Framing Systems)*

The energy-intensive means of producing steel will cause environmentalists to question the true efficiency of such a product. In theory, the recyclability of steel spreads the actual first-run energy costs over several generations of use. The average 2000-ft² steel-framed house can generate as little as 1 yd³ of recyclable scrap, mainly due to the precise lengths available for steel studs. 60 million tons of steel are recycled each year. This amount is greater than the combination of all recycled paper, aluminum, glass, and plastic.[29]

Miscellaneous

The general public has many other misconceptions about steel-framed homes. There is no additional radio or TV interference and homes are actually better grounded in the event of a lightning strike. According to the American Iron and Steel Institute, scientists recommend seeking shelter in steel-framed homes during lightning storms because the steel frame provides a secondary path to the ground.[30]

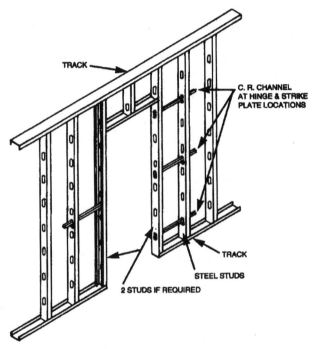

TRACK

C. R. CHANNEL
AT HINGE & STRIKE
PLATE LOCATIONS

TRACK

STEEL STUDS

2 STUDS IF REQUIRED

Figure 4-32   Door opening. *(Clark Steel Framing Systems)*

Summary

Hawaii has the highest percentage (25 to 30 percent) of steel-framed houses being constructed anywhere in the world. Perhaps it is the limited resources of wood or the superior strength properties of steel that has caused a boom in its popularity. In either case, the major barrier that prevents widespread acceptance by the residential construction industry is that the materials, tools, and methods seem, at first, alien to seasoned builders in the traditional methods of wood framing. One builder described his first steel-framing experience best: "Suddenly everything in my tool pouch was wrong. For 20 years I had clanked and jingled around job sites like someone in the infantry, ready for anything. I could chalk, nail, clamp, chip, pry, measure, shave, square, and punch, drawing the right tool like a gunslinger. Sometimes I carried more nails than Home Depot and my pants would fall down. Now I felt like a rookie. I missed my hammer."[31] But like so many things new, the anticipatory anxiety is always worse than the reality. As the same builder reflects on his experience, an admission is presented. "After a while it started to click. It was still new but not foreign. It felt different but the moves were basically the same. Sure there are different details and names for things...but a carpenter's sense for order and logic are not lost or wasted with steel framing. Loads are loads, layout is layout, and aside from learning new details and fastening requirements, this is familiar territory for a wood framer."[32] It will eventually be for most everyone.

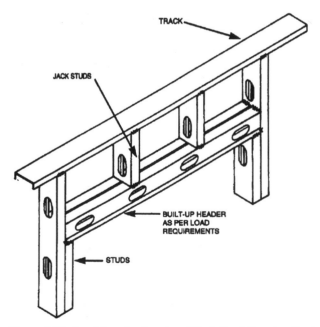

Figure 4-33 Load-bearing header. *(Clark Steel Framing Systems)*

PRECAST CONCRETE UNITS

As mentioned in Chapter 2, the intent of this book is to discuss the means, methods, and materials in a nonproprietary manner, although it is not possible with all construction products. autoclaved aerated concrete (AAC) units are a lightweight, structural, precast concrete building material of a uniform porous (cellular) structure. Two such manufacturers are achieving growing acceptance in this country. The Hebel and YTONG proprietary products include units analogous to unit masonry as well as concrete panel units for use in walls, floors, and roofs.

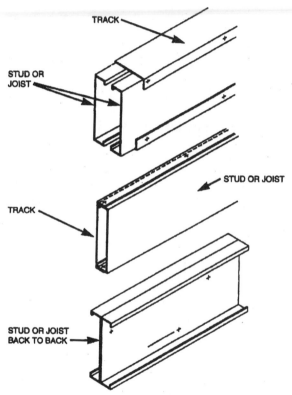

Figure 4-34   Header configurations. *(Clark Steel Framing Systems)*

Hebel

Josef Hebel began producing AAC in a factory in Munich in 1943. The innovative, integrated system allows a house's walls, floors, and roofs to be fully constructed of AAC panels or units. Over 50 years later, The Hebel Group has grown to 45 plants around the world, producing 8 million cubic yards of AAC annually. Although headquartered in Germany, the United States has one production facility, located in Adel, Georgia, and plans for a new plant in Texas are to be underway by the end of the decade.

The use of AAC is relatively unknown in the residential market in the United States. However, AAC accounts for 60 percent of the Japanese wall construction market and 15 percent of the German market.

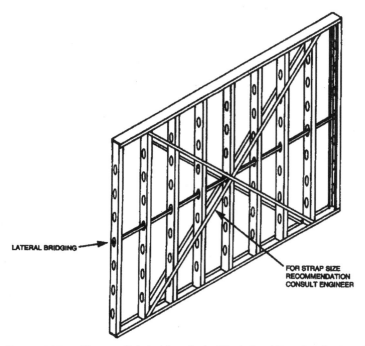

Figure 4-35   Shear wall (wind bracing). *(Clark Steel Framing Systems)*

Material Properties

Hebel panels and Hebel units are composed of sand, cement, lime, gypsum, water, and a secret expansion agent. The manufacturing process may be analogous to that of baking bread. First of all, the raw materials are mixed and placed into a mold and then allowed to expand (or rise). A chemical reaction occurs when the molded panels are cured under pressurized steam for 10 or 12 hours in a device called an autoclave, creating millions of microscopic air bubbles. These air bubbles thus create the cellular structure that provides the lightweight characteristics as well as the thermal and acoustic properties of the units.

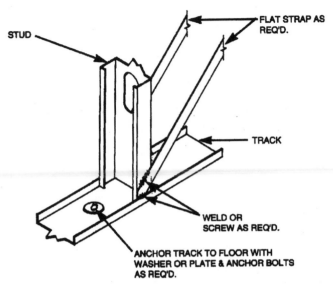

STUD

FLAT STRAP AS REQ'D.

TRACK

WELD OR
SCREW AS REQ'D.

ANCHOR TRACK TO FLOOR WITH
WASHER OR PLATE & ANCHOR BOLTS
AS REQ'D.

Figure 4-36 Shear wall connection detail. *(Clark Steel Framing Systems)*

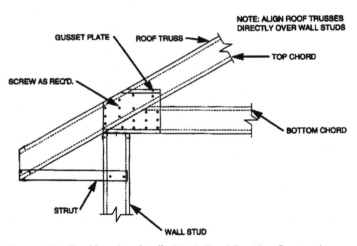

NOTE: ALIGN ROOF TRUSSES
DIRECTLY OVER WALL STUDS

GUSSET PLATE

ROOF TRUSS

TOP CHORD

SCREW AS REQ'D.

BOTTOM CHORD

STRUT

WALL STUD

Figure 4-37 Roof bearing detail. *(Clark Steel Framing Systems)*

Hebel panels can be manufactured for wall, roof or floor applications (Fig. 4-39). All Hebel panels have some steel reinforcing for transportation concerns. Wall panels intended for load-bearing walls, floors, and roofs are cast with steel reinforcing bars and classified as reinforced. Reinforced wall panels can be

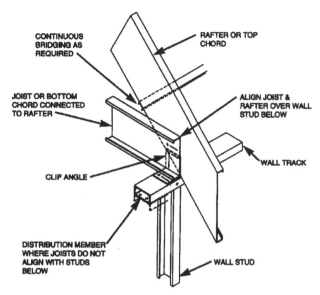

Figure 4-38   Roof eave detail. *(Clark Steel Framing Systems)*

Figure 4-39   Aerated autoclaved concrete. *(Hebel)*

used for exterior and interior walls whether load-bearing or non-load-bearing, as well as lintel blocks. Wall panels that are used in loadbearing applications cannot be field cut. This is not true of non-loadbearing wall panels. Wall, roof and floor panels range in size from 3" - 12". Each panel is 2' in height and lengths can range up to 20'. The manufacturers provide construction drawings for each specific design application. Each panel is numbered and installed per the shop drawings. Although floor, wall, and roof panels can be used for residential structures, AAC wall units will be the focus of this text due to their "unit masonry" type construction techniques.

Nonreinforced AAC wall units are more common for residential applications than are the panels. Hebel units are available in the following nominal sizes: 4" × 8" × 24", 6" × 8" × 24", 8" × 8" × 24" to 10" × 8" × 24". 2" and 12" thick units are also available. The units are available in three different types based on the compressive strength desired. HBL-33 (360 psi), HBL-38 (725 psi) and HBL-44 (1090 psi) are the different classifications and are similar to the panel classifications (Figs. 4-40 and 4-41).

Figure 4-40   AAC wall units. *(Hebel)*

Thermal Performance

A house built with an 8" wall unit thickness outperforms a home with an equivalent R-value greater than R-30. Although the actual R-value of the 8" unit is R-9, the thermal mass and reduced air infiltration of the wall system provide a more resistant wall than wood frame construction. These same properties provide a sound transmission class (STC) rating up to 47 for the 8" unit.

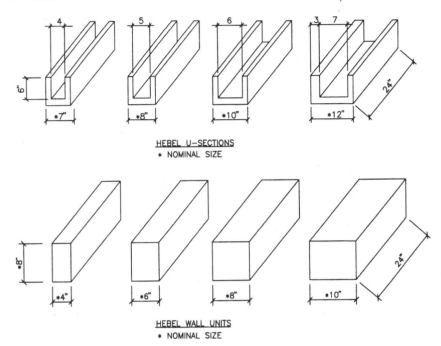

HEBEL U-SECTIONS
* NOMINAL SIZE

HEBEL WALL UNITS
* NOMINAL SIZE

Figure 4-41   AAC wall unit sizes. *(Hebel)*

Fire Rating

The AAC units are noncombustible and achieved test results of 2 hours for the 4" unit and 4 hours for the 8" unit.

Construction Application

As mentioned before, the installation of AAC wall units is similar in technique to that of masonry unit construction. The individual units are laid up, in a running bond, and set in $1/2$" mortar joints. Unlike CMU or brick, however, AAC units can be cut with a handsaw or bandsaw. AAC units are also lightweight, which typically requires fewer laborers and/or worker-hours to erect a wall.   The 8" × 8" × 24" unit is the most common block size. Although routing and/or notching is allowed up to about two-thirds of the unit's width, it is advised to use a smaller width unit when possible for plumbing or other chases. U-section units and lintel units are also available.

Exterior Finishes

Premixed acrylic coatings are acceptable if a synthetic stucco finish is desired. Brick veneer and horizontal siding products are also appropriate exterior finishes.

Interior Finishes

Any finish must be of a breathable nature to protect against mildew. According to the manufacturer's literature, a Hebel-approved water-based acrylic paint or one that has high vapor permeability may be used.

Single-coat, premixed, gypsum plasters are recommended by Hebel as an interior finish. Other finishes, such as gypsum wallboard, can be attached directly to the wall with screws and adhesive or on furring strips. Ceramic tiles can be set using thin-bed, cement-based mortar.

Masonry cut nails or other screws in combination with Fischer nylon wall inserts are to be used for any other interior attachments.

Environmental Attributes

Hebel products are made of environmentally safe materials. No pollutants or toxic by-products are produced in the manufacturing process or are present in the final product.

YTONG

Another AAC manufacturer, although not as widely distributed in the United States as Hebel, is YTONG. YTONG, a word combination of "Yxhult" — the location of its development — and "betong" the Swedish word for concrete, was developed by the Swedish architect Johan Axel Eriksson and was patented in 1924. At the time, Eriksson was looking for a building material which has the thermal properties of wood with good workability but also is noncombustible and resistant to decay. Erikson's developments produced a highly cellular material from a purely mineral-based building material, made from sand, water, limestone, and a very small amount of aluminum powder. The product is noncombustible and no toxic fumes can be generated in the event of fire. The exceptional thermal properties of YTONG, in large part due to the cellular air pore structure, also provide excellent sound insulation properties.

According to the manufacturer's reports, no pollutants or hazardous waste are generated in the manufacturing process. Maximum efficiency is obtained during the low-temperature-steam curing process with the recovery of the thermal energy. Production trimmings are also recycled back into the next "batch." Similar in process to the aforementioned Hebel block, the YTONG batched mixture of raw materials "rises" during curing, which creates five units of finished volume from one unit of volume of raw materials.

YTONG is available with tongue-and-groove joints in several different load-bearing and non-load-bearing forms. These include:

- Large blocks with handholds
- Lightweight partition panels
- Lintels
- Reinforced slabs for floors and roofs
- Load-bearing wall-panels

Summary

Christopher Alexander, author of *A Pattern Language*, the second volume in a three-volume series exploring methods of alternative architectural thought, materials, and construction, derives a "class of good materials" for all building construction. He writes that it is best "to find a collection of materials which are small in scale, easy to cut on site, easy to work on site without the aid of huge and expensive machinery, easy to vary and adapt, heavy enough to be solid,...not needing specialized labor...light in weight, easy to work with...can be nailed with ordinary nails, cut with a saw, drilled with wood-working tools, easily repaired."[33] It appears that Hebel and other AAC units are almost such a material.

CONCLUSION

SIP, steel framing, and precast AAC are but three alternatives for wall and wall-framing systems for residential applications. Each of these materials is an engineered derivative of the traditional systems of stud walls, wood studs, and concrete block or brick masonry. The physical properties, the environmental sensibilities, and the systematic methodology behind the implementation are sound reasons for residential use. However, it is their growing market share in the 1990s that serves as an indication of their predicted success in the next century.

APPENDIX

AFM Corporation
Box 246
24000 W. Highway 7
Excelsior, MN 55331
(800) 255-0176
"R-Control"

American Iron and Steel Institute
1101 17th Street, NW, Suite 1300
Washington, DC 20036-4700
(800) 79-STEEL

Classic Steel Frame Homes
7301 Fairview
Houston, TX 77041
(713) 896-7425

Fischer SIPS Incorporated
1843 Northwestern Parkway
Louisville, KY 40203
(502) 778-5577

Hebel Southeast
3340 Peachtree Road
Suite 150
Atlanta, GA 30326
(800) 99-HEBEL

Structural Insulated Panel Association
1511 K Street NW
Washington, DC 20005
(202) 347-7800

Tri-Steel Structures, Inc.
5400 S. Stemmons Frwy.
Denton, TX 76205
(800) TRI-STEEL
Fax: (940) 497-7497

REFERENCES

1. Morris Hicky Morgan (trans. and ed.) *Vitruvius, The Ten Books of Architecture* (New York: Dover Publications, 1960), p. 39.
2. Structural Insulated Panel Association and Society of the Plastics Industry, *Strength and Energy Performance Properties of Foam Core Sandwich Panels* (1994), p.2.
3. Perma R website washington.xtn.net/~SIP
4. Murray State University website.
    //msumusik.mursuky.edu/~tphilpot/http/SIP.htm
5. Building Systems Magazine, Vol. 18, No. 3 (May/June 1997)
6. R-Control Promotional Literature, AFM Corporation
7. Structural Insulated Panel Association and Society of the Plastics Industry, *Strength and Energy Performance Properties of Foam Core Sandwich Panels* (1994), p. 5.
8. Ibid., p. 6.
9. Ibid., p. 6.
10. Ibid., p. 6.
11. Ibid., p. 7.
12. Ibid., p. 7.
13. Steve Andrews, "All in the Wall," *Builder Magazine*, May 1989, p.221.
14. Merle Henkenius, "Steel Framing," *Popular Mechanics*, August 1997.
15. Ibid.
16. Classic Steel Frame Homes Promotional Literature, NCI Building Systems, Houston, TX, p. 2.
17. Raul Barreneche, " Framing Alternatives," *Architecture*, October 1994, p. 104.
18. David F. Seiders, "Lack of Labor Hinders Steel Use," *Builder Magazine*, October 1997, p. 76.
19. Ibid., p. 76.
20. American Zinc Association Brochure.
21. 1983-1987 NFIRS, NFAA Survey.
22. Merle Henkenius, "Steel Framing," *Popular Mechanics*, August 1997.
23. Today's Steel Industry Internet Website, American Iron and Steel Institute, October 1997.
24. Merle Henkenius, "Steel Framing," *Popular Mechanics*, August 1997.
25. Ibid.
26. Steve Andrews, "Cold Facts About Steel Framing," *Builder Magazine*, February 1996, p. 177.
27. Ibid., p. 180.
28. Merle Henkenius, op. cit.
29. Steel Recycling Institute Brochure # BH 100 10/96
30. American Iron and Steel Institute Brochure # AISI RG-9401 0194-10M-RI
31. Rick Schwolsky, "Steel Crazy After All These Years," *Builder Magazine*, December, 1994, reprint.
32. Ibid.
33. Christopher Alexander, *A Pattern Language*, (New York: Oxford University Press, 1977), pp. 956-957.

5

Siding, Cladding, and Roofing

INTRODUCTION

"Consider a variety of natural organisms: trees, fish, animals. Broadly speaking, their outside coats are rough, and made of large numbers of similar but not identical elements. And these elements are placed so that they often overlap: the scales of a fish, the fur of an animal, the crinkling of natural skin, the bark of a tree. All these coats are made impervious and easy to repair. In simple technologies, buildings follow suit. Lapped boards, shingles, hung tiles, and thatch are all examples. Even stone and brick, though in one plane, are still in a sense lapped internally to prevent cracks which run all the way through. And all of these walls are made of small elements, so that individual pieces can be replaced as they are damaged or wear out."[1] So wrote Christopher Alexander in *A Pattern Language*, the second volume in a three-volume series exploring alternative methods of architectural thought, materials, and construction. Alexander's illustration cuts straight to the heart of the true function of exterior cladding. The reality of weather, wind, sun, and decay poses threats to the integrity of the exterior shell every single day the building stands. Cladding materials, when chosen for their "appropriateness," will not only perform well functionally but will also be aesthetically pleasing.

Historically, the consumer has seen a plethora of exterior cladding materials used in residential construction. Brick, stone, horizontal wood boards, vertical wood boards, aluminum siding, vinyl siding, synthetic stucco, tabby stucco, wood shakes and shingles, and concrete masonry units, are a few. The dilemma in selecting such a material for exterior use is that there are inevitable disadvantages with each selection. The wood siding products need regular maintenance and the vinyl siding products telegraph substrate irregularities. Likewise, the quality of brick veneer work can only be achieved by well-trained masons, and even synthetic stucco can cause substrate water damage if incorrectly installed and sealed. Similar compromises are realized with the widespread use of standard three-tab asphalt shingles. Besides being vulnerable to wind uplift and water infiltration, the material is subjected to sun damage and must be replaced approximately every 15 years.

Three types of cladding products for wall and/or roof application will be discussed here. These products: fiber cement siding and roofing, laminated high-density wood composites, and manufactured stone veneer are made from inorganic or composite technologies. They also provide a lower life-cycle cost and reduced maintenance for the homeowner than the aforementioned materials while being pleasing to the eye.

FIBER CEMENT SIDING AND ROOFING

Cellulose fiber–reinforced, asbestos-free, cementitious building products have been growing in popularity in residential applications over the past two decades. Fiber cement products feature the long life and low maintenance of concrete while having a more user-friendly workability not unlike that of wood. Traditional users of wood, masonite, hardboard, or OSB clapboard sidings will find fiber cement products have superior weathering capabilities and provide the look of textured, painted wood products. These products are manufactured for use as horizontal lap siding, exterior panels, and exterior soffits. The superior performance of these products especially suits them for residential applications in high-humidity coastal environments although they are available in almost any climate or region.

Material Properties

The basic composition of fiber cement products (with minor variations between manufacturers) is portland cement, ground sand, cellulose fiber, selected additives, and water. These ingredients are mixed into a slurry and deposited in layers on a roller. The sheets are cut by high-pressure water jets and then cured in an autoclave. (An autoclave is a high-temperature oven that reduces the curing time of concrete.) Fiber cement products can be formed into siding, planks, panels, or tiles. Depending upon the form (or the manufacturer) most products are $^1/_4$" or

$^5/_{16}$" thick and are extremely impact resistant. These materials are also relatively lightweight, weighing between 2 and 3 lb/ft². These products retain a paint finish without cracking or blistering. (The autoclave forces any free lime out of the product, allowing a better bond of paint to the substrate.)

All products are cut to shape on site by one of a variety of methods. Most manufacturers can supply cutting tools specifically designed for fiber cement products. Electric and pneumatic shears, a hand guillotine or a "score-and-snap" knife are the best methods. (Many contractors mistakenly use a circular or hand saw utilizing either a carbide or diamond blade, which is why "cutting" seems to be the most common complaint about these products.)

Figure 5-1   Fiber cement siding. *(FCP)*

Fire Resistance

Fire resistance is typically expressed by an index called the *flame spread*. The flame spread index is a numerical designation classifying a material's ability to resist the spread of flame over its surface. The smoke development index is a numerical classification based on ASTM E84.[2] For each of these classifications, the lower the number, the better. Fiber cement products are noncombustible, having a flame spread rating of 0 and a smoke density rating of 0 to 5, depending upon the manufacturer. The products comply with ASTM C1186, Standard Specification for Grade II, Type A, Non-Asbestos Fiber-Cement Flat Sheets.

Cost

Although specific pricing is not guaranteed, a cost comparison with other materials is possible. Fiber cement siding, for example, is more expensive than vinyl, but less expensive than brick or stucco, and similar to most wood or hardboard siding products.

Warranty

Fiber cement products will not rot or decay. These materials resist permanent damage from water and salt spray, making them advantageous for use in coastal environments. This class of products can withstand hurricane force winds up to 120 mph. (See manufacturer's literature for specific fastening requirements for maximum wind pressure ratings.) Hence, the typical warranty against defects, rot, termites, and workmanship for these products is 50 years. Since fiber cement products absorb moisture, one concern is their performance during freeze/thaw cycles. This is more a critical issue with roofing products. One fiber cement manufacturer has restricted roof product sales in the extreme northeast United States and Colorado; however, most manufacturers report this is not a significant problem.

Maintenance

Boards and panels may be supplied primed or unprimed, depending upon the manufacturer. Painting is required and typically should be a water-based exterior-grade acrylic paint, although some manufacturers recommend an alkali resistant paint. (Some products can be stained, too.) It is recommended that unprimed fiber cement products be painted within 90 days of installation. Paint finishes on fiber cement products should last from 10 to 15 years as compared to 5 years for painted wood cladding.

Limitations

Fiber cement products in their manufactured state do not present any known health hazards. However, the dust created when sawing, cutting, sanding, or drilling these products may cause coughing or lung irritation. This is due to the calcium silicate, cellulose fiber, and silica dust released into the air during such activity. Although calcium silicate and cellulose fiber are not known to cause long-term or chronic health effects, respirable silica dust (specifically respirable crystalline quartz) seems to generate conflicting reports. The International Agency for Research on Cancer (IARC) has labeled respirable silica dust a carcinogen, while OSHA (Occupational Safety and Health Administration) and NTP (National Toxicology Program) have issued no such warnings.[3] Any construction personnel involved in such activities should wear a mask to avoid breathing the dust. The dust is also known to irritate or cause redness in the eyes. In any event, the fiber-cement material safety sheet should be recognized and respected.

Lap Siding

Fiber cement lap siding products, typically $5/16$" thick, are available in a wide variety of finish textures, including smooth, woodgrain, or Colonial styles. The typical dimensions are 6", $7^1/2$", 8", $9^1/2$" and 12". Siding typically is available in lengths of 12'. Lap siding products can be installed directly to wood or steel framing members up to 24" o/c. If installed over foam sheathing, manufacturers recommend installing batten strips over the foam at each stud. Trim material can be fiber cement, wood, vinyl, aluminum, or PVC (Figs. 5-2 and 5-3).

Lap Siding Installation Techniques

It is important to consult the specific manufacturer's installation directions during construction. The following are general guidelines for information purposes only. (See the Appendix at the end of the chapter as well as the manufacturer directory for specific manufacturers.) Lap siding can be applied to wood or light gauge steel framing with studs spaced at 16" o/c or 24" o/c. Wall assemblies, including a vapor barrier, should be per local codes or requirements. Prior to starting the installation of horizontal lap siding, install a shim (or starter) strip behind the base of the first plank in order to achieve a consistent beveled appearance. (This is not needed up the wall since each subsequent plank provides the bevel thickness.) All flashing and stops should be installed as well.

A minimum of 6" clearance should be maintained between the lowest edge of the bottom plank and the finished grade. The siding is applied horizontally, commencing from the bottom course of a wall with minimum $1^1/4$"-wide laps at the top edge. When installed on wood framing members, the siding shall be fastened either through the overlapping planks with corrosion-resistant (galvanized or stainless steel) nails at each wood framing member or through the top edge of single planks with $1^1/4$"-long corrosion-resistant roofing nails into each wood framing member. Predrilling is not necessary. The lap conceals the fasteners in the previous course. As a general rule, nails should penetrate 1" into a wood stud.

Figure 5-2   Fiber cement siding. *(James Hardie Building Products)*

When attached to metal framing members, the siding is fastened either through the overlapping planks with self-drilling, corrosion-resistant, ribbed buglehead screws (as specified) at each metal framing member or through the top edge of single planks self-drilling, corrosion-resistant, ribbed Phillips waferhead screws (as specified) at each metal framing member. As a general rule, screws should penetrate three threads into a steel stud. As before, the lap conceals the fasteners in the previous course.

Blind nailing is allowable for most installations although some restrictions apply to 24" o/c stud spacing and/or 12" planks. Vertical joints shall butt over studs of framing members when possible. Fasteners shall be no closer than $^3/8$" from the plank side edge or $^3/4$" from the plank bottom edge. Different manufacturers have differing recommendations regarding the flush butting of planks. Some recommend a $^1/8$" gap between planks filled with a latex caulk (Fig. 5-4).

Figure 5-3   Fiber cement siding textures. *(FCP)*

When the vertical joints of the planks butt between the framing members, a metal joining type accessory is needed, called the "off stud splice device" (Fig.5-5). The device, placed at each plank end, is positioned so that the bottom lip is resting on the adjacent solid course of planks. The plank is then fastened to the

WOOD STUD NAIL INSTALLATION

BLIND NAILING

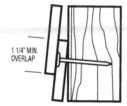

Figure 5-4   Nailing options. *(James Hardie Building Products)*

framing. The abutting plank is positioned and fastened into place, ensuring that the lower edges of the two planks align. The metal device is located centrally over the joint. Restrictions on the "off-stud splice device" locations are as follows:

- All splices shall be located a minimum of two stud cavities from wall corners.
- Successive splices within the same plank course shall be located no closer than 48" from one another.
- All splices shall be staggered at minimum of 24" intervals when located in the same wall cavity.
- Splices shall be at least one stud cavity away from door or window openings.

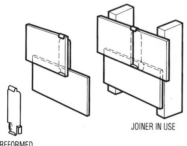

JOINER IN USE

PREFORMED
OFF-STUD METAL JOINER

Figure 5-5   Off-stud splice device. *(James Hardie Building Products)*

Siding Panels

Panel products are available in $^1/_4$" and $^5/_{16}$" thick sheets of varying sizes and a variety of textures (Fig. 5-6). 4' × 8', 4' × 9' and 4' × 10' are typical dimensions. All panel joints should fall at a framing member or have blocking installed. Panels must be fastened no closer than $^3/_8$" from the panel edge.

Figure 5-6   Fiber cement panel textures. *(James Hardie Building Products)*

Soffit Boards

Exterior soffits boards are available from some manufacturers and are typically $^3/_{16}$" or $^1/_4$" thick. They are available in varying sheet sizes ranging from 8' × 16" to 10' × 48". The soffit boards have a smooth, unsanded surface and are shipped already primed with an opaque acrylic paint, ready to receive a finish coat of high-quality exterior-grade acrylic, latex, PVA, semigloss, or flat paint. Soffit boards are typically applied to nominal 2 × 4 framing members spaced up to 24" o/c, with the long panel dimension perpendicular to the framing. Fasteners are installed with a minimum $^3/_8$" edge distance and minimum 2" clearance from corners. Joints are fastened at abutting sheet edges.

Figure 5-7   Fiber cement roofing. *(Eternit)*

Roofing Tiles

Fiber cement roofing products are of similar composition to the aforementioned products, except a color pigment is added (Fig. 5-7). Integral colors typically available are brown, green, cedar, gray, and pewter. When installed, the panels have an appearance of wood shakes with the textured wood-grain relief molded into the top face. The "shake-type" panels are approximately 22" long, $1/4$" thick, and 6", 8", or 12" wide (Fig. 5-8). The "slate-type" panels are 18" long and 8" wide and have a slate-relief texture (Fig. 5-9). Each installed roofing system weighs approximately 400 lb per square. (A square, or roofer's square, is 100 ft^2).

Efflorescence and color variation are common in cement-based products. Different bundles should be intermixed to ensure a varied and even color distribution. The roofing products are typically covered by the same 50-year warranty as the siding products but are not covered against freeze/thaw damage or other problems associated with ice or snow. The maximum wind uplift rating is 75 mph. Class A and Class B fire ratings can be achieved when proper assemblies are installed.

Roofing Tile Installation Techniques

The slate/shake-type roofing products are typically installed over nominal 1" × 4" or 1" × 6" sheathing boards spaced 7" or 11" o/c, (maximum, respectively), or solid sheathing. The minimum and maximum roof slopes are 3:12 and 24:12, respectively (Fig. 5-16). The maximum rafter spacing is 24". When setting the panels, care shall be taken to avoid the use of cut panels less than 4" wide or small pieces.

Figure 5-8   Fiber cement roofing shakes. *(James Hardie Building Products)*

A Class A fire rating consists of No. 40 x 36"-wide roofing felts on 1 × 4, 1 × 6 or $7/16$" OSB sheathing. A Class B rating uses No. 30 × 36" wide roofing felts with an 18" No. 30 interlayment.

Figure 5-9   Fiber cement roofing shakes. *(James Hardie Building Products)*

A $^1/_4$" thick starter strip is installed and spaced to allow any accumulated moisture to drain. Along the eave line, a 36"-wide strip of No. 30 roofing felt is laid over the sheathing. An eave starter course is laid projecting $1^1/_2$" to 2" beyond the edge of the sheathing to facilitate drainage into the gutter. Butt joints in the starter course shall be centered under a covering shake. An 18"-wide strip of No. 30 roofing felt is laid over the top portion of the starter course. This should extend onto the sheathing with the bottom edge of the felt positioned a distance equal to the weather exposure of the panel from the leading edge of the starter sheet.

The first panel course is laid over the starter sheet with the leading edges flush with the leading edge of the starter course. Panels are spaced $^3/_8$" to $^1/_2$" apart and fastened with two corrosion-resistant (galvanized or stainless steel) No. 11 roofing nails. Nails must not be overdriven or underdriven.

An 18"-wide strip of No. 30 roofing felt is laid over the top portion of the panels, extending onto the sheathing. The bottom edge of the felt is positioned a distance of twice the weather exposure of the panel from the leading edge of the roofing material. The next course of panels is then laid, ensuring that the joints between panels are offset at least 2" in adjacent courses and not in alignment with alternate courses. This procedure is repeated to complete the roof (Fig. 5-10).

Hips and ridges are fabricated by installing a 9"-wide piece of No. 30 roofing felt to cover 4" each side of the center of the ridge, over a full piece of No. 30 roofing felt. The fiber cement hip piece is fastened using two corrosion-resistant roofing nails of sufficient length to fully penetrate the sheathing $^3/_4$" or the full thickness of the sheathing, whichever is less (Fig.5-11).

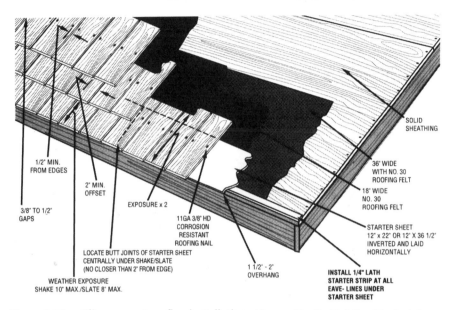

Figure 5-10   Fiber cement roofing installation. *(James Hardie Building Products)*

Roof valleys shall be flashed with minimum No. 28 gauge galvanized steel or corrosion-resistant metal such as copper or stainless steel. The flashing extends 11" each way from the center line and is applied over an underlayment of not less than No. 30 roofing felt. Flashing sections shall overlap 4" minimum (Fig. 5-12).

Base and counter flashing at any wall is formed to run a minimum of 3" up the wall with 6" horizontal legs. The flashing is placed between the exposed panel and the covered portion of the lower adjacent course and must be fastened through the panel into the sheathing. Stepped counter flashing, built into the wall, is placed over the wall flashing described above and shall be cut $^1/_2$" short of the horizontal surface. Any horizontally placed siding should start a minimum of 1" above the roof surface (Fig.5-13).

To prevent water penetration at overhangs, a $^1/_2$"-thick self-adhesive bitumem-impregnated foam strip is placed between the barge board top and the panels. Other details are contained in the manufacturer's installation specifications.

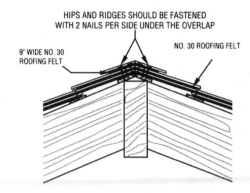

Figure 5-11   Ridge detail. *(James Hardie Building Products)*

As mentioned earlier, freeze/thaw cycles can be a problem with some roofing products. Some manufacturers are currently introducing new fiber cement products with a polymer additive to prevent water absorption and alleviate the problems associated with freezing water.

Figure 5-12   Valley detail. *(James Hardie Building Products)*

LAMINATED HIGH-DENSITY WOOD COMPOSITE

Also known as resin-bonded cladding, laminated high density wood composite products are a unique type of lap siding. These products have the appearance and appeal of wood, restrained textures, clean lines and designer colors (Fig. 5-14). Weather, harsh environments, moisture, and impacts will not affect the appearance or structure of the cladded material. It is asbestos free and readily cleaned of graffiti. It is designed for easy installation and is compatible with standard construction materials and practices. The cladding does not require pre- or postinstallation application of primers, paints, surface sealants, or special finishes. The performance has been proven in Europe for several decades and for more than 10 years in this country.

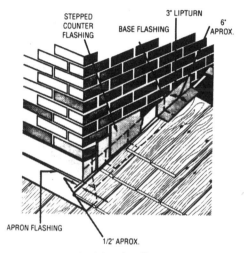

STEPPED COUNTER FLASHING

BASE FLASHING

3" LIPTURN

6" APROX.

APRON FLASHING

1/2" APROX.

Figure 5-13   Flashing detail. *(James Hardie Building Products)*

As mentioned in Chapter 2, the intent of this book is to discuss the means, methods, and materials in a nonproprietary manner. However, it is not possible with all construction products. This propriety cladding, manufactured by Werzalit of America, was developed by Werzalit AG & Co., a group that has an established 65-year reputation for creating resin-bonded building products. The lap siding products, installed in Europe for 35 years, have been in the United States since 1987.

Material Properties

Seasoned hardwoods, primarily black cherry and maple wood flakes, are shredded, sieved, dried, then combined with resins and preservatives. The mix is molded into preshaped blanks then sandwiched with phenolic surface/reinforcing sheets and compressed under extreme heat and pressure. Panels are color-coated with a thermoset acrylic finish on a Melamine paper and baked to a final cure. Lap siding panel widths are 4", 6" or 8" with four different textures are available (Fig. 5-15). All siding boards have a tongue-and-groove bottom edge. The lapped application of horizontal siding allows all fasteners to be concealed. Twelve standard colors are available. Custom colors are also available at no extra charge or minimum quantity. The cladding has a 15-year warranty against defects, damage, or finish problems. According to the manufacturer, these products are cost-competitive with other high-quality wood cladding systems while having a lower life-cycle cost.

Figure 5-14   Laminated high-density wood composite. *(Werzalit)*

Weather Resistance

Werzalit cladding is designed to be resistant to damage by ultra-violet rays. The manufacturer states that it will not blister, flake, or peel. It maintains its original texture, color, and structural integrity despite being subjected to heat, snow, rain, salt water, and environmental pollutants.

Moisture Resistance

The core of Werzalit cladding is more resistant to changes in moisture content than natural wood, hardboard, or particleboard. It is manufactured to prevent warping, checking, or buckling with changes in humidity, temperature, or freeze/thaw cycling.

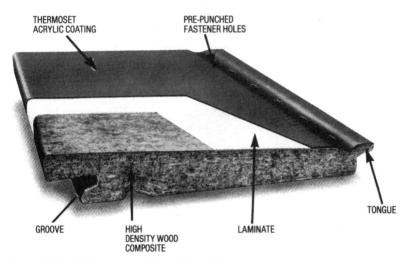

THERMOSET
ACRYLIC COATING

PRE-PUNCHED
FASTENER HOLES

TONGUE

GROOVE

HIGH
DENSITY WOOD
COMPOSITE

LAMINATE

Figure 5-15   Siding composition. *(Werzalit)*

Damage Resistance

Werzalit cladding withstands splitting, cracking, splintering, most installation abuse, and moderate vandalism. According to the manufacturer, hail, ice, or everyday wear and tear will not dent, chip, or nick the shell of the cladding.

Stain/Scuff Resistance

The abrasion-resistant acrylic surfaces are easily cleaned and are impervious to acids, alkalines, and cleaning solutions.   Graffiti and other stains or scuffs are removable.

Installation

The tongue-and-groove siding boards come with predrilled fastener holes that are elongated to allow for expansion and contraction. Boards are compatible with all typical wall assemblies that are used for wood or fiber cement siding attachment: The length and rigidity of the panels are designed for a one-man installation. No special tools, primers, paint, sealants or special finishes are required (Fig. 5-16).

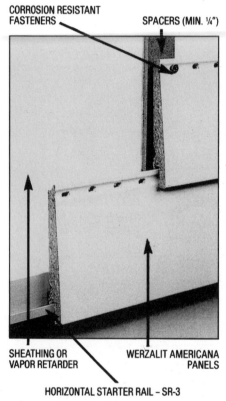

CORROSION RESISTANT
FASTENERS   SPACERS (MIN. ¼")

SHEATHING OR   WERZALIT AMERICANA
VAPOR RETARDER   PANELS

HORIZONTAL STARTER RAIL – SR-3

Figure 5-16   Siding installation. *(Werzalit)*

It is important to consult the manufacturer's installation directions during construction. The following are general guidelines for information purposes only:

• First of all, fasten ventilation spacers and starter rail on the wall support.

- Position the initial panel on the starter rail. Insert fastener in center of predrilled holes and secure panel to wall.
- Slip subsequent tongue-and-groove panels into adjoining panels and fasten to wall.
- Install Werzalit-supplied accessories as required.

According to the manufacturer, additional or new paint can be easily applied to the prefinished panel. Werzalit products are also being used as window sills in some proprietary window units.

MANUFACTURED STONE VENEERS

Manufactured stone veneer is a lightweight and easy-to-install alternative to authentic quarried stone (Fig. 5-17). These veneers can be used for exterior or interior surfaces and are installed at a fraction of the cost of full-thickness natural stone. Another advantage to using stone veneers is that these can be used where full-thickness natural stone won't work due to structural inadequacies. The stone is lightweight and adheres quickly for fast, easy installation with no additional footings or wall ties required.

Figure 5-17   Manufactured stone veneer. *(Stone Products Corporation)*

Simulated stone products were first popularized in the 1930s. Many of these products were very labor intensive to install, usually requiring specially trained technicians or contractors. Two methods were generally available: off-site prefabrication of stone panels or on-site forming using a wet finish coat similar to stucco.[4]

Manufactured stone veneer is cast in molds taken from natural stone, using a process that faithfully reproduces even the faintest detail. One proprietary product, Cultured Stone® by the Stone Products Corporation, casts stones from thousands of individual molds, essentially eliminating repetition. The manufacturer also claims that no two stones are ever reproduced with the exact same coloring, also eliminating the possibility of repetition.

Depending upon the manufacturer, these products are covered by up to a 30-year warranty. Although wall veneers are the focus of this text, brick veneers and landscape brick or stone pavers are also available from some manufacturers.

Material Properties

Manufactured stone veneer is produced by placing a mixture of portland cement, mineral oxide pigments (for color) and lightweight aggregates into a mold. Although thicknesses may vary from 1" to 3" depending on the texture, the average thickness of stone veneer is $1^3/_4$". Stone sizes can range from 2" to 30" in diameter. Manufactured stone veneer weighs approximately 8 to 12 lb/ft² (Fig. 5-18).

Although the base color is blended throughout the entire product, color overtones are applied and integrated into the product during the casting process. Existing applications show no undesirable change in color after years of weathering.

Thermal Characteristics

Manufactured stone veneer is noncombustible with zero flame spread and zero smoke development (UL Classification #209T). Manufactured stone veneer can be used on fireplace facings or behind free-standing stoves.

Efflorescence

Efflorescence is an encrustation of water-soluble salts, typically white, that may appear on the surface of stucco, concrete, brick, and other masonry products. This occurrence is typically caused by the evaporation of water that has penetrated the wall. There is little one can do except remove the source of the water (sometimes a poor seal or an open-capped wall allows water to work its way through the assembly) or wait an unspecified amount of time until the problem remedies itself. If mild efflorescence is to be removed, allow the stone to dry thoroughly and scrub vigorously with a stiff bristle brush (do not use a wire brush). Finally, rinse thoroughly using clean water.

Figure 5-18   Manufactured stone veneer types and sizes.
(Stone Products Corporation)

Maintenance

Manufactured stone veneer products are typically maintenance-free. Occasional washing to remove surface dust and dirt is all that is required. Simple scratches or scuff marks can generally be removed by using a strong solution of granulated soap or detergent and water with a bristle brush, then rinsing immediately with fresh water. Do not sandblast or wash with acid, abrasives, or high-pressure water. Replacement is the best option if the materials are damaged or marred by graffiti.

Cost

Cultured Stone® by Stone Products Corporation typically costs $7.50 to $12.00/ft². The current national average installed cost is $8.50/ft².[5] The increased speed of installation over real stone is fairly evident. A mason can typically lay 40 ft² of stone a day. Manufactured stone veneer products can be set at a rate of 80 to 250 ft² per day.[6]

Installation

Manufactured stone veneers may be applied over any clean, untreated, structurally sound wall such as wood, wallboard, masonry, or metal. Depending upon the substrate, various material-specific preparations will need to take place. Metal lath on waterproof building paper or building felts lapped 4" is needed for any sheathed surfaces. Open-stud systems require a paper-backed metal lath with a $1/2$" to $3/4$" scratch coat applied (allow to dry for 48 hours). New and clean concrete or masonry surfaces do not need any preparation work. Existing painted or dirty concrete masonry surfaces will need to be sandblasted or covered with metal lath (Fig. 5-19).

Before starting, spread the stones out at the job site and review the range to ensure a good variety of sizes, shapes, and colors from which to choose. Plan some variety and contrast in the overall design. For example, use small stones next to large ones, heavy-textured pieces next to smooth, and thick stones next to thinner ones. Mixing manufactured stone veneer from different boxes during application will also allow a desirable balance of individual stones on the finished project.

Each piece of manufactured stone veneer is applied individually and attached permanently to the wall surface with Type N portland cement mortar. First, mix the mortar to a firm, moist consistency as specified in the manufacturer's literature. Mortar that is too dry and crumbly will not provide a proper bond. Mortar that is too wet will be weak and messy. It is important to note that applications should be protected from temperatures below freezing as mortar will not set up properly under such conditions. Do not use antifreeze compounds to lower the freezing point of mortar.

If stone is being applied in hot or dry weather, the back of each piece should be moistened with a fine spray of water or a wet brush to adequately prevent excessive absorption of moisture from the mortar. If being installed over concrete, masonry, or scratch coat substrate, the substrate surface area should also be dampened before applying mortar.

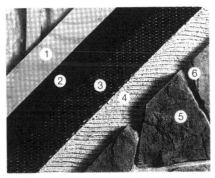

In sequence: (1) sheathing, (2) weather resistant barrier, (3) galvanized metal lath, (4) mortar, (5) Cultured Stone®, (6) mortar joint.

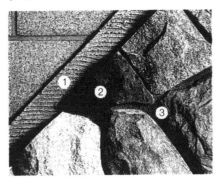

In sequence: (1) mortar applied directly to untreated, unpainted masonry, concrete or stucco, (2) Cultured Stone®, (3) mortar joint.

Figure 5-19   Manufactured stone veneer installation. *(Stone Products Corporation)*

Using a plasterer's or mason's trowel, apply $1/2$" to $3/4$" thick bed of mortar to the prepared surface area. Do not spread more than what is considered a workable area, usually 5 to 10 ft² at a time. This should prevent the mortar from "setting up" before the stone is applied. Apply mortar and stone working from the bottom up or most stones can be applied from the top down. (Consult the manufacturer's literature for specific instructions.)

Working from the top down may help avoid splashing previously applied stone with dripping mortar.

Press each stone into the mortar setting bed firmly enough to squeeze some mortar out around the stone's edges. Apply pressure to the stone to ensure a good bond and complete coverage between the mortar bed and back surface of the stone. This is accomplished by "wiggling" the stone while applying light pressure. Mortar may also be applied to the entire back of the stone.

One manufacturer recommends that in order to obtain the most natural look, mortar joints should be as narrow as possible. On average, joints should not exceed $1/2$" in width. Joints should be tooled and finished once the mortar begins to stiffen. An attractive look can also be achieved by fitting stones tightly together. Care must be taken to avoid smearing mortar on surface of stone. Accidental smears should be removed using a whisk broom only after the mortar has become crumbly. It is imperative to never use a wet brush to treat the mortar joints due to the probability of undesirable staining.

Manufactured stone veneers can be cut and shaped for a better fit. A variety of tools can be used, including wide-mouth nippers, a hatchet, with a circular saw fitted with a masonry blade, or a masonry saw. Some broken stones may be found in the box. These may also be used in filling gaps between large stones. In most cases cut or trimmed edges will be covered by mortar joints. If recommended by the manufacturer, use a mortar coating to cover exposed cut edges. Position cut edges up when they are above eye level, and down when below eye level. Always use safety glasses when cutting and trimming (Fig. 5-20).

Stone Products Corporation, makers of Cultured Stone®, also provide corner pieces. According to their literature, these should be applied first. Since the corner pieces have a long and a short leg, these should be alternated in opposite directions. After the corner pieces are in place, flat pieces are applied working toward the wall center. Place the individual stones close together, creating uniform joints between them. Cut and trim as required to achieve consistent width in the mortar joints. Then trim and fit small pieces into any remaining voids.

A poured-in-place concrete cap should be used to provide adequate runoff protection on horizontal or sloping top areas of exterior walls, piers, retaining walls, chimneys or other surfaces. Caps should extend approximately 1" to 2" beyond the finished stone surface. Some manufacturers also supply prefabricated caps (Figs. 5-21 and 5-22).

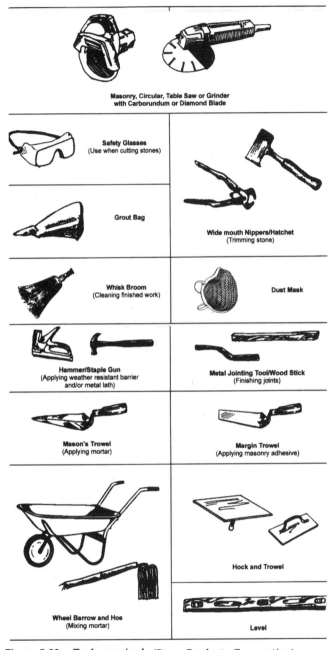

Figure 5-20   Tools required. *(Stone Products Corporation)*

All retaining walls should be damp-proofed at the fill side and proper weep holes or other suitable drainage provided. Keep the finished edge of the manufactured stone veneer a minimum of 4" above ground level (finished grade) to avoid possible staining of the stone by soils containing alkali or other minerals. This can be achieved by the use of a 2" × 4" leveling strip (straight-edge).

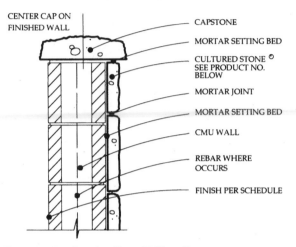

Figure 5-21   Cap detail on CMU wall. *(Stone Products Corporation)*

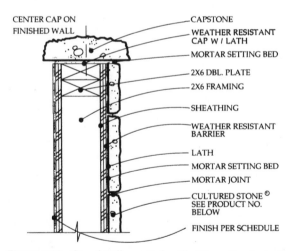

Figure 5-22   Cap detail on stud wall. *(Stone Products Corporation)*

Limitations

Manufactured stone veneer wall veneers are not suitable for foot traffic. Manufactured stone veneer should not be used below water level as in swimming pool liners. As with any concrete or natural material, continued exposure to chlorine and other chemicals may discolor or adversely affect manufactured stone veneer products. If manufactured stone veneer is installed close to the pool where it will be frequently splashed, one manufacturer recommends protection with a non-film-forming breather-type masonry sealer applied on a regular basis. Similarly, most manufactured stone veneer products are not warranted against damage incurred from salt or other chemicals used to remove snow or ice.

On exterior applications, the incorrect installation or absence of flashing, cant strips, gutters, and downspouts may result in diversion of water runoff onto finished surface areas. Masonry and other building products subjected to these conditions may develop staining, and when combined with severe freeze/thaw conditions, may eventually cause surface damage. The application of manufactured stone veneer under these conditions is not recommended.

The National Evaluation Service Committee recommends that manufactured stone veneer applications not exceed 30' in height above grade when used as an exterior veneer attached to wood frame construction.[7]

CONCLUSION

Mimesis, the technique of reinterpreting or imitating a traditional material in the form of a new material, has been employed in works of architecture dating back to the ancient times of the Egyptians. For example, the triglyphs located on the stone frieze of the Greek temple, the Parthenon, were reinterpretive expressions of the heavy timber framing used on similar structures prior to the use of stone. Similarly, the stamped aluminum skirting made to look like a concrete masonry unit foundation found under many mobile homes incorporates the same philosophy. This technique of new technology improving on the old is equally evident in fiber cement siding, wood composite cladding, and manufactured stone veneer products. Each of these products are designed to give the comfort and aesthetic value of traditional materials while improving on their original compositions. Purists may reject these products, but homeowners interested in improved durability, reduced maintenance, longer warranties, all at competitive or lower costs have already demonstrated that a need has been filled.

APPENDIX

Stone Products Corporation
PO Box 270
Napa, CA 94559-0270
(800) 225-7462
Fax: (707) 255-5572

James Hardie Building Products
26300 La Alameda
Suite 250
Mission Viejo, CA 92691
(800) 348-1811

Werzalit of America, Inc.
PO Box 373
40 Holley Avenue
Bradford, PA 16701
(800) 999-3730

REFERENCES

1. Christopher Alexander, *A Pattern Language*, (New York: Oxford University Press, 1977), p. 1094.
2. Harold J. Rosen and Tom Heineman, *Architectural Materials for Construction* (New York: McGraw-Hill, 1996), pp. 5-6.
3. Fiber Cement Material Safety Data Report, James Hardie Building Products, Inc.
4. Thomas C. Jester, ed., *Twentieth-Century Building Materials* (New York: McGraw-Hill, 1995), pp. 176-177.
5. Cultured Stone® Literature, page AB 1/96 9000A22B, Stone Products Corporation.
6. "Faithful Usonian, *Custom Builder Magazine* reprint, May/June 1997.
7. The National Evaluation Service Committee Report No. NER-358, May 1, 1996.

6

Exterior Doors and Windows

INTRODUCTION

John Ruskin (1819 to 1900), a professor of fine arts at Oxford during the second half of the 19th century, published *The Seven Lamps of Architecture* in 1848. In it he said "Houses with windows which are merely holes in the walls are like empty skulls."[1] Although Ruskin's criticism (albeit contradictory at times) was a discussion on the importance of expressing truth in ornament, he also implies that a sense of appropriateness be applied in the design of all architectural elements. One hundred fifty years later, that same logic should be undertaken by the designer, builder, or homeowner when selecting such seemingly rudimentary objects as doors and windows. To merely select a unit based on convenience or habit is to ignore the significant improvements that technology has made in the production of doors and windows.

Frame and sash construction, muntins and lite proportions, dual or triple glazing, impact resistance, coatings, and wood, vinyl or aluminum claddings are but a few of the traditional choices. New technologies are now producing composite frame materials and highly efficient glazing systems that are not only superior in construction and energy efficiency but are priced competitively against traditional choices.

GLASS

Although the origins of glass may date back some 4500 years, historians claim it was first used in windows by the Romans. Archeologists have found evidence of a 3' × 4' sheet used in a public bath in Pompeii in AD 79. Plate glass, first produced by the French in the late 1600s, was imported into the United States until the 1850s. Plate glass was produced by casting and rolling large sheets which were then ground and polished. This popular method was especially suited for large shop windows.[2] The Pilkington Brothers introduced a new method of glass production in England in 1959. Float glass was invented to combine the fire polish and low cost of sheet glass with the flatness and low distortion properties of plate glass.[3] Float glass is made by floating molten glass on a bath of liquid tin in a furnace. Float glass has been produced in the United States since 1963 and accounts for over 90 percent of domestic flat glass production.[4]

The physical properties of float glass can be modified for a specific end use. Patterned, spandrel, reflective-coated, security, obscure, tinted (bronze or gray), spandrel, and wire glass are typically available form various manufacturers. This discussion will study typical residential applications of insulating glass, gas-filled chambers and low-E glass coatings.

Window Glass Terminology

Due to the extensive number of varieties and assembly combinations possible with glass units, window and door specifications can be difficult to compare. A number of methods for quantitative analysis have been devised to assist in the task of comparing similar products.

- Unit thickness: The total overall thickness of the insulated glass unit.
- U-value: The heat flow, or thermal conductivity rate through a given construction. The lower the U-value, the less heat is transmitted through the glazing material.
- R-value: This measures the insulation effectiveness, or resistance to heat flow, of the glass. The higher the R-value, the better the insulating performance. (R-value is the reciprocal, or inverse, of the U-value.)
- Shading Coefficient (SC): A measure of the heat gain through glass from solar radiation. Specifically, it is the ratio of the total solar heat gain through the glazing compared to $1/8$" clear glass under the same design conditions. It includes both the solar energy transmitted directly plus any absorbed solar radiation that is re-radiated as heat into the interior. The number ranges from 0.0 to 1.0 The lower the shading coefficient, the lower the heat gain. The higher the number,

the better for passive heat gain. For example, standard insulating glass has an SC of 0.81.

- Relative Heat Gain: The total heat gain through the glass for a specific set of summer design conditions. This value considers indoor/outdoor temperature differences and the effect of solar radiation.
- Solar Heat Gain: This unit measures the sun-shielding properties of the product and its ability to absorb or reflect solar heat. The lower the solar heat gain, the better the product is at protecting against heating caused by sunlight.
- Visible Light Transmittance: This unit signifies the percentage of light in the visible spectrum that a glazing transmits through the window. The number ranges from 0 to 100 percent. The higher the number, the more visible light that gets in. Standard clear insulating glass has a daylight transmission of 82 percent.
- Solar Energy Transmittance: The percentage of ultraviolet, visible, and near-infrared energy that is transmitted through the glass. The higher the number, the greater the amount of energy.

Types of Glass

As mentioned earlier, there are an extensive number of varieties of glass that can be used in the home. The following are the most common examples.

Annealed Glass

Annealed glass is float glass that is cooled in a controlled manner as it leaves the bath in the float glass furnace. This procedure minimizes residual internal stresses.

Tempered Glass

Tempered glass is four to five times stronger than annealed glass. If broken, tempered glass breaks into innumerable small cubed fragments, minimizing the chance of injury on personal impact. Since tempered glass falls out of its opening in interlocking clumps, manufacturers recommend against its use for glazing in residential skylights. Tempered glass is available in practically every thickness that is used for flat glass products and is required by most building codes in applications where human impact is possible.

Heat-Strengthened Glass

Heat-strengthened glass increases resistance to thermal shock and is about twice as strong as annealed glass. Heat-strengthened glass is made by cutting annealed glass to size, heating to near its softening point, then cooling faster than normal, but not as quickly as when producing fully tempered glass.

In general, heat-strengthened glass is specified where thermal stresses are high, such as solarium and skylights or where climates may be severe. Properly applied, the glass will resist most normal thermal and wind loads, and virtually eliminates the risk of spontaneous breakage. Unlike tempered glass, heat-strengthened glass will not pulverize into a crystal-like form. If heat-strengthened glass should break, the pieces will be larger and tend to stay in the frame until removed.

Laminated Glass

Laminated glass consists of two or more layers of glass sandwiching a vinyl interlayer to form a single laminated unit. The plastic interlayer produces a unit that will prevent sharp fragments from shattering and flying about when a sharp impact and breaks occur, since the glass adheres to the vinyl interlayer. Typical applications include burglar-resistant units, skylights, solariums, atriums, as well as safety glazing when approved by building codes.

Insulating Glass

There are many factors which affect the thermal performance of windows. These include the local climate, the framing material, the window construction, and the quality of installation. Since glass represents up to 85 percent of any window, the quality and properties of that glass are extremely important in measuring overall window performance.

Window glass is a very poor thermal insulator. In fact, a single sheet of glass conducts heat about five times as fast as an inch of polystyrene foam insulation. A second sheet of glass installed with an airspace, or cavity between, known as insulating glass, cuts the extreme rate of heat loss by 50 percent.[5] Insulating glass is available in two configurations, double glazed (Fig. 6-1) and triple glazed (Fig. 6-2), and is separated by a hermetically sealed airspace. Insulating glass, with its inherent high performance in thermal resistance and shading coefficient, is especially effective and thus primarily used to control heat transfer. Insulating glass windows are even far superior in energy performance than standard windows with storm windows.

Figure 6-1 Double-glazed insulating glass unit. *(Marvin Doors & Windows)*

Triple-glazed units provide a greater R-value than double-glazed window units but are more expensive. This cost difference may be justified if the home is in a relatively colder climate. Generally speaking, double-glazed units will provide sufficient R-value for the cost of the window in most locations.

Gas-Filled Chamber

Air is the typical filler in lower-cost residential windows. Unfortunately, air has a high conductivity, which contributes to the windows's total heat loss. According to one manufacturer, a large portion of ambient heat is lost by contact between the inside air and the surface of the internal pane. Energy then dissipates toward the external pane through the interpane air. This unavoidable effect, known as conduction, is usually responsible for two-thirds of heat losses.[6]

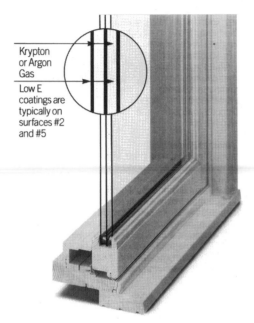

Krypton
or Argon
Gas

Low E
coatings are
typically on
surfaces #2
and #5

Figure 6-2 Triple-glazed insulating glass unit. *(Marvin Doors & Windows)*

Instead of air, the insulated glass cavity may be filled with a heavier gas (greater molecular mass) than air. A heavier gas moves more slowly than a lighter gas. This reduces the conductive heat transfer across the airspace, improving (lowering) the U-value. The gas layer also acts as a sound absorber, reducing unwanted outside noise. Argon, xenon, or krypton are the gases used to fill the cavity in lieu of air, with argon being the most common gas used in residential applications.

Argon is a colorless, odorless gas that is chemically inactive. Argon makes up approximately 1 percent of the world's atmosphere, making it the most abundant of all the noble (inert) gases.[7] Argon, because of its natural abundance, costs less than other gases, including many manufactured compounds. It is also very stable, so there is no concern over its reactions with other materials used in insulating glass systems.

Gas-filled insulating glass units have 1.4 times the insulating value of air-filled units.[8] In fact, one manufacturer states that the U-values obtained with an argon gas–filled chamber is the equivalent of a quadruple-glazed window unit in the winter time.[9]

Low-E Glass

One researcher discovered that 1 ft^2 of single-pane glass "leaked" the equivalent of 1 gallon of heating oil each winter.[10] Although insulating glass units dramatically improve the thermal efficiency of residential windows, the use of a low-E coating on at least one of the glass faces will even further improve the performance of the window.

In order to minimize the transfer of radiant heat through glass, a revolutionary product was invented in the early 1980s, called low-E glass. (Low-E is an abbreviation for low emissivity. Emissivity is a measure of how much a glass surface transfers radiant heat.) Low-E glass allows natural light to enter while reflecting indoor heat energy back into the home in winter. Likewise, it reflects outdoor heat energy back to the outside in summer[11] (Fig. 6-3).

Figure 6-3 Low-E glass. *(PPG)*

Types Of Low-E Glass

There are two types of low-E coatings, softcoat and hardcoat. Softcoat low-E coatings are vacuum-deposited on the glass after it comes off the float glass manufacturing line. These coatings are created as the room temperature glass passes through a series of vacuum chambers where metallic particles are deposited onto the glass surface.

Hardcoat low-E coatings are applied in a pyrolytic process on the float glass manufacturing line before the glass has cooled. This means the coating is sprayed on the molten glass and is fused to the glass as it cools, creating a permanent bond. Although not as thermally effective as softcoat, this process produces a coating that is as durable as the glass itself.[12] For the text discussed herein, the softcoat process (also known as sputter coating or off-line coating) will be referred to as "vacuum low-E" and the hardcoat process (also called on-line process) will be referred to as "pyrolitic low-E".[13]

How Low-E Glass Works

The sun radiates energy in the form of short-wave rays. When the sun shines directly through the windows of a home, short-wave rays enter the room, providing visible light and invisible heat. The rays strike objects like the floor, walls, and furniture, and subsequently warm them. These sun-warmed objects then reradiate invisible infrared heat in the form of long-wave rays. Long-wave radiant heat is provided within the home from other sources such as heating systems, fireplaces, appliances, lightbulbs, and human bodies. It is the long-wave radiation that low-E glass is designed to control.

So what does this mean? Since ordinary clear glass has no coating, it absorbs and transmits heat very readily. For example, in the winter, clear glass absorbs heat from the inside of your home and transfers it to the cold exterior.

Once the sun's heat is inside a home, the low-E coating works to reduce the amount of heat transferred through the glass to the colder exterior. This means that less indoor heat, whether provided by the sun or a furnace, is transmitted back through the glass to the outside. (One manufacturer claims low-E glass insulating units are more than three times better than single-pane, clear glass at keeping heat inside in winter.)[14]

In the summer months, heat enters a house through ordinary clear glass to the cooler interior. This happens not only by direct short-wave sunlight but also by long-wave radiation generated by the hot exterior environment such as sidewalks, driveways, and other elements which have absorbed heat from the sun. Low-E glass effectively reduces the amount of heat transmitted through the glass by reflecting a significant portion of the long-wave radiation back to the outside.[15] (It is important to note that direct short-wave sunlight transmission can best be minimized through overhangs, awnings, and window coverings.)

The most appropriate combination for homeowners that have more heating days than cooling days is to have window units that have a high R-value and a relatively high shading coefficient. While ordinary clear glass allows more solar energy into your home than low-E glass does, clear glass has such a low R-value that it allows not only the solar energy gain but any furnace-generated heat (during the winter) to escape. A high shading coefficient indicates that more heat can penetrate through the window unit is also desirable in northern climates, since this area typically desires more solar heat gain for passive solar heating in the winter.

The low-E coating should typically be on the surface that faces the air space in an insulating glass unit. The coating on the No. 3 surface maximizes the passive solar heat gain. When the coating is on surface No. 2, the shading coefficient and passive solar gain are lower. In either case, the U-value is the same[16] (Fig. 6-4).

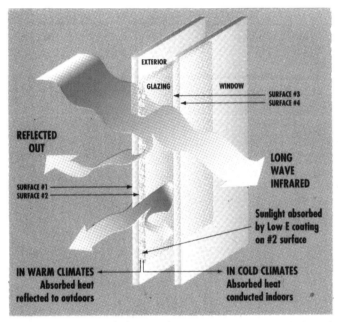

Figure 6-4   Insulated glass surfaces. *(Marvin Windows & Doors)*

Low-E windows can achieve R-values as high as R-5, a marked improvement over the R-1 single-pane, or even R-2 double-pane windows. Low-E windows cost a little more than standard windows and allow slightly less light to enter, but are often cost effective in extremely hot or cold climates.[17]

Reasons To Use Low-E Glass

In addition to lower utility bills, there are a number of advantages to having low-E windows installed in the home. Some of these include increased comfort near windows, greater design freedom, ultraviolet ray reduction, and reduced condensation.

Heat energy always flows from warm objects to cool objects. For example, when a person picks up a cold can of soda, his or her hand feels cold because heat is transferring from the warm hand to the cold soda can. In winter, when someone is standing near a poorly insulated window, the drafty feeling is caused by the person's body heat leaving his or her skin. Windows with low-E glass help keep the inside surface temperature of the glass warmer.[18] Human comfort is improved during the winter months; between 70 and 75 percent of the heat that would otherwise escape from the house is reflected back into the home for energy savings.[19]

The energy efficiency of low-E glazing also counteracts the typical problem of energy loss associated with large windows. This means that the designer has a greater latitude in selecting fenestration choices since the disadvantage of increased energy inefficiency is no longer an issue. Another factor is the glass appearance. Low-E glass is predominantly color-neutral by most manufacturers, making it appear virtually the same as clear single-pane glass.

Ultraviolet rays can cause premature fading and degrading of fabrics, upholstery, carpeting, and artwork. Low-E glass significantly reduces transmission of the sun's damaging ultraviolet rays when compared to clear glass.

Condensation is another common nuisance that can be minimized with low-E glass. Condensation is created when moisture vapor in the air is cooled to its liquid state. This happens when the surface temperature of a solid, such as the frame or glass, is lower than the dew point of the humid air in its immediate vicinity. This is most obvious on ordinary clear glass windows in the winter, because of the dramatic temperature difference between the heated air in the home and the inside surface temperature of the glass.

Condensation is minimized on window surfaces since Low-E glass helps keep the inside glass surface temperature warmer. One manufacturer claims that in order for condensation to appear on their low-E glass product, humidity levels must be four times higher than on single-pane clear glass windows.[20]

Low-E glass is not limited to new construction applications. For existing windows, low-E coatings are also available on films which can be applied to the inside surfaces. This film application can be a good investment.[21] According to a recent survey done by *Remodeling Magazine*, real estate agents nationally estimate a new set of energy-efficient windows returns 75 percent of your money invested.[22]

Standards for Window Comparisons

The extensive variety of glass types and manufacturers' products can make educated window selections difficult. A process is being implemented that should remove some of the confusion of comparing various characteristics of residential windows. The National Fenestration Rating Council, (NFRC) created under the Energy Policy Act of 1992, has been establishing a program to standardize the reporting of various energy factors. These include: solar heat gain, optical properties, air infiltration, condensation resistance, and long-term and annual energy performance. Unlike the typical task of comparing specifications of individual components, this new system will account for whole product performance for the energy-related effects of all of the window components. The standard label is designed to provide consumers, architects, builders and code officials with energy performance ratings in a comparable, easy-to-read format (Fig. 6-5).

The manufacturer's name section displays the name of the window, door, or skylight manufacturer. The certificate will also display the product's U-factor, solar heat gain coefficient, air leakage rating, and visible light transmittance rating.[23] The independent agency designation area is reserved for the name and logo of the independent agency which certifies that the product meets the NFRC program's requirements. NFRC licenses these agencies and inspects them to make sure their work conforms to NFRC's rigorous testing and certification procedures. The product description describes the characteristics of the window, door, or skylight.[24] Several states, including California, Oregon, Washington, and Massachusetts, as well as many local jurisdictions, require NFRC labels on all new windows and skylights.

FIBERGLASS WINDOWS AND DOORS

Fiberglass provides excellent physical and mechanical properties desired in windows and doors, including low thermal conductivity, dimensional stability over the temperature spectrum, resistance to moisture and corrosion, and ready acceptance of colored finishes. These characteristics make pultrusions attractive for use not only as a single window framing material, but also in combination with other traditional materials such as wood, PVC, and aluminum. These designs allow full utilization of the specific advantages of various materials, resulting in significantly improved windows that feature unique qualities and would be impossible to obtain with a single material.[25]

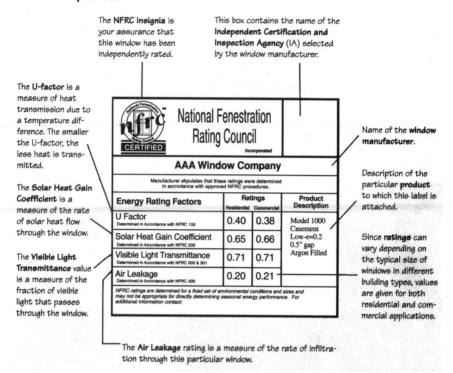

The **NFRC Insignia** is your assurance that this window has been independently rated.

This box contains the name of the **Independent Certification and Inspection Agency** (IA) selected by the window manufacturer.

The **U-factor** is a measure of heat transmission due to a temperature difference. The smaller the U-factor, the less heat is transmitted.

The **Solar Heat Gain Coefficient** is a measure of the rate of solar heat flow through the window.

The **Visible Light Transmittance** value is a measure of the fraction of visible light that passes through the window.

Name of the **window manufacturer**.

Description of the particular **product** to which this label is attached.

Since **ratings** can vary depending on the typical size of windows in different building types, values are given for both residential and commercial applications.

National Fenestration Rating Council
Incorporated
CERTIFIED

AAA Window Company

Manufacturer stipulates that these ratings were determined in accordance with approved NFRC procedures.

Energy Rating Factors	Ratings		Product Description
	Residential	Commercial	
U Factor Determined in Accordance with NFRC 100	0.40	0.38	Model 1000 Casement
Solar Heat Gain Coefficient Determined in Accordance with NFRC 200	0.65	0.66	Low-e=0.2 0.5" gap Argon Filled
Visible Light Transmittance Determined in Accordance with NFRC 300 & 301	0.71	0.71	
Air Leakage Determined in Accordance with NFRC 400	0.20	0.21	

NFRC ratings are determined for a fixed set of environmental conditions and sizes and may not be appropriate for directly determining seasonal energy performance. For additional information contact:

The **Air Leakage** rating is a measure of the rate of infiltration through this particular window.

Figure 6-5 NFRC label. *(NFRC)*

Production of Pultruded Fiberglass

Pultrusion is an automated process for the manufacture of constant volume profiles made from composite materials. These materials can be formulated to meet severe chemical, flame-retardant, electrical or environmental requirements while possessing high strength-to-weight ratios, high heat distortion temperatures, moisture resistance, and low thermal conductivity. These lightweight, continuous-length, high-strength profiles are used in various applications such as construction ladders, sporting goods equipment, bridges, garden tools, and medical devices.

By definition, pultrusion is the process of "pulling" resin and reinforcing fiber through a die to produce a continuous, high-strength composite material. In the fabrication process, continuous fiber reinforcing strands, mats, and woven cloths of glass, graphite, and a range of other fibers can be combined with thermosetting resins and continuously formed on-line. The dry fibers are first pulled from racks to a wet-out bath where the fibers are thoroughly impregnated with resin. Next, the wet fibers are brought together and formed into a preliminary shape by a preform tool. The wet, uncured package then enters the special pultrusion die. This die is a precision mold, machined and ground to exacting tolerances. Cure of the thermosetting resin is activated by heat in the die and catalyst in the resin mix, causing the resin to crosslink or cure (Fig. 6-6).

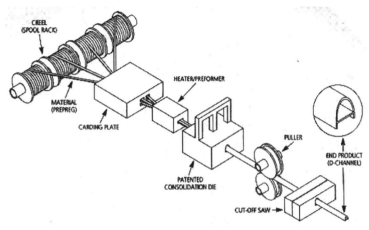

Figure 6-6   The pultrusion process. *(Thermoplastic Pultrusions, Inc.)*

Unlike aluminum or PVC, which are pushed through a die and then worked at the exit end, the pultrusion process pulls the material, hence the name, through the die and the resulting profile is cut to length as it leaves the die. It is then ready for use without further forming or other treatment.

Pultruded Fiberglass Properties

A number of properties inherent to fiberglass make it a superior choice for windows and doors. For example, pultruded fiberglass has a low coefficient of thermal conductivity similar to other low-conductivity materials such as PVC and wood. Pultruded profiles can be made very thin, which eliminates all but a narrow heat path for thermal bridging, resulting in excellent thermal performance.

Pultruded fiberglass is virtually impervious to moisture. This eliminates problems associated with rotting, warping, cracking, or twisting. Similarly, pultruded fiberglass is corrosion-resistant and is unaffected by the chemicals, salt air, and acid rain which affect window frames in harsh coastal environments. The tensile and flexural strength characteristics of pultrusions permit stiffness in window designs similar to those of conventional metals without the inferior thermal characteristics.[26]

Pultrusion, like glass, has a very low coefficient of thermal expansion/contraction, thereby minimizing any distortion caused by extreme hot or cold temperatures. Window frames of pultruded fiberglass hold their original shape, are impervious to temperature changes, and maintain their initial air infiltration rates. This quality of dimensional stability also allows fiberglass to be laminated with vinyl or polyester woodgrains.[27]

Figure 6-7 Pultruded fiberglass window. *(Accurate Dorwin Industries)*

Pultruded Fiberglass Windows

Although the pultrusion technology has been available for over 40 years, it was not until the early 1980s that the industry saw the development of forming technology that permitted the production of the thin-wall complex shapes necessary for the window industry. The superior dimensional stability, strength, and thermal performance of fiberglass windows is reported to have been first exhibited by Accurate Dorwin Industries and Omniglass Ltd. in Canada in 1984.[28] Since that time, improvements have been made; however, the basic properties and their inherent advantages are still significant (Fig. 6-7).

Fiberglass window frames usually exhibit higher R-values than frame profiles of other materials. For example, in a comparison of similar frames by one manufacturer, the fiberglass window frame had an R-value of R-10, while the vinyl window frame was R-6, the wood was R-5, and the aluminum frame was R-0.2.[29] The high tensile strength of the material allows it to be used in relatively thin-walled hollow profiles which are completely foam-filled, resulting in superior thermal resistance. Pultruded fiberglass windows have a lower expansion coefficient, somewhat close to flat glass, which helps maintain airtightness throughout the unit.[30] Depending upon the manufacturer, units can have an integral finish, a baked-on enamel finish, or can be painted.

A look at activity among window and door manufacturers across North America reveals a growing array of styles, designs, and compositions of fiberglass windows. Although some manufacturers are fabricating window frames of monolithic construction, some are producing units consisting of composite or multimaterial designs that incorporate fiberglass with aluminum, PVC or wood. (Figs. 6-8 through 6-10) Two examples are noteworthy:

- A combination of pultruded fiberglass, on the exterior, and wood on the interior.

- The intricate frame and sash components are made completely of pultruded fiberglass frame and sash with an interior veneer of a thin layer of real wood applied by a process known as profile wrapping.

Both of these examples are capitalizing on the durable maintenance-free properties of fiberglass for the exterior and the aesthetic and tactile qualities of wood on the interior. Industry professionals suggest that design trends indicate window units will continue to incorporate a variety of materials based on their physical and economic properties as well as their availability. These factors are influenced further by the perception of consumers about the material's environmental impact.[31]

At present, fiberglass and composites are slightly more expensive than other window units. Industry sources recommend to expect to pay 15 percent more for a fiberglass casement window.[32] Technological advances and rising lumber prices suggest this cost difference will eventually level off.

Figure 6-8 Composite window unit. *(Andersen Windows and Patio Doors)*

Figure 6-9 Composite window sash. *(Marvin Windows and Doors)*

Warranty

Frames are constructed of low-maintenance fiberglass that can also be painted. Fiberglass frames are most compatible with glazing, offering the lowest range of expansion and contraction. This enables some fabricators to offer a lifetime warranty against warping, twisting, rotting, shrinking, denting, or bowing.

Figure 6-10   Composite patio door section. *(Marvin Windows & Doors)*

FIBERGLASS DOORS AND FRAMES

The front entry door provides the "first impression" of a home to a new visitor. Unfortunately, the front door, by virtue of its size, orientation, and/or lack of maintenance is all too often in poor shape. Swelling, shrinking, warping, and inferior paint are factors that also contribute to the poor performance of wood doors. As mentioned earlier, the inherent properties of fiberglass eliminate many of these problems, which is why fiberglass composite entry doors and patio doors (or sliders) are gaining popularity. Many have a realistic wood grain that can be stained to imitate a variety of popular wood finishes.

The performance of various fiberglass doors demonstrates superior characteristics when compared to wood or steel doors. For example, test results show that under identical loading conditions, one manufacturer's pultruded fiberglass patio door, when compared to a solid wood door, experienced about 75 percent less deflection. Another door manufacturer's composite design, combining pultruded fiberglass, aluminum, granite, structural foam, and wood, avoids both moisture-related warp and the phenomenon of "cold weather bowing," a characteristic of steel doors in winter. [33]

Some manufacturers produce a product consisting of fiberglass compression-molded panels. These fiberglass doors are available in the same styles as wood doors with competitive prices. Many doors are available with warranties that range from 30 years to "a lifetime" (Fig. 6-11).

Figure 6-11 Molded fiberglass door. *(Therma Tru)*

Environmental Attributes

An environmental assessment was produced by an independent agency for a specific fiberglass window manufacturer. In this specific case study, the window composition possesses the following materials:

- Fiberglass for window frames is 65 to 85 percent glass fibers and 15 to 35 percent resin.
- Silica sand is melted and spun into glass fibers.
- The resin is a thermoset polyester which is a petroleum-based alkide containing styrene, glycols, and acids.
- The insulation in the frames is expanded polystyrene.

According to the report, the raw material reserves for silica sand are very large at present and are not expected to be exhausted. In-plant waste resins for fiberglass are reused and reblended. The raw material reserves are based on the limits of petroleum products. The amount of petroleum is relatively small and contributes to a durable product that has a long life and energy efficiency not available from other products. The polystyrene insulation, also a petroleum product, is a durable insulation that has advantages in energy use reduction during the life of the window when compared to other window products.

Vinyl windows require a large quantity of polyvinyl chloride resins, which use petroleum as feedstock. Wood windows require clear heartwood for visible components, placing a strain on old-growth forests. The production of aluminum releases two fluorine gasses with potent greenhouse warning potential.

Glass fiber production and resin manufacture is said to be a closed process, with few emissions escaping into the environment. (There is a chemical risk from the resins, but it is less than that of PVC production. The production of PVC releases petroleum by-product into the atmosphere.)

According to the report, there are no ozone-depleting chemicals used in the manufacture of fiberglass windows. The expanded polystyrene, however, uses pentane as a blowing agent, which is a greenhouse gas.

From this analysis, fiberglass windows were found to have the lowest overall environmental impact when compared to other residential windows. The high energy use, resource depletion, and (to a lesser extent) the emissions created during the production of aluminum-clad wood and vinyl windows were the principle negative factors.[34]

CONCLUSION

The popularity of windows with low-E glass installed in argon filled, insulating glass units is quickly growing. Similarly, a recent study by a Cleveland-based survey group predicted pultruded fiberglass will soon enjoy a tenfold increase in its annual growth rate from that of the 1983-1993 period. Demand in the United States is also expected to advance at more than double the rate of growth of the window industry as a whole.[35] These technological advances demonstrate that a window is no longer "just" a window, nor is a door "just" a door. Different climates, varying solar exposures, as well as aesthetic issues can be addressed with the *appropriate* combination of some or all of these components.

APPENDIX

Accurate Dorwin Industries
660 Nairn Avenue
Winnipeg, Manitoba, Canada R2L0X5
(204) 982-4640
Fax: (204) 663-0020

National Fenestration Rating Council
1300 Spring St., Suite 120
Silver Spring, MD 20910
(301) 589-6372
Fax: (301) 588-0854

Omniglass Ltd.
6 Neville Park Blvd.
Toronto, Ontario, Canada M4E3P6
(416) 699-4552
Fax: (416) 699-2073

PPG Industries, Inc.
One PPG Place
Pittsburg, PA 15272 USA
(412) 434-3131
(412) 434-2858
Fax: (412) 434-3991

Therma-Tru Corp
1687 Woodlands Dr
Maumee, OH 43537
(419) 891-7400
(800) 537-8827
Fax: (419) 891-7411

REFERENCES

1. Thomas Thiis-Evenesen, *Archetypes in Architecture* (Oslo: Norwegian
    University Press, 1987), p. 259.
2. Thomas C. Jester, ed., *Twentieth-Century Building Materials* (New York:
    McGraw-Hill, 1995), p. 182.
3. Harold B. Olin, *Construction — Principles, Materials and Methods* (Chicago:

U.S. League of Savings Associations, 1980), pp. 207–208.
4. Edward Allen, *Fundamentals of Building Construction* (New York: John Wiley & Sons, 1990), pp. 604–606.
5. Ibid.
6. "How Superinsulating Gases Work," Northern Windows website, 1/10/98.
7. "Gas Filling," Westmark, Inc. website, 1/10/98.
8. Northern Window Manufacturing Limited website, 1/10/98.
9. Eagle Windows and Doors Product Literature, p. pd.2, 11/96.
10. "Roy Gordon and the Search for Low-E Glass," Planet Neighborhood website, 1/9/98.
11. PPG Product Literature, 5067P, 10/96, p. 22.
12. Allen, op. cit., p. 616.
13. PPG Glass website, 1/9/98.
14. "Everything You Always Wanted to Know about Low-E," Pilkington / Libbey-Ownes-Ford website, 1/10/98.
15. Ibid.
16. "Why Successful Window Manufacturers Use ... Low-E Glass," Pilkington / Libbey-Owens-Ford website, 1/10/98.
17. "Low-E Window Glass" SCANA company/SCE&G website, 1/9/98.
18. "Everything You Always Wanted to Know about Low-E," Pilkington/Libbey-Owens-Ford website, 1/10/98.
19. "Low-E Window Glass" SCANA Company/SCE&G website, 1/9/98.
20. "Everything You Always Wanted to Know about Low-E," Pilkington / Libbey-Owens-Ford website, 1/10/98.
21. "Low-E Window Glass" SCANA Company/SCE&G website, 1/9/98.
22. "Everything You Always Wanted to Know about Low-E," Pilkington / Libbey-Owens-Ford website, 1/10/98.
23. "Energy Performance of Fenestration Products," *Architectural Specifier Magazine*, July/August 1997, pp. 14–17.
24. "How to Read the Label," NFRC website, 1/12/98.
25. Phillip Wake, "Pultruded Fiberglass Provides a Window Frame for the 90's and Beyond," *Fenestration Magazine*, September/October 1995.
26. Ibid.
27. Ibid.
28. Ibid.
29. "Insulation Value," Fibertec Window Manufacturing Ltd. Website, 1/12/98.
30. "Fiberglass Fever: Window Manufacturers are Turning on to Composite Windows," Pilkington / Libbey-Owens-Ford website, 1/10/98.
31. Wake, op. cit.
32. "Fiberglass Fever: Window Manufacturers are Turning on to Composite Windows," Pilkington / Libbey-Owens-Ford website, 1/10/98.
33. Wake, op.cit.
34. "Environmental Assessment of Fiberglass Window Systems," Omniglass Ltd. Website, 1/12/98.
35. Wake, op. cit.

Chapter

7

Interior Doors and Hardware

INTRODUCTION

There are few elements in architecture that possess the poetic, metaphorical, musical, or even the literal significance like that of a door. "Open door policy," "the girl next door," "behind closed doors," "door to the future," and even Alice's struggles to pass through the door in Lewis Carroll's *Alice's Adventures in Wonderland* demonstrate the multilevel significance of this seemingly rudimentary object. Unfortunately, objects so common in the built landscape are all too often taken for granted or even neglected. This may be true with household doors however the reality is that the typical interior door is run into, drilled, swung on, and of course slammed. Technology has not ignored the interior door and has responded to this type of use and abuse with engineered compositions and finishes. This chapter will discuss some of these new products, including solid core molded interior doors, plastic laminate clad doors, and nylon finished hardware. Lever-type door handles, as earlier discussed in Chapter 1, will also be discussed.

INTERIOR DOORS

Swinging, pocket, surface sliding, bypass and bifold are various types of interior doors found in the home. The solid wood panel door, also referred to as a stile and rail door, have been the prevalent style in the United States since the 18th century. Typically, this door is a framework of vertical and horizontal wood members, interlocked and glued together. Whether ponderosa pine, douglas fir, or a hardwood veneer, the finish or style of the door can define the character of a home's interior. The solid-core flush door, absent of the character and relief of the panel door, is faced with a hardwood or plastic laminate veneer. The typical core construction of a solid flush door can be glued blocks (stave) or particle board. Hollow-core interior doors, with molded woodgrain-like facings can be satisfactory in appearance but provide relatively little acoustical insulation. The core of this type of door can be lightweight acoustical dampening material or a uniform grid of honeycomb fiber or corrugated cardboard. The absence of a continuous, solid substrate also makes the door vulnerable to punctures.

The popularity of each of these door types demonstrate apparent advantages. A recent introduction into the door market assembles the positive attributes of each type into a single door unit. Molded core doors, also called solid-molded interior doors, possess the solidity and acoustical properties of a solid-core door as well as the tactile qualities (wood texture and raised panels) of a solid wood door at a reduced cost.

Solid-Core Molded Interior Doors

A typical solid-core molded door has four parts:

- An internal door solid "core"
- The door frame surrounding the core
- Two molded door facings that are affixed on either side of the door's frame.

Molded Door Facing

The molded interior door facing, or skin, is a panel of high-density fiberboard that gives the appearance of wood. Textured "oak" panels have been the predominant embossed wood grain pattern. Some companies are now manufacturing skins with a smooth texture to create a high-quality painted appearance and to make cleaning easier.

Although the intent of this book is to discuss the means, methods, and materials in a multiproprietary manner, this is not always possible given the nature of innovation and the reality of patents. This applies in the scope of this text to Masonite®.

William Mason invented the process of molding wood fiber under intense heat and pressure. He founded the Mason Fiber Company in 1924 (which later became the Masonite Corporation) as a vehicle for manufacturing hardboard panels.[1] This text is not to be construed as an advertising medium for one specific manufacturer; however, the Masonite® brand door facing, due to the sheer volume of market share, has almost become synonymous with interior hollow-core doors, not unlike the way Xerox® is synonymous with the term for photocopiers. Masonite Corporation manufacturers a proprietary door facing, Craftmaster® brand, as well as a proprietary CraftCore® brand core. These two components are shipped to door manufacturers throughout the United States who in turn fabricate the final product. The doors are subsequently sold and shipped under various proprietary names. There are also other manufacturers in the industry that fabricate their own molded wood door facings. Although specifications were not available, visual inspections suggest that the properties are somewhat similar.

The molded door facing is a $1/8$"-thick, wood fiber sheet molded under intense heat and pressure into one of a variety of designs. Each design creates the look of a solid wood panel door (Fig. 7-1), complete with raised panels and fine detailing in smooth or wood-grain textured surfaces.

Figure 7-1 Solid-core molded interior doors. *(Masonite Craftmaster)*

According to the Masonite Corporation, this process begins when the wood chips are broken down into fiber when conveyed into machines called "defibrators." The interlocking fiber is then mixed with wax to provide water resistance and resin to enhance the wood's natural bond. The fiber is formed into uniform mats and then pressed under intense heat and pressure into sheets that are harder and denser than wood, without knots and imperfections. Dies or molds are used to create the three-dimensional raised-panel designs (Fig. 7-2). After pressing, the door facings are humidified with water to stabilize them. They are then cut to size and coated with primer that prepares the door facing for painting.[2] Prestained molded facings are also available. (Specifications for other manufacturer's molded facings were not available.)

Figure 7-2 Door facing production. *(Masonite Craftmaster)*

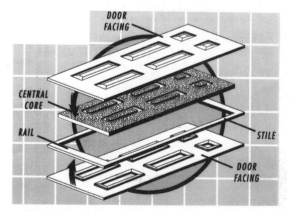

Figure 7-3 Door fabrication. *(Masonite Craftmaster)*

Molded Door Cores

During door fabrication, the door facing is bonded to each side of a substrate. The substrate, (or core) can be hollow, semi-solid or solid (Fig. 7-3). (Semi-solid and hollow are beyond the scope of this text.) Solid-core interior doors, depending upon the manufacturer, can be of a variety of compositions. Particleboard is typically used in commercial applications but can be manufactured for use in $1^3/_8$" residential doors. The additional weight of the particleboard core may require larger-capacity hinges and should be verified with the manufacturer. Some manufacturers are using a substrate similar to particleboard, but significantly lighter. CraftCore® brand door cores by Masonite® and Elite Interior™, by Jeld-Wen use a lower-density (than particleboard) wood fiber core (Fig. 7-4). Lighter than conventional particleboard core, the manufacturer claims this door replicates the weight of a solid pine door.

Figure 7-4 Door core and facing. *(Masonite CraftCore)*

Performance

The solid-core substrate provides equal support for the facing material. According to one manufacturer, doors made with facings are actually superior to solid wood doors in that they are far more resistant to cracking, swelling, shrinking, and warping, and more affordable.[3] A $1^3/_8$" interior solid-core molded door has a STC of 33.

Environmental Attributes

According to the Masonite Corporation, no old-growth timber is harvested solely to supply wood for these doors. The manufacturers utilize 100 percent of harvested timber to obtain the wood chips used in the production of door facings. The manufacturers also use wood that is a by-product of other manufacturing processes, such as saw milling operations. In fact, CraftCore® brand door cores by Masonite® are constructed of up to 15 percent waste recycled material.

Weight

For comparison, a $1^3/_4$" × 3'-0" × 6'-8" interior door was surveyed by the Masonite Corporation. The hollow-core door weighed 34 lb, while the solid pine door weighed 56 lb. The CraftMaster® brand door facing with the solid-core door was 56 lb while the solid oak door was 76 lb. The Craft Master® brand door with a particleboard core weighed 83 lb.

Size and Styles

Standard passage and bifold styles with two-, three-, four- and six-panel designs are common among most door manufacturers. Thicknesses are $1^3/_8$" or $1^3/_4$". Widths typically range from 1'-4" to 3'-0". 1'-0", 1'-2" and 3'-4" door widths are also available from select manufacturers. Heights are typically 6'-8", 7'-0" and in some styles, 8'-0". Fire-rated doors are also available with 20-minute ratings from most molded solid-core door manufacturers. Doors tested are typically $1^3/_4$" thick and 6'-8" or 7'-0" in height. Doors with a heavier-weight particleboard core are rated at 45, 60, and even 90 minutes (Fig. 7-5).

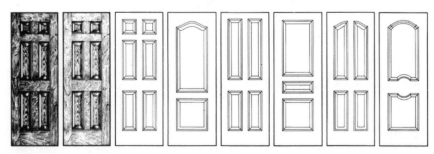

Figure 7-5 Door styles *(Masonite Craftmaster)*

Durability Testing

The Masonite Corporation's proprietary product, CraftMaster brand door facings and CraftCore™ brand solid cores undergo a rigorous testing process. Information as provided by the manufacturer indicate the following examples:

- The Cleavage Test. Doors are torn apart to verify the strength of the glue bond between the facing and the frame.
- The Slam Test. Doors are slammed against a steel stop 24 times per minute and must withstand more than 100,000 slams to pass.
- The Soak Test. Sections of door facings are submerged in water for 24 hours to assure they meet or exceed NWWDA (National Wood Window and Door Association) water repulsion standards.
- The Environmental Chamber. After a week in the chamber, where the humidity fluctuates between 30 and 90 percent, the door must show less than 6.35 mm of lengthwise distortion.
- The Paint Adhesion Test. 3M #250 tape is applied to a primed door. When the tape is removed, the primer adherence must meet standards.
- The Modulus of Rupture (Bending Strength) Test. Ensures that door facings meet or exceed the 2,268 kg/in^2 standard.

Warranty

Solid-core molded interior doors usually have lengthier warranties than other interior doors. Typically, solid-wood stile-and-rail doors come with a 2-year warranty, whereas hollow-core doors have a 1-year warranty. Jeld-Wen's Elite Door™ as well as Premdor's Safe n'Sound™ Door offers a limited 5-year warranty on solid molded interior doors.

General Notes on Storage, Handling, and Installation

As with most interior building products, improper storage, handling, finishing and installation of wood doors may result in severe damage to the doors or the facing. As a precaution, always store doors flat on a level surface in a dry, well-ventilated building. Doors should be kept at least 3$^1/_2$" off the floor and should have protective coverings under the bottom door and over the top. Although the covering should protect doors from dirt, water, and abuse, it should allow for air circulation under and around the stack of doors. Interior doors should be protected from extremes of heat and/or humidity or stored in buildings with excessive moisture content. Finally, doors should be lifted and carried when being moved, not dragged across one another.[4]

General Notes on Painting and Staining

Most doors are shipped ready to paint after having been primed at the factory. First of all, the surface must be clean and dry prior to any painting or staining. It is also important to note that application methods may vary slightly among manufacturers, so it is important to follow the manufacturer's recommendations. Generally speaking, most facings will accept a top quality gloss or semi-gloss paint.

Staining, on the other hand, is more involved and proprietary product sensitive. One manufacturer (Masonite) states that due to the formulation of their facings, it is more like "antiquing" and warns that it is not a project for beginners. Smooth doors should not be stained. Choose an opaque, solid body, or pigmented solid-color stain (oil-based liquid or gelled stain; water-based liquid). In any event, it is recommended not to use transparent or semi-transparent stains. As a precaution, the applicator should test or even "practice" on the back side of door first[5] (Fig. 7-6).

Figure 7-6   Staining. (JELD-WEN)

Plastic Laminate Clad Doors

Plastic laminate clad doors have been around for many years, but have been predominantly used in commercial applications. Plastic laminate doors have been especially effective in hospitals or other high-traffic environments. Dimensional stability, as well as superior resistance to abrasion, alcohol, many solvents, and moisture are some of the reasons for this door's popularity. This type of door finish is relatively new to residential applications, but in addition to the aforementioned properties, these doors are durable and easy to clean (Fig. 7-7).

Figure 7-7   Plastic laminate–clad door. *(VT Industries)*

Plastic laminate-covered doors for residential use are cladded with a high-pressure decorative laminate (HPDL) face (Fig. 7-8). The HPDL is .050"-thick and bonded to a hollow-core or solid-core substrate and wood frame. The rails and stiles are typically $1^3/8$" hardwood or engineered wood.[6]

Manufacturers will apply any HDPL that is commercially available and meets the necessary specifications. In other words, the selection available is as extensive as the variety of laminate choices. Solids, patterns, woodgrains or custom stencils are possible finish choices (These are the same plastic laminate companies that supply countertops, i.e., Nevamar, Wilsonart, Formica, etc.) (Fig. 7-9). The stiles can be painted or stained to match the HPDL faces or HPDL covered.

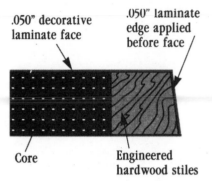

.050" decorative laminate face

.050" laminate edge applied before face

Core

Engineered hardwood stiles

Figure 7-8   Plastic laminate–clad door section. *(VT Industries)*

Figure 7-9   Custom plastic laminate clad designs. *(Wilsonart)*

Typical warranty for plastic-laminate hollow-core doors is 1 year. The cost is about the same as a field-finished solid wood doors.

LEVER HANDLE LOCKSETS

As first mentioned in Chapter 1, the door knob, or handle, is another element that deserves attention. Any operating mechanism that requires tight grasping or twisting of the wrist can be difficult for a person of limited mobility. This can be easily avoided by choosing a door-opening device that is lever-operated and easily opened with one hand.

The reasoning implemented in many barrier-free design strategies can also be applied to many able-bodied design issues. For example, it could be suggested that if a lever is easier to use, it would make sense to use lever handles in lieu of knobs for all door applications.

All of the hardware manufacturers reviewed for this text produce a wide variety of styles of levers and lever trim sets. These are available for entry handlesets, keyed entry locksets, interior latchsets and even deadbolts (Fig. 7-10). Handles are forged of solid brass and ergonomically designed for a comfortable grip (Fig. 7-11). Finishes come in many standard styles such as bright brass, satin brass, satin bronze, bright chrome, and satin chrome.

Figure 7-10   Lever trim sets. *(Baldwin Hardware Corporation)*

Figure 7-11   Lever styles. *(Baldwin Hardware Corporation)*

Some of the typical applications and functions of lever-handled hardware are as listed below:

- Entrance Lock: Unlocked by key from outside when outer lever is locked by turn-button in inside lever. Inside lever is always unlocked.
- Single Cylinder Deadbolt Lock: Deadbolt thrown or retracted by key from outside or by turn unit inside. Bolt automatically deadlocks when fully thrown.
- Double Cylinder Deadbolt: Deadbolt thrown or retracted by key from either side. Bolt automatically deadlocks when fully thrown.
- Door Bolt: Deadbolt thrown or retracted by turn unit only. No outside trim. Bolt automatically deadlocks when fully thrown.
- Passage Latch: Both levers always unlocked.
- Patio Lock: Push-button locking. Turning inside lever releases button. Closing door also releases button.
- Bath/Bedroom Privacy Lock: Push-bottom locking. Can be opened from outside with small narrow circular tool. Turning inside lever releases button. Closing door may also release button.
- Dummy Trim: Single dummy lever for one side of the door. Used for door pull or as matching inactive pull.
- Closet Latch: Outside lever and inside turn unit are always unlocked.

Warranty

Although warranties will vary among manufacturers, a number of premium hardware manufacturers offer a lifetime mechanical and finish warranty. Many of the midrange manufacturers of lever hardware sets come with a 10-year mechanical warranty and a 5-year finish warranty.

NYLON LEVERS AND LOCKSETS

Another option for residential door hardware are nylon levers and locksets (Fig.7-12). These architectural hardware products, made of high quality nylon are formed by an injection molding process (Fig. 7-13). Unlike many products in the commercial market which are nylon-coated steel, the residential levers are solid nylon. A number of manufacturers make nylon handles and drawer pulls around the world; however, HEWI, Inc., is the only manufacturer in the United States at the time of this writing.

Figure 7-12   Nylon lever handle and latch. *(HEWI)*

Nylon handles provide a number of physical properties that are unavailable with brass and chrome locksets. For example, nylon hardware is integrally colored, which promises excellent color retention. Nylon products will not tarnish or rust. Nylon handles are hygienic, since the material is nonporous and does not support the growth of bacteria. A damp cloth is usually all that is necessary for proper cleaning. It is also a good insulator, since nylon does not transmit static electricity or changes in temperature. Finally, solid nylon hardware is durable, "impact resistant and virtually unbreakable in ordinary use."[7]

Nylon locksets are available in red, white, gray and black. Additional colors are available in the commercial line of hardware and may be substituted for an additional cost. Lever handles are available in two basic shapes, either U-shaped or half-circular (Fig. 7-14).

The third shape is a rectangular variation of the U-shaped style. All lever handles should comply with ANSI A117.1 and/or be ADA-compliant.

Several fastening methods and spindle variations make door trims compatible with most mortise lock types. The fastening screws and the bearing area are concealed by a nylon cover cap.

Figure 7-13   Injection mold. *(HEWI)*

Warranty

HEWI, Inc. offers a 2-year warranty on all nylon levers and locksets.

CONCLUSION

The 1997 Standard Building Code has a number of requirements regarding doors. The width, hardware operation, and direction of doorswing are delineated, but any discussion of aesthetics, maintenance, durability, and finish is appropriately omitted. The building codes are a minimum standard, but the same attention to detail is necessary to make informed decisions regarding all aspects of a home's design. Solid-core molded interior doors, plastic laminate–cladded doors, lever handles and nylon hardware are products that exceed any minimum standard. For homebuilders striving to improve an image by providing quality products, an architect trying to stay on the cutting edge, or a homeowner demanding superior performance, these products are well worth the consideration.

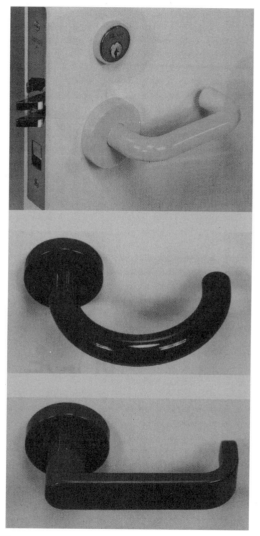

Figure 7-14   Nylon lever handle styles. *(HEWI)*

APPENDIX

HEWI, Inc.
2851 Old Tree Drive
Lancaster, PA 17603
(717) 293-1313
Fax: (717) 293-3270

Masonite Corp.
1 S. Wacker Dr., Suite 3600
Chicago, IL 60606
(800) 255-0785
Fax: (312) 263-5808

Schlage Lock Co.
2401 Bayshore Blvd.
San Francisco, CA 94134
(415) 467-1100
Fax: (415) 330-5626

VT Industries
1000 Industrial Park
Holstein IA 51025 USA
(800) 827-1615
(712) 368-4381
Fax: (712) 368-4320

REFERENCES

1.   Masonite Craftmaster Door Facings Product Literature, #95411, 1996.
2.   Ibid.
3.   Ibid.
4.   JELD-WEN, Inc./Elite Doors website, 1/14/98.
5.   Ibid.
6.   VT Industries Product Literature, PermaClad, Publication No. VT014-1/95.
7.   HEWI, INC. Product Description, Buildcore website (www.buildcore.com), 1/14/98.

8

Interior Partitions

INTRODUCTION

As evidenced in the 17th-century frontier days of the United States, the European settlers used a mud plaster that was applied as a finish for the interior faces of walls. This type of plasterwork consisted of clay or earth, which was mixed with water to give it a plastic or workable consistency. If the clay mixture was too plastic, it would shrink, crack, and distort on drying and sometimes drop off the wall. Sand and fine gravels were added to reduce the concentrations of fine clay particles, which were the cause of the excessive shrinkage. Straw or grass were sometimes added as reinforcement and sometimes supplemented with cattle manure, which not only provided fiber reinforcement to cracked plasters, but also natural protein adhesives. "With a bit of luck and some assistance from holes hacked in logs surfaces...these early plasters managed to stay on the walls."[1]

These humble yet resourceful beginnings of interior finishing yielded to many refinements and technological improvements throughout the ensuing years. Mud plaster eventually gave way to systems of smooth plaster on lath followed by gypsum wallboard on wood and metal studs. The end of the 20th century is continuing to "reinvent" materials that are similar in form and function, yet superior in quality. Fiber-reinforced gypsum wallboard, metal studs, and laminated-strand lumber products demonstrate that residential partitions can be straighter, more durable, and more fire resistant than ever before.

FIBER-REINFORCED GYPSUM BOARD

The first gypsum board was patented in 1894 by Augustine Sackett. It consisted of five thin layers of gypsum separated by six layers of felt and weighed approximately $1^1/_2$ lb/in^2. This product slowly grew in popularity and by World War I was beginning to displace wood and metal lath as a plaster backing. The United States Gypsum Company, having acquired Sackett's company some years earlier, began producing standardized 48"-wide panels of sheetrock in the early 1920s. Unlike Sackett's earlier gypsum product, sheetrock panels could be used as a finished wall surface. In 1927, the National Gypsum Company began manufacturing a lighter wallboard that further increased its use in residential and commercial applications. The 1950s witnessed another dramatic improvement with the introduction of fire-rated gypsum wallboard.[2] The 1990s saw the basic composition of gypsum wallboard modified once again with the introduction of fiber-reinforced gypsum panels.

Although the intent of this book is to discuss the means, methods, and materials in a multiproprietary manner, this is not always possible given the nature of innovation and the reality of patents. This text is not to be construed as an advertising medium for one specific manufacturer; however, FiberBond, by US Gypsum (USG) Corporation, is the only proprietary product for fiber-reinforced gypsum panels. It had been previously produced until 1998 under the same name by Louisiana Pacific. (Another similar product, Gypsonite recycled- fiber wallboard was manufactured by Highland American Corporation but is no longer available). It is also noted that the majority of information evaluated in the preparation of this text was provided by FiberBond and has not been independently verified.

Product Description

FiberBond fiber-reinforced gypsum panels are designed to outperform conventional gypsum panels when used in interior walls and ceilings. They are strong, solid, and durable, and resist denting, breaking, and puncturing even in high-traffic areas. Conventional drywall products, such as Georgia Pacific's GyProc and Fireguard, USG's Sheetrock and Firecode as well as Gold Bond's Gypsum Wallboard and Fire Shield wallboard, have paper facings surrounding a core of pure gypsum. FiberBond fiber-reinforced gypsum panels are solid panels and have no paper face.

FiberBond wallboard has three distinct layers. The two outer layers are fiber-reinforced gypsum (gypsum and recycled newspaper). The middle layer is a core of gypsum, recycled newspaper, and perlite (Fig. 8-1). FiberBond wallboard is installed and finished in a manner similar to regular gypsum wallboard and does not require specialized labor or tools.

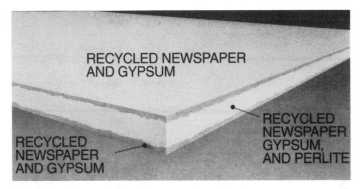

RECYCLED NEWSPAPER AND GYPSUM

RECYCLED NEWSPAPER AND GYPSUM

RECYCLED NEWSPAPER GYPSUM, AND PERLITE

Figure 8-1 Fiber-reinforced gypsum board. *(USG)*

The absence of a paper face has some significant advantages for a gypsum wallboard panel. Typical problems associated with paper-faced gypsum panel products such as bubbles or blistering are virtually eliminated, as well as any failures by delamination. All FiberBond panels are "Type X," or fire-resistant, resulting in a Class 1 rating for flame spread, smoke developed, and fuel contribution. (Type X is formulated by adding noncombustible fibers to the gypsum. These fibers help maintain the integrity of the core as shrinkage occurs, which provides greater resistance to heat transfer during fire exposure.) When properly installed, the manufacturer claims that FiberBond will provide equal or better sound transmission reduction than that offered by regular gypsum wallboard assemblies. It is also more moisture tolerant than regular drywall and may be used in "dry areas" of bathrooms.

FiberBond has a higher density than standard gypsum wallboard resulting in higher impact values. Harder ends and edges also account for less damage to the wallboard. Higher density also means that it is a little heavier than regular drywall; $1/2$" FiberBond weighs 2.3 lb/ft^2 while $5/8$" FiberBond weighs 2.9 lb/ft^2. Competitive Type X products weigh approximately 2 lb/ft^2 for $1/2$" wallboard and between 2.2 and 2.5 lb/ft^2 for $5/8$" wallboard.

The superior strength characteristics are also noteworthy. Since FiberBond wallboard panels are reinforced throughout the panel, they posses higher racking and sheer strengths than standard gypsum wallboard and have less sag. The increased strength and stiffness allow kitchen cabinets to be mounted directly to the drywall. According to the manufacturer, locating a wall stud for typical cabinet installations is not necessary.

The increased rigidity will also allow additional construction cost savings. The spans for fiber-reinforced panels are greater, which means fewer studs are needed for interior partitions. The recommended framing spacing for $1/2$" Type X gypsum wallboard is 16" o/c, $1/2$" FiberBond fiber-reinforced gypsum panels can be placed on studs with a 24" o/c spacing. (Both $5/8$" fiber-reinforced panels and gypsum wallboard can be placed on 24" o/c stud spacing.)

Fire Resistance

As mentioned earlier, both $1/2$"- and $5/8$"-thick fiber-reinforced gypsum panels are equivalent to Type X–rated wallboard when tested in accordance with ASTM E 119. FiberBond wallboard has a Class 1 (Class A) rating for flame spread (5) and smoke development (0) when tested in accordance with ASTM E 84. Other gypsum wallboard products are also Class 1, with an identical rating of 0 for smoke developed, but the flame spread index is 15.

Sizes

Fiber-reinforced gypsum panels are available in the following sizes:

$3/8$" Thick	4'-0"Wide	Length – 8', 9', 10', or 12'
$1/2$" Thick	4'-0"Wide	Length – 8', 9', 10', or 12'
$5/8$" Thick	4'-0"Wide	Length – 8', 9', 10', or 12'

It is noted that several gypsum wallboard manufacturers provide panels in lengths from 6' to 16' and in an additional thickness of $1/4$".

Physical Properties

The following information has been provided by Louisiana Pacific and other sources to provide a comparison between fiber-reinforced wallboard panels and Type X gypsum wallboard per ASTM C36, Specifications for Gypsum Wallboard. Some quantities may vary slightly depending upon the manufacturer.

Nail pull resistance (units are lb/ft)		
Thickness	FiberBond	Gypsum wallboard
$3/8''$	75	60
$1/2''$	120	80
$5/8''$	145	90

Screw withdrawal (units are lb/ft)		
Thickness	FiberBond	Gypsum wallboard
$1/2''$	79	24
$5/8''$	96	37

Humidified deflection (units are inches)		
Thickness	FiberBond	Gypsum Wallboard
$3/8''$	—	$15/8''$
$1/2''$	$3/8''$	$10/8''$
$5/8''$	$1/4''$	$5/8''$

Core, end, and edge hardness (units are lb/ft)		
Thickness	FiberBond	Gypsum wallboard
$3/8''$	40	15
$1/2''$	40	15
$5/8''$	40	15

Flexural strength (units are lb/ft)			
Thickness	FiberBond each direction	Gypsum wallboard Width	Length
$^1/_2$"	120	110	40
$^5/_8$"	155	150	50

"R" Values		
Thickness	FiberBond	Gypsum wallboard
$^1/_2$"	0.42	0.45
$^5/_8$"	N/A	0.56

Racking Resistance

According to the manufacturer's literature, $^1/_2$" FiberBond wallboard has demonstrated a 42 percent increase in racking resistance and a 57 percent increase in maximum racking load compared to conventional gypsum wallboard when tested according to ASTM E 72. "Wet" racking resistance tests demonstrated $^1/_2$" FiberBond has a 46 percent increase in racking resistance and an 82 percent increase in corresponding values compared to conventional gypsum wallboard.

Environmental Impact

One hundred percent of the cellulose fibers used in the manufacture of FiberBond fiber-reinforced gypsum panels are obtained from recycled newspaper. FiberBond's fiber content is about twice that of conventional products.[3]

The actual recyclability of FiberBond is under some debate. At present, gypsum wallboard may be disposed of in landfills permitted to accept gypsum waste only. This is primarily due to the toxic gases emitted during decomposition. According to one environmental analysis, FiberBond's mixture of gypsum and perlite is not readily recyclable. This is not as significant as it sounds, since drywall recycling facilities are limited. This may become more of an issue as drywall recycling becomes more prevalent in the future.[4]

Limitations

Fiber-reinforced gypsum panels are more rigid than conventional drywall panels. Although this contributes to greater strength and impact resistance, this also limits bending. Typically, $1/2$" drywall panels can be bent lengthwise on a 10' radius. Some manufacturer's $5/8$" panels can be bent on a 15' radius. Bending of FiberBond panels is not recommended.

FiberBond is more moisture tolerant than conventional drywall. Although manufacturer's literature claims it can be used as a base for tile and wall in dry areas, FiberBond wallboard should not be used in wet areas or in locations where exposure to temperatures in excess of 125°F for extended periods of time occurs.

When working with power-driven cutting tools and during sanding operations, an approved OSHA respirator or dust mask should be worn by the mechanic to avoid the nuisance dust.

Referenced Standards

FiberBond fiber-reinforced gypsum panels meets the requirements in the following standards as published by the ASTM:

- ASTM C 1278-94: Specification for Fiber Reinforced Gypsum Panels.

- ASTM C 475-89: Specification for Joint Compound and Joint Tape for Finishing Gypsum Board.

- ASTM C 840-94: Specification for Application and Finishing of Gypsum Board.

- ASTM C 36-93: Specification for Gypsum Wallboard.

- ASTM E 119-88: Test Methods for Fire Tests of Building Construction and Materials.

- ASTM E 695-79: Method for Measuring Relative Resistance of Wall, Floor and Roof Constructions to Impact Loading.

FiberBond fiber-reinforced gypsum panels meets and/or are to be installed and finished per the requirements in the following standards as published by the Gypsum Association:

• GA 214-90: Levels of Gypsum Board Finish.

• GA 216-89: Application and Finishing of Gypsum Board.

• GA 600-94: Fire Resistance Design Manual.

General Handling and Installation Guidelines

The following guidelines are provided for a general understanding of the product. Manufacturer's literature and applicable building codes should be referenced. FiberBond fiber-reinforced gypsum panels can be installed over wood framing, steel framing, furring channels, and concrete walls.

FiberBond fiber-reinforced gypsum panels are to be delivered to the project site in the manufacturer's original packaging with labels intact. The panels must be kept off of the floor, stacked on pallets, in a dry, clean, well-ventilated area. The panels are to be protected from direct moisture. Temperatures in excess of 125°F are to be avoided for extended periods of time.

When working in cold weather, wallboard and joint treatment should not be applied to surfaces that are damp or contain frost. Heat should be provided to maintain a controlled temperature between 50°F and 70°F for at least 48 hours before installation. This temperature range should be maintained during the application of FiberBond fiber-reinforced gypsum panels and joint treatment, and for at least 48 hours after completion or until the permanent heating system is in operation. In summer weather, provide suitable ventilation to ensure normal drying conditions and prevent high humidity conditions.

The scoring and snapping method for FiberBond panels is different from that of standard paper-faced gypsum wallboard. Some labor and time savings can be realized since the FiberBond is only scored on one side of the panel. After scoring twice, the panel is snapped away form the cut face. The backside of the panel is broken by snapping the panel in the reverse direction. This is contrast to paper-faced drywall, which must be scored on one side, snapped, and then scored (or cut) on the other side.

Fasteners are to be corrosion-resistant nails, screws or staples with $7/16"$ crown as specified in ASTM C 840. FiberBond wallboard can be installed with standard gypsum board corner beads, studs, furring channels, door jambs and other gypsum board accessories. Joint tape, taping compound, and finishing compound shall comply with ASTM C 475. Consult with the specifications for acceptable adhesives, control joint location requirements and application of taping compounds.

After the taping compound has dried completely, apply additional coats of a high-quality, ready mix finishing compound until the required level of finish is achieved. Do not begin application of coatings or other finishes such as paint, texturing, wallpaper, or wall coverings until the finishing compound coats are completely dry. The surfaces are to be free from dust and other impurities that could impair proper bonding.

Summary

According to USG, the company will continue to produce FiberBond for an indefinite period of time. The product will eventually be converted, with minor modification of composition intended to enhance the existing properties and performance, and sold under the name FiberRock. Other drywall manufacturers are in the research and development stage of producing similar products in order to capitalize on the advantages associated with fiber reinforced gypsum wallboard.

METAL STUD FRAMING

As discussed in the Steel Framing Systems section of Chapter 4, metal stud framing systems are becoming more widely accepted in the residential construction industry. The most recent statistics from the American and Iron Steel Institute indicate the popularity of residential steel framing is growing at a dramatic rate. Estimates show that galvanized steel framing may be in as many as 325,000 new homes by the year 2000 as opposed to the 50,000 homes in 1995.[5]

Advantages

High strength to weight ratios allow steel framing members to be more lightweight than wood framing members. Metal studs are not only noncombustible, but a zinc coating provides corrosion resistance. This coating minimizes rust and protects the steel from air, moisture, salts, acids or other contaminants. Steel framing is free from weaknesses caused by knots and will not warp, shrink, or crack. This dimensional stability also helps reduce nail pops and helps prevent squeaks from developing. Problems associated with rotting, attacks by termites or vermin are also avoided.

Physical Properties

All steel framing members should be in compliance with ASTM C754, Gypsum Wallboard Steel Studs. These interior, non-load bearing steel studs, commonly referred to as drywall studs, are available in 20, 22 and 25 ga. The sizes include $1^5/_8$", $2^1/_2$", $3^5/_8$", 4" and 6". Although sizes vary per each manufacturer, studs are typically available in lengths up to 20' for 25 ga studs and 28' for 20 ga. As discussed earlier, load-bearing steel studs (or joists), referred to as C-sections, can be 14, 16, 18, or 20 ga. The sizes available include $3^5/_8$", 4", 6", $7^1/_4$", 8", $9^1/_4$", $11^1/_2$" and $13^1/_2$".

Steel studs are now being produced to accurately reflect the actual dimensions of wood framing members. Studs are available in widths of $3^1/_2$", $5^1/_2$" as well as 8", 10" and 12". The flange is $1^5/_8$". Nomenclature is also being revised to avoid the confusion associated with gauge thickness. Studs can now be specified using mils (1/1000 of an inch). For example, 33 mils is 20 ga, 43 mils is 18 ga and 54 mils is 16 ga.

$1^1/_2$" × 4" slotted holes, referred to as "knockouts" or "cutouts" are typically located at 24" o/c along the length of the steel member. Knockouts are especially convenient when accommodating electrical runs or horizontal bracing channels.

Deflection is a major consideration in designing framing system members. Even though an assembly is structurally capable of withstanding a given load, the amount of deflection incurred may be greater than the tolerance of the corresponding veneer or sheathing materials can withstand without damage. For any horizontal load, the amount of deflection increases as the height of the partition increases. This is expressed as a ratio of the length of the span (L) divided by a specific criteria as established by the applicable building codes. For example, a $3^5/_8$" metal stud at 16" o/c can be 13'-2" in height if the deflection is limited to L/120. If the stud spacing is 24" o/c, 10'-9" is the maximum height. The maximum deflection allowed for a 10'-high wall at L/120 is 1". If the deflection was limited by L/360, then the maximum deflection would be about $5/_{16}$". (This example is for illustration purposes only. Local building codes will determine the appropriate deflection limits.)

Accessories

Many accessories available include flat strapping, self drilling, self tapping screws and metal angles. Miscellaneous hold-downs, floor ties, mudsill anchors and bracing are available from a variety of manufacturers.

THE CARPENTER'S STEEL STUD

A "cousin" to the aforementioned drywall stud is a modified steel framing member manufactured and sold under the name, The Carpenter's Steel Stud by the HL Stud Corporation (Fig. 8-2). The Carpenter's Steel Stud may actually be the bridge that wood-framing contractors need before making the holistic transition to light-gauge steel framing. The unique attribute of this steel member is that it will allow partitions to be built using the same labor force the wood-frame builder has on the payroll while implementing the inherent advantages of light-gauge steel framing. The tools, such as the hammer and staple gun, are also the same.

System Description

The framing system is very simple. As mentioned earlier, steel framers typically use a 25-ga steel stud set in a steel track for non-load-bearing interior partitions. The Carpenter's Steel Stud, also made from 25-ga steel, utilizes a wood sill plate, as in conventional wood framing, for the bottom track. The flange (side) on the Carpenter's Stud makes the stud positioning simple. The

Figure 8-2 The Carpenter's Steel Stud. *(HL Stud Corporation)*

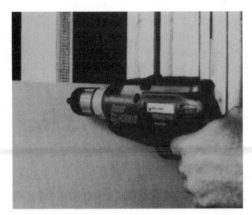

Figure 8-3   Hanging drywall. *(HL Stud Corporation)*

flange sits down on each side of the wood sill plate and is subsequently nailed or stapled (a screw gun will be required for drywall application) (Fig. 8-3).

The metal studs are prepunched to facilitate wiring and plumbing runs. Each prepunched hole is then fitted with a grommet (unless conduit is being used) to protect the wire's sheath (Fig. 8-4).

The reduced material weight of the steel studs will provide some advantages to the labor force. According to the manufacturer, a bundle of 14 Carpenter's Steel Studs weighs approximately 40 lb. This should translate, however modestly, to increased speed of partition construction.

The Carpenter's Steel Stud is made from galvanized recycled 25-ga prime steel that doesn't need cover; is rust-resistant; will not rot, warp or split; and is noncombustible.

Figure 8-4   Plumbing run and grommet. *(HL Stud Corporation)*

Cost Savings

The economic advantages of using this product may be threefold. First of all, The Carpenter's Steel Stud costs less than wood. The dimensional stability of the steel product should reduce nail-pops and subsequent callbacks. Finally, the price of steel is typically more stable than that of wood. This should mean that the price quoted during estimating should be approximately the same price when purchased.

Physical Properties

The Carpenter's Steel Stud is $3^1/_2$" wide and available in heights of up to 10'. The deflection limit is L/240. The end attachment is with (2) 6d common nails with a minimum penetration of $1^1/_8$" or (2) No. 16 ga staples with a minimum penetration of 1" (Fig. 8-5). All material meets the requirements of ASTM A446. Load bearing studs and floor joists are also available.

Environmental Attributes

According to the manufacturer, 1 trillion lb of steel scrap has been recycled in the last decade.[6] The Carpenter's Steel Stud is made from recycled steel, of which 70 percent of comes from salvaged cars. The manufacturer estimates this product could replace approximately 1.8 billion board-feet of lumber per year.

Figure 8-5 Staple connection. *(HL Stud Corporation)*

LAMINATED-STRAND LUMBER

Chapter 3 has already discussed the benefits of using engineered wood products for residential applications. Aside from Wood-I-Joists and oriented-strand board (OSB), the predominant engineered wood components in use are glued laminated timber (glulams), parallel-strand lumber (PSL) and laminated-veneer lumber (LVL). At first glance these products may appear quite similar however, there are significant differences.

The philosophy of engineered wood products is that each composition and subsequent physical product are combined to create the most efficient structural member for the appropriate application. Glulams are produced by gluing together horizontal layers of dimensional lumber that are to be used as headers, beams, girders, and columns. PSL products are made from strands of wood glued together into long, wide members. These are especially suited for beams, columns, posts, headers and lintels. PSL products are sold under the name Parallam® PSL by Trus Joist Macmillan. The LVL, not unlike plywood, is a layered composite of wood veneers and adhesive. The grain of each piece runs in the long direction making it strongest when edge loaded as a beam or face loaded as a plank. These are also used as headers, beams and Wood-I-Joists' flanges.

LSL is another type of engineered wood product. At the time of this writing, LSLs are produced by the Trus Joist MacMillan company and sold under the proprietary name of TimberStrand. TimberStrand® LSL (Fig. 8-4) was first introduced in 1990.

Applications

TimberStrand® LSL is produced for a variety of applications such as studs, headers, and beams, and core material for windows and doors, furniture frames, and specialty millwork. This text illustrates the possibility of using the TimberStrand® LSL for interior bearing or non-load-bearing wall framing as well as plates when used with a SIPs wall system.

TimberStrand® LSL wall framing is manufactured in 2 × 4's and 2 × 6's (Fig. 8-6). The lengths that are available range from 16" to 48' (the maximum length allowed for vertical stud wall framing is 14' for 2 × 4's and 22' for 2 × 6's). The manufacturer provides literature demonstrating nailing requirements, assembly instructions and design tables for exterior and interior loadbearing walls.

Figure 8-6   LSL plate and studs. *(Trus Joist MacMillan)*

Columns are available in sizes of $3^1/2$" × $3^1/2$", $3^1/2$" × $5^1/4$", $3^1/2$" × $7^1/4$" and $3^1/2$" × $8^5/8$". Column lengths range from 3'-0" to 14'-0" (Fig. 8-7).

Figure 8-7   LSL column. *(Trus Joist MacMillan)*

Production

TimberStrand® LSL does not rely on old-growth timber, but is manufactured from readily available small-diameter trees that are easily renewed on a 20- to 30-year cycle to provide long-term availability and a more stable economic solution to fluctuations of commodity lumber.[7]

The LSL manufacturing process begins when 8' tall aspen and yellow poplar logs are cleaned, debarked, and cut into strands up to 12" long. The strands are dried in order to guarantee uniform moisture content. The strands are coated with a formaldehyde-free adhesive, which means post production off-gassing should not be an issue. (Before it is cured, the adhesive is highly toxic. This requires all pressing processes to be remotely controlled.[8]) The exterior-grade adhesive will not degrade or fall apart when exposed to moisture.

The coated strands are aligned parallel (see Fig. 8-5) to each other to take advantage of the wood's natural strength. Then, steam injection pressing process laminates the strands into solid billets of wood up to 48' long, 8' wide and $5^{1}/_{2}$" thick. (Bark from the trees is burned to generate the necessary heat.[9]) Billets are then cut to exact specifications per the appropriate end use.

Performance

TimberStrand® LSL is engineered to resist or eliminate common problems associated with solid sawn lumber such as warping, splitting, twisting and wane (see Fig. 8-6). The dimensional stability of TimberStrand® LSL guarantees that this product is consistently straight and true. A better quality-controlled product also means fewer culls and less waste. TimberStrand® LSL can be ripped, cut, chopped, resawn, drilled, or molded with conventional equipment. In some cases, it may be advantageous to use carbide tooling.

Cost

TimberStrand® LSL studs are more expensive than regular solid dimensional lumber. The price difference varies depending upon the region. Sources say the average cost is twice that of S-P-F studs; however, this could be less in some parts of the country.[10] The cost increase can be partially offset in lieu of the system as a whole. The manufacturer states that typical 8' and 9' stud walls can have 24"-o/c spacings if the local region is subject to 80 mph or less wind speeds. This will produce some cost savings over conventional 16"-o/c spacings since less material is required.

Limitations

The basic premise with engineered wood products is that the manufacturer's literature and directions must be followed. Engineered wood products, by virtue of their efficient design properties, are less tolerant of unintended uses and applications (as opposed to solid dimensional lumber.)

Limitations for holes and notches in TimberStrand® LSL studs are not too dissimilar from CABO One and Two Family Dwelling Code requirements for solid dimensional lumber (consult the manufacturer's literature and the applicable building code for all specific requirements). For example, notches may be cut anywhere along the stud except the middle $1/3$ of the length. The notches must be no larger than $7/8$" deep for 2 × 4's and $1^3/8$" for 2 × 6's. Holes, no larger than $1^3/8$" in diameter for 2 × 4's and $2^3/16$" for 2 × 6's and have a minimum of $5/8$" clearance from the edge. Notches and holes must not occur in the same cross section (Fig. 8-8).

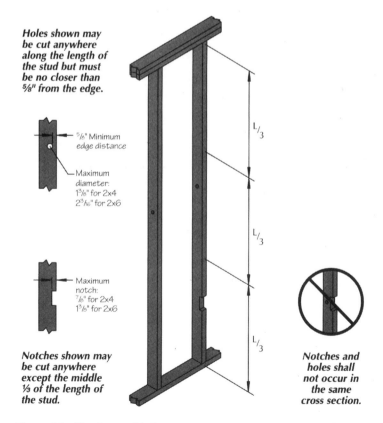

Holes shown may be cut anywhere along the length of the stud but must be no closer than ⅝" from the edge.

⅝" Minimum edge distance

Maximum diameter: 1³/₈" for 2x4 2³/₁₆" for 2x6

Maximum notch: ⁷/₈" for 2x4 1³/₈" for 2x6

Notches shown may be cut anywhere except the middle ⅓ of the length of the stud.

Notches and holes shall not occur in the same cross section.

Figure 8-8   Notches and holes. (Trus Joist MacMillan)

Manufacturer's recommendations for nailing patterns must also be followed. 16d nails must be no closer than $1/2$" from the edge of the narrow edge of the stud and o/c spacing must not be closer than 6"; 8d nails can be within $3/8$" from the outside edge and no closer than 3" o/c.

Studs and plates are not pressure-treated and are intended for use in a location where maximum moisture content does not exceed 19 percent. TimberStrand® LSL may not be substituted for plate material when studs are conventional sawn lumber.   Consult the manufacturer's literature for complete descriptions, instructions, and exclusions.

CONCLUSION

From mud plaster on logs to fiber-reinforced gypsum wallboard on metal studs, the construction and design industries have historically searched for ways to improve on the existing or invent the new. The difficult task has always been in obtaining the public's acceptance of "something different." Perhaps the similarities between fiber-reinforced gypsum wallboard and conventional, between LSL and solid wood will put the user at ease. Anxiety is a minor discomfort to endure in order to obtain straighter, more fire-resistant, more durable interior walls.

APPENDIX

American Iron and Steel Institute
1101 17th Street, NW
Suite 1300
Washington, DC 20036-4700
(800) 79-STEEL

TimberStrand® LSL
Trus-Joist MacMillan
200 E. Mallard Drive
PO Box 60
Boise ID 83707
(800) 628-3997

United States Gypsum Company
125 South Franklin Street
PO Box 806278
Chicago, IL 60680-4124
(800) 874-4968

REFERENCES

1. Martin E. Weaver, *Conserving Buildings*, (New York: John Wiley & Sons, Inc., 1997), p. 149.
2. Thomas S. Jester, ed., *Twentieth-Century Building Materials*. (New York: McGraw-Hill, 1995), pp. 269-270.
3. "FiberBond Gypsum Wallboard," *Environmental Building News*, Vol. 2, No. 3, May/June 1993.
4. Ibid.
5. "Consumers Rediscover Steel's Many Strengths," American Iron and Steel Institute website, 1/18/98.
6. "The Carpenter's Steel Framing System," HL Stud Corporation
7. Timberstrand LSL product literature, #3200
8. "Laminated Strand Lumber Product Introduced," *Environmental Building News*, Vol. 1, No. 3, November/December 1992.
9. Ibid.
10. "Engineered Lumber Studs from TJM," *Environmental Building News*, Vol. 5, No. 3, May/June 1996.

Chapter

9

Heating and Air Conditioning

INTRODUCTION

The previous three decades have seen the typical consumer slowly develop a new awareness and understanding of not only the limits of our environmental resources but a responsibility toward the need to preserve these resources. It may have been the energy crisis of 1973 that served as the major catalyst, or "wake-up" call. Coupled with growing insurance premiums and new emission controls, the gas-guzzling muscle cars of the 1960s and early 70s were supplanted by fuel-efficient vehicles. Single-pane windows are now replaced by a variety of insulated units: argon gas–filled chambers, triple pane units or even glazed with low-E coatings. The lighting industry is still in the midst of technological change, with electronic ballasts, more efficient tubes, and redesigned reflectors all contributing to products far superior to their standard fluorescent fixture counterparts of several years ago.

Years of excess and waste have made people realize that conventional energy resources are limited and must be conserved. One major culprit has been our growing dependence on environmental control systems. The 1930s saw kerosene and fuel oil begin to displace wood as the primary fuel for residential systems followed by the prominence of electricity and natural gas in the 1950s.[1] As heating and cooling costs have skyrocketed, the demand for alternative heating and cooling methods has increased, creating a demand and desire to use renewable and sustainable energy sources in lieu of fossil fuels (coal, natural gas, and oil).

Even as today's traditional systems have become more efficient, the basic operating principles have remained the same. The most common of these systems are (but not limited to):

- Air-to-air heat pumps for heating and cooling.
- Electric resistance heating with window air conditioners.
- Gas furnaces with electric air conditioning.
- Oil furnaces for heat and electric air conditioning.
- Wood-burning stoves.

There are many drawbacks to each of these systems. For example, the air-to-air (air source) heat pump, popularized during the 1970s, draws heat from the outside air in the winter. In the summer, it draws the heat out of the home and rejects the heat into the air. Unfortunately, when the outside winter air drops below 20°F, resistance heating coils must provide additional makeup heat, which greatly increases the user's cost. This inefficient shortcoming is one reason why air-to-air heat pumps are more commonly used in the southern states. Regular maintenance is also required due to the outdoor location of the unit.

Electric resistance heat is commonly used in smaller homes. The individual thermostat in each room is a convenient zoning tool but the cost to operate this system is undesirable. During the summer, an equally inefficient cooling solution is often used. This unitary cooling system, commonly known as the "window air conditioning unit," drives electrical power bills up, and is noisy and unappealing to the eye.

Gas furnaces with electric air conditioning are probably the most common combination of systems outside the northeastern United States. It is also the most economical of the aforementioned systems. The biggest drawback is that natural gas, a nonrenewable energy source, is subject to inflationary costs as supply gets more and more scarce. This system also relies on electric air conditioning for summer cooling. Safety hazards originating from the pilot light, the ignition system, combustion gases, and carbon monoxide are additional disadvantages.

Oil heat is most prevalent in the northeast region of the United States. Oil is also not a renewable resource and its cost can fluctuate depending on how much oil is imported in any particular year. An additional undesired aspect of oil as a heat source is the maintenance of the oil furnace. The "dirty" burning characteristic of oil creates a never-ending problem.

Wood-burning stoves became chic in the 1980s. The ecologically minded 1990s are aware that this heat source depletes our forests, is very messy in the home, and requires someone to maintain the fire. If you leave for a short trip, even for a couple of days, you will lose heat.

This analysis can lead to only one logical conclusion. An alternative system must be implemented that is efficient, uses a renewable energy source and is easy to maintain. The geoexchange heating and cooling system is one such system. As you read this chapter, you will see how this energy source will provide for your needs today and can be enhanced tomorrow as the development of photovoltaics solar cells, thereby eliminating an electrical energy source necessary to run the system.

GEOEXCHANGE HEATING AND COOLING SYSTEMS

The basic premise of geoexchange heating and cooling is very simple. Below the earth's surface, the temperature remains fairly consistent relative to a specific geographic region (Fig. 9-1). This temperature will remain constant in the same location regardless of the air temperature at the surface.

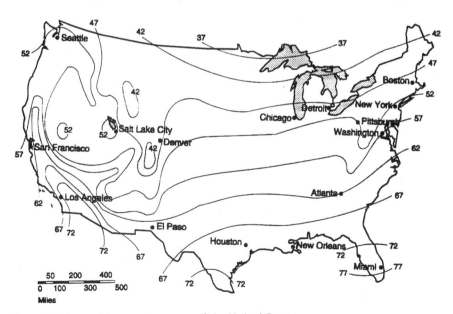

Figure 9-1 Ground temperature map of the United States.

The typical heat pump unit uses a refrigeration system that extracts heat from the outdoor air, pumps it through the heat pump unit, heats the air to the desired temperature, and forces the air via a fan (air handler) into the home. The geothermal heat pump works under the same principle except that:

1. Heat is absorbed from water in lieu of outdoor air.
2. The earth is used as the heat source.

The geoexchange heat pump transfers heat from a building into the earth when cooling or from the earth into a building when heating. Water is used to carry this heat through pipes to and from the earth. Since the thermal mass of the earth is providing the heat energy, less energy is expended by the heat pump. Electricity is used only to move the heat, not to produce it. For example, in the winter, when the air temperature at the earth's surface is very cold, the heat pump will take advantage of the warmer subsurface temperatures to heat the home. The decreased temperature differential improves efficiency. Similarly, in the summer months, when the earth's surface air temperature is very hot, the heat pump will take advantage of the cooler subsurface temperatures to draw heat out of the home.

Geothermal heat pumps have been receiving more attention for both commercial and residential applications across North America every year since their introduction. With a successful track record of having worked successfully in thousands of facilities including schools, hospitals, and offices, the U.S. market alone is growing quickly as customers realize the benefits of geothermal.

When it comes to efficient, low-cost residential heating and cooling, the geothermal heat pump has no equal. According to a report from the Environmental Protection Agency (EPA), the geothermal heat pump is the most energy-efficient, least-polluting HVAC system on the market today. While geothermal heat pumps cost slightly more to install than some systems, the performance benefits are superior. For example:

• Geothermal Systems are 400 to 500 percent more efficient than fossil heating systems and provide 25 to 30 percent more efficient air conditioning.

- Because mechanical noise is reduced, the public is less aware of the presence of the unit, thus improving architectural aesthetics.

- Operating costs are 25 to 35 percent less than comparable systems since a majority of heat is transferred from the ground.

- Supplemental backup heat is often not required, as opposed to traditional air source heat pumps.

- Since the components of the system are indoors and underground, a decrease in vandalism is likely.

- Geothermal is an environmentally friendly system due to the sustainable nature of the earth's energy.

- The manufacturer warrants the geothermal ground loop systems for 50 years. The geothermal heat pump, being located indoors, has a life expectancy up to 20 years.

- The system reclaims heat to produce a significant percentage of hot water at no additional cost.

The Components of a Geoexchange System

The three main components of the geoexchange system are the heat pump unit, the ground heat exchanger, and the air delivery system. Since the ductwork system is the same as those in other traditional forced-air systems, it will not be discussed in this chapter.

The Heat Pump

As mentioned earlier, the heat pump operates on the principle of transferring heat rather than creating it. The heat pump does not produce heat by burning fuel. Instead, it transfers heat from the outdoor air, water, or earth into the indoor air of the home. During the summer, the cycle reverses and the heat pump serves as the central air conditioner. In this case, the heat from the indoor air is transferred outdoors.

The most common type of electric heat pump is the air source unit. In the winter, it absorbs heat from the outdoor air using a refrigerant fluid flowing through a coil in the outdoor unit. The refrigerant then flows into the house and through another coil in the furnace where the heat is transferred to the indoor air.

The heat pump provides all of the heat needed until the home reaches the "balance point," which generally occurs between temperatures of 25° to 35°F. (The outdoor temperature below which a heat pump requires a supplemental heating source.) Below the balance point, the supplemental heating source automatically comes on to assist the heat pump to maintain indoor comfort. This arrangement allows both the heat pump and supplemental heating source to operate when each is most efficient. The supplemental heating source may be one of several alternatives, depending on the region of the country and its associated climate.

During the summer, the heat pump is simply a central air conditioner. The operating cycle of the heat pump reverses, absorbing heat from the indoor air and transferring it through the refrigeration system to the outdoor air. It can provide for all of the air conditioning needs in the home.

Heat pumps do not typically cycle on-and-off as often as fossil fuel systems. This means a more comfortable and even flow of conditioned air throughout the home. Heat pumps also eliminate the hot, dry air of other heating systems.[2]

The federal government requires manufacturers of heating and cooling equipment to provide consumers with information about the efficiency of their equipment. Heat pump manufacturers provide a seasonal energy efficiency ratio (SEER) for air conditioning (the cooling efficiency rating), and a Heating Seasonal Performance Factor (HSPF) for heating (heating efficiency rating). The higher the SEER and HSPF numbers, the more efficient the heat pump.

The geoexchange heat pump units, located indoors (as opposed to the traditional HVAC outdoor unit or split system), can be suspended from a structure above, with horizontal air inlet and discharge, or floor-mounted with horizontal air inlet and vertical upflow/downflow air discharge. The residential units have a microprocessor control, compressor, evaporator, condenser, reversing valve, and expansion device. Options include a desuperheater (a device for recovering superheat from compressor discharge gas of a heat pump) for heating hot water, multistage electronic digital thermostat, and an electrostatic air filter (Fig. 9-2).

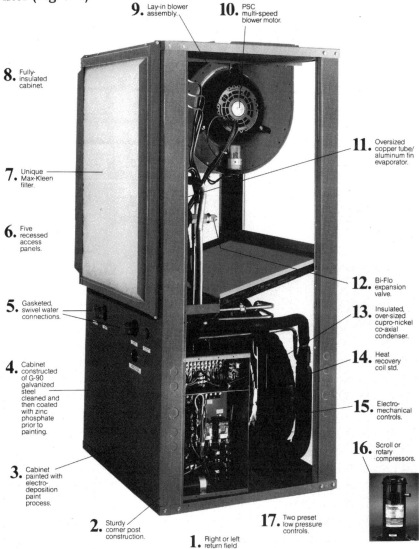

9. Lay-in blower assembly.

10. PSC multi-speed blower motor.

8. Fully-insulated cabinet.

7. Unique Max-Kleen filter.

6. Five recessed access panels.

5. Gasketed, swivel water connections.

4. Cabinet constructed of G-90 galvanized steel cleaned and then coated with zinc phosphate prior to painting.

3. Cabinet painted with electro-deposition paint process.

2. Sturdy corner post construction.

1. Right or left return field convertible.

11. Oversized copper tube/aluminum fin evaporator.

12. Bi-Flo expansion valve.

13. Insulated, over-sized cupro-nickel co-axial condenser.

14. Heat recovery coil std.

15. Electro-mechanical controls.

16. Scroll or rotary compressors.

17. Two preset low pressure controls.

Figure 9-2 Water source heating and cooling unit. *(Addison Products Company)*

The Heat Source (Ground Loop)

The heat source in a geoexchange system is the earth. The thermal mass of the earth functions as a virtually limitless heat source (heat is extracted by a heat pump) and heat sink (rejected heat is received from a heat pump). There are two geothermal systems available: the open loop and the closed loop.

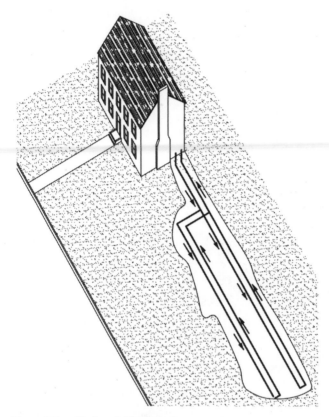

Figure 9-3 Horizontal loop system.

The open loop draws water from wells, lakes, or ponds and returns the water back to the same or a nearby source (discharge point). Open-loop systems are often restricted by local regulations and occasionally have water-quality problems, which may sometimes result in the scaling of the pipe system. According to WaterFurnace International, Inc., 90 percent of the systems installed are closed-loop systems. For this reason, we will limit our discussions to the closed-loop system.

The closed-loop system uses an extended heat exchanger constructed of an underground network of high-quality sealed plastic pipe. Chemical treatment is not necessary once it has been initially charged with treated water. The method of closed loop piping in the heat exchanger can be one of three types: horizontal loops (Fig. 9-3), vertical loops (Fig. 9-4), or pond loops (Fig. 9-5). The horizontal loop, least expensive when adequate land surface is available, requires piping to be installed at a depth of 5' to 6' below the surface. The horizontal heat exchanger is a continuous trench dug for each loop, which establishes a series of parallel circuits (Fig. 9-6). (The length of pipe depends on the calculated required load for the home, generally 300' to 600' per system ton.) It is important to note that seasonal temperature variation can be considerably greater with shallow ground (and pond) heat exchangers, sometimes requiring fluid antifreeze protection in extreme climates.

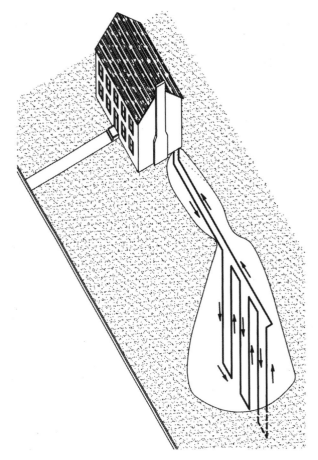

Figure 9-4   Vertical loop system.

Vertical loop systems require a minimum amount of land but are more popular for nonresidential applications. The same field principle used in horizontal-loop systems applies to the vertical loop except boreholes are drilled to an engineered depth. Two pipes are placed in each hole with a U-bend at the bottom of the borehole to complete the loop. Although this system may be more expensive to install, it requires less land area and reduces the chance of accidentally damaging a pipe. The typical installation depths range from 75' to 300'.

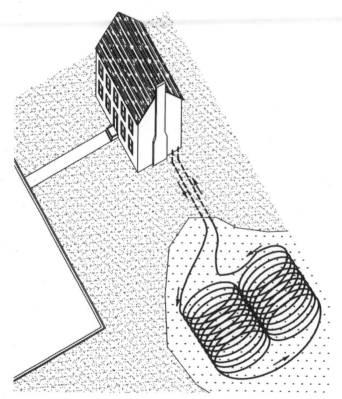

Figure 9-5   Pond loop system.

The pond-loop system is similar to the horizontal loop except a pond, lake, or even a retention basin is the heat sink. The only requirement is that the pond be of a minimum depth in order to maintain a relatively consistent temperature around the submerged pipe. This system is very economical to install since the cost of excavation is virtually eliminated.

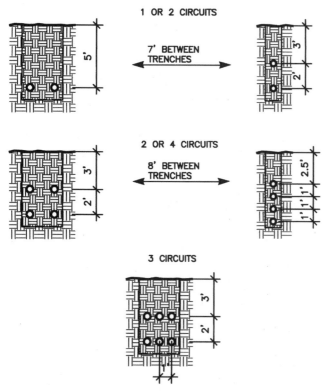

Figure 9-6   Typical horizontal heat exchanger configurations.

Thermal Characteristics

The thermal and geographic characteristics of the earth must be considered in the design of ground heat exchangers. For example, soil and/or rock conditions may not only determine the size of the field, but also dramatically increase (or reduce) the cost of drilling and trench digging. Factors that affect the ground's ability to absorb, store, and release heat include soil porosity, rock content, moisture content, and soil type. For horizontal loops, the required pipe length for a light dry soil can be over two times that required for a heavy damp soil. In vertical loops, the required length of bore increases by 35 percent in ordinary rock over dense rock.

For large commercial projects, the thermal properties of the soil of a specific site are best determined through test bores where samples of the earth are brought to the surface for inspection and evaluation. The test boreholes should be at least as deep as the bore holes for the proposed design.

The scale of the ground loop system in residential applications does not require test boreholes. Although it is important to note that there may be instances of geologic obstructions such as bedrock, qualified local contractors are able to provide general information necessary for loop layout based on experience and knowledge of the area.

Loop Design

The design of the heat exchanger may require the use of two separate computer programs: one to evaluate the building loads and the response of the HVAC systems to the loads; and the other to develop ground heat exchange specifications. As heat pump performance varies with loop temperature, the load calculations should be adjusted to account for actual heat exchanger performance.

The most popular pipe material for ground fields is a specific type of high-density polyethylene pipe, similar to that used in the natural gas industry. This material has been field-tested for this application, and has been found to be durable, easy to work with, relatively inexpensive, and acceptable in terms of thermal performance. As described by the IGSHPA (International Ground Source Heat Pump Association), the pipes are joined by socket fusion or butt fusion (heat fusion). Vertical boreholes must be backfilled with grout or other acceptable materials suitable for groundwater protection and good heat transfer (Fig. 9-7). Sources of installation guidelines are listed in the Appendix B in the back of the book.

Loop Heat Recovery for Hot Water

Once a geothermal heating and cooling system is installed, hot-water generation is the single highest remaining utility cost item for the homeowner. (The actual cost has been estimated to be the equivalent to approximately 15,000 miles of vehicle commuting.)[3] These costs can easily be reduced. The financial and ecological benefits of the ground source heat pump for space conditioning are well-documented. The geoexchange system can also be applied to hot-water generation, thereby further utilizing the system to peak efficiency. A heat recovery coil is installed to heat the domestic water with heat that would have been thrown away in the summer. In the winter, the coil saves over 50 percent compared to a regular water heater.[4]

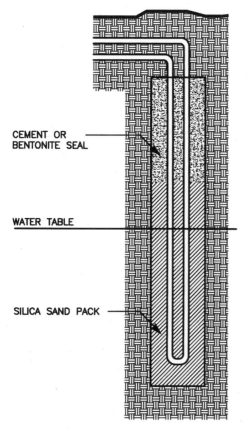

Figure 9-7 Typical installation—closed loop system with vertical riser.

The ground source heat pump water heater provides a significant improvement over other water-heating technologies. Ground loop length for space-conditioning equipment is primarily determined by conditioning loads. By connecting the heat pump to the earth loop, the same heat source that conditions the home can now heat water for domestic use without lengthening the ground loop. In the summer months, the unit extracts waste heat that originated in the home and is essentially moving excess summer heat from the home directly into the hot water. This increases the cooling efficiencies of the space-conditioning unit since the water heater also assists in removing the heat.

Cost

The first cost of a geothermal heating and cooling system is typically greater than conventional systems due to the additional costs of the ground heat exchanger. Although site specifics may cause construction costs to vary, the horizontal loop field (in 1997) will cost approximately $750 per ton. A vertical loop field will cost approximately $900 to $1400 per ton, depending on the subsoil conditions. Even though the vertical loop system costs more, it is more efficient to operate. It is important to note that only a certified installer can give an accurate construction estimate. (A typical 2000-ft^2 home will require a $3^1/_2$- to 4-ton unit.) A number of studies demonstrate these systems will typically save 50 to 60 percent over conventional heating and air conditioning systems. The National Laboratory of Renewable Energy estimates that geothermal systems can produce savings between $300 and $1000 per year in the average 2,000-ft^2 home. For example, a 2100-ft^2 home in Charlottesville, Virginia reported an annual heating and cooling cost of $180; a 2750-ft^2 home in Kansas City, Missouri reported a cost of $294 while the harsh winter of a 2750 ft^2 home in Indianapolis, Indiana resulted in an annual cost of $496.[5] The recovery (payback) of the additional cost should be possible within 3 or 4 years. Additional savings will also be realized from the hot-water heating loop recovery.

ULTRAVIOLET LIGHT HVAC FILTERING SYSTEMS

"Sick building syndrome" (SBS), "building-related illness" (BRI) and poor "indoor air quality" (IAQ) have become all-too-familiar terms to facility managers and office dwellers. Unfortunately, the same viruses, bacteria, yeast, mold and mildew are also unwelcome inhabitants of the home and are not controlled by HVAC filters. A revolutionary air disinfection system, using ultraviolet light, has the ability to "kill" all of these microorganisms and is now available for use in residential HVAC applications.

Artificially generated ultraviolet light in the C band (UVC) has been used extensively for disinfection purposes in still-air applications such as the Centers for Disease Control (CDC) in Atlanta. Recent technological improvements have now made these products applicable for residential HVAC systems. The concept was first discovered in the 19th century when a Danish physician, Niels Finsen, employed the sun's rays for treating disease. He discovered that bacterial infections, when exposed to the sun, healed much more rapidly than conventional. By the start of World War II, many manufacturers of fluorescent tubes, such as Westinghouse and GE, were also manufacturing UV tubes for still-air applications such as meat processing, dairies, breweries, and hospitals. In the late 1950s, with the increased spread of tuberculosis, UVC was considered for HVAC equipment. The inefficiency of these moving-air installations delayed consumer acceptance. New improvements have now produced systems that are equally effective in warm or cold moving air. These newer and higher-output UVC lamps produce no ozone or other harmful products, do not pose a risk to home inhabitants, and can be retrofitted into existing or installed in new HVAC systems.

As mentioned earlier, UVC is especially effective against microorganisms but is also effective on other organic compounds such as VOCs and food odors. Microorganisms are measured in microns (a micron is 1/25,400 of an inch). Bacteria range in size from 0.5 to 4 microns, mold range in size from 1 to 5 microns and viruses can be as small as .02 microns. Besides the small size, the ability to quickly reproduce makes the control of microorganisms especially difficult. Bacteria and viruses can double every 20 minutes. This means that one microbe can become 70 trillion in a 24-hour period. [6]

UVC is biocidal (capable of killing living organisms) toward many contaminants of the home which include:

- Viruses which cause influenza, colds, mumps, and chickenpox
- Bacteria which cause sinusitis, tuberculosis, and strep
- Mold which cause histoplamosis, aspergillosis, and other fungal infections
- Cell fragments, including spores and toxins from microbes that cause allergies, headaches and allergy asthma. VOCs and musty odors are also eliminated.

Although products will vary among manufacturers, it is recommended to consult manufacturers that make commercial equipment and residential equipment. One such product, the SteriLight™, by Steril-Aire™, Inc., is easily installed at the downstream side of the cooling coil (Fig. 9-8). The Emitters™ (tubes) are available in 20" or 24" lengths and on centers of 10" or 14". The manufacturer states that these units will fit almost any existing or new residential HVAC system.

Figure 9-8   UVC emitter. *(Steril-Aire, Inc.)*

Advantages

Most airborne viruses and bacteria are too small to be captured by the average filter but are easily killed by UVC. The mold and bacteria found on cooling coils and in drain pans are completely eliminated. The nonchemical energy of UVC kills microorganisms without endangerment to the HVAC equipment, the environment, or the inhabitants of the home.

Disadvantages

The cost is the only real disadvantage. Although prices will vary depending on the model and manufacturer, most residential units start at $600. The cost for annual relamping can range from $250 to $350. The steadying increase in popularity (demand) should continue to lower these prices.

PHOTOVOLTAICS

The growing emphasis on renewable energy resources has seen the development of photovoltaic (PV) power systems as a method of harnessing the power of the sun. In fact, PV systems installed since 1988 provide enough electricity to power 150,000 homes in the United States (or 8 million homes in the developing world).[7] Often referred to as solar electricity, the principle of PV power is the conversion of light energy (from the sun) directly into electricity. Today's technology is not only reliable, it is clean, silent, nonpolluting, virtually maintenance free, and requires no fuel. Photovoltaics afford energy producers and consumers the opportunity to tap into a secure, economical, essentially inexhaustible and widely available resource—sunlight. In a few short years, it will be economically viable to create a hybrid system of using the photovoltaic solar cells with a geothermal heat pump system. For more information on photovoltaics, see Chapter 11, Electrical Systems and Accessories.

CONCLUSION

As one can see, geoexchange heating and cooling is a common sense alternative to the conventional types of HVAC systems generally used. They are more than three times as efficient as the most efficient fossil fuel furnace.[8] Some states even have tax credits available for installing geothermal systems. The U.S. General Accounting Office estimates that if geothermal systems were installed nationwide, they could save several billion dollars annually in energy costs and substantially reduce pollution.[9] Energy-efficient, aesthetically unobtrusive, lower life-cycle cost, extended warranties, and environmentally friendliness are qualities of geothermal systems and photovoltaics that cannot be ignored.

APPENDIX

Geothermal Heat Pump Consortium, Inc.
701 Pennsylvania Ave. NW, 5th Floor
Washington, DC 20004-2696
(202) 508-5512

Steril-Aire™, Inc.
11100 E. Artesia Blvd.
Suite D
Cerritos, CA 90703
(562) 467-8484
Fax: (562) 467-8481

WaterFurnace International, Inc
9000 Conservation Way
Fort Wayne, Indiana 46809
(219) 478-5667

CASE STUDY 9-1*

Background

Ron Dickey has been with PR&W Electric Cooperative in Wamego, Kansas, for 23 years and has served as Member Services Director for the past 3 years. He approached the U. S. Department of Agriculture's Rural Housing Service (formerly the Farmers Home Administration) about an idea that would help rural Kansans with modest incomes buy homes with energy-efficient thermal envelopes and geoexchange systems. Mr. Dickey convinced the Rural Housing Service that more home buyers would be able to qualify for Rural Housing Service mortgages if the homes were highly efficient. Also, a well-built home would cost less to renovate should the Rural Housing Services need to resell the house in the future.

Charles Burger's New Home

A prime example of this coming to fruition is a new 2600 ft^2 house in Wamego, Kansas. The home is 1-year old and occupied by Charles Burger's family of 6, including three teenagers and one 7-year old child. The Rural Housing Service specified a comprehensive weatherproofing and insulation package, and worked with PR&W and the heating and cooling contractor, Tim Dugan of Bill's Electric in Holton, Kansas, on the design of the $2^1/2$ ton WaterFurnace geoexchange heat pump. The heating load of the house is 26,478 Btu/hr. In addition to heating and cooling the home, the geoexchange system provides the majority of Burger's domestic water-heating needs.

The ground loop is a horizontal, multiple-pipe configuration with six pipes per trench. The trenches at the Burger home are 2' wide, average 5' in depth, and total 285' in length. Three pipes lay on the bottom. Each trench is then backfilled with 2' of dirt and three more pipes are laid before backfilling is completed. A total of 1710' of polyethylene tubing was used. The loop was designed for a minimum of 100°F. The loop is filled with a 25 percent solution of Environolen, an ethanol-based antifreeze, and water. The balance point of the system (outside temperature below which back-up heat is needed) averages −7°F.

*Text Provided by Geothermal Heat Pump Consortium, Inc.

Capital and Operating Costs

The actual heating, cooling, and water-heating cost for 1996 was $432 (see Table 1). The first cost of the geoexchange system was $10,245. The estimated cost of a natural gas furnace/electric air conditioning system for the Burger house is $4597 and projected heating, cooling, and water-heating energy bills are $1174. Incorporating the first-cost premium of $5648 to a 30-year mortgage at 8 percent will add just $31 to the monthly payment after taxes, while saving an average $62 in monthly utility bill, a positive cash flow of $31 per month.

The total cost of the Burger's house was $108,200. This includes $6000 for water hook-up and the $12,000 cost of the lot.

CASE STUDY 9-2*

The Palmer Residence

The Palmer residence is in East Hampton, Connecticut. It is a two-story colonial with 2987 ft² of conditioned space and 3537 ft² total. Wall insulation is sprayed foam with an R-value of 20. Blown cellulose gives the attic an R-50, fiberglass bats in the floors over the unconditioned basement result of R-19. The double-pane, low-E, argon-filled windows boast a U-value of 0.36. Air sealing is verified by blower door testing, which discovers where the leaks are, so they can be sealed.

To ensure air quality in their well-sealed home, the Palmers installed a heat recovery ventilator that provides fresh outside air without the usual energy penalties by tying into the air distribution side of the geoexchange heat pump. The ECH (Energy-Crafted Home, Northeast Utilities) measures result in a heating load of 49,614 Btu/hr and a cooling load of 30,568 Btu/hr. Dr. Palmer says, "From a health and ecological perspective, using ECH design strategies and techniques is the only responsible way to build a new home."

Geoexchange System

The house is heated and cooled by a 4.2-ton WaterFurnace geoexchange heat pump. The closed-loop ground heat exchanger

*Text provided by Geothermal Heat Pump Consortium, Inc.

uses two vertical 250' wells and 1000' of polyethylene tubing. A desuperheater preheats the domestic hot water to dramatically reduce propane consumption of the traditional water heater. The propane water heater also provides back-up space heating via a hot-water coil mounted in the geoexchange heat pump.

In the event of an electrical power outage, the circulation pump for the coil, air handler blower, and controls are connected to an emergency generator. While prepared for any situation, Dr. Palmer has rarely had to rely on his backup system.

The Geoexchange System Cost

The geoexchange equipment and ductwork cost the Palmers $10,541, and the ground loop ran $8742. The total geoexchange system cost of $19,283 reflects the high prices experienced in the northeast United States. However, competing HVAC systems are also more expensive than in other areas of the country. The Palmers received a quote of $16,200 for an oil-fired furnace and electric central air conditioning system. The Palmers received a rebate from Northeast Utilities of $713 per ton for a total of $2971.

Operating Cost

The geoexchange system provides a comfortable climate year-round for Dr. Palmer and his family at an average cost of $93.52 per month based on submeter readings and an electric rate of 9.884 cents/kWh. According to Dr. Palmer, "It's healthier, more comfortable home to live in while using perhaps half the energy of a conventional house."

CASE STUDY 9-3*

Piper Glen Subdivision

From a homeowner's point of view, geothermal heat pumps (GHPs) are attractive because operating costs are lower than other electric heating and cooling technologies. Electric utilities are interested in promoting GHPs since they have substantially lower peak demand that other technologies during periods when

*Text Provided by Geothermal Heat Pump Consortium, Inc.

systemwide utility demand is high — the coldest and hottest days of the year.

The heat transfer performance of a GHP earth loop is highly dependent on the loop configuration as well as the characteristics of the local soil. But there's very little data on GHP performance in the Southeastern United States, and this NRECA–sponsored research project will quantify the performance of modern GHP systems over a 12–month period with various loop configurations.

The loop configurations under evaluation include horizontal slinkys, vertical slinkys, and vertical bore loops. Jackson EMC will compare them to see which is most cost-effective. Other items to be examined and evaluated are the measured performance of the GHP units compared to the manufacturer's expected performance data, measured energy use (kWh) and demand (kW) versus other standard technologies, the energy use and demand savings associated with de-superheater operation, and the economic potential of GHPs from the perspective of the customer and the electric utility. Meters will enable Jackson EMC to collect data and monitor 16 to 18 sensor points on each home.

Test bores were done on the subdivision to determine the depth of the rock table. Dr. Marvin Smith of Oklahoma State University, an expert on geothermal technology, designed the loops based on this information, soil type characteristics in the area, and heat loss/gain requirements for the homes. Horizontal and vertical slinky loops and vertical bores were being installed, but the objective was to use slinkys for the majority of homes because of the lower installation cost. However, the vertical slinkys proved difficult to install because the soil characteristics caused the trenches to cave in on the loops before they could be adequately backfilled in a controlled method. The horizontal slinkys also proved difficult to install because the rock table was actually at a much shallower level than the original test bores indicated. Thus the remaining lots have vertical bores. This method can be made cost effective by hiring a loop contractor who owns a drilling rig designed for the local rock type.

Location in Gwinnett County, GA
33, ½-acre lots
1600 ft² (approx.) homes
Prices: high $90s to low 100s
Competing fuel is natural gas

Heating/cooling components in each home:
3-ton Addison heat pump, 15 kW auxiliary heat
Closed loop
Central thermostat

Thermal envelope of each home:
R-30 ceilings
R-13 walls
R-13 floors
Double glass windows
Metal-insulated doors

Installation costs:
$4700 increment over comparable system
$3600 indoor hard cost
$2766/ton
$1800/house incentive from Jackson EMC

Operating cost (air source/water source):
Heating $307/$211
Cooling $252/$230
Water heating $270/$136
Annual total $1073/$577
5.84 year payback to recover $2900

Energy savings:
Heating   40%
Cooling   25%

REFERENCES

1. National Renewable Energy Laboratory, *Renewable Energy Annual.*
2. Lincoln Electric System, Energy Conservation & Applications Division, 11th & "O" Street, P.O. Box 80869, Lincoln, NE 68501 (402) 475-4211
3. The Energy Service Company, Eugene, Oregon.
4. *Addison Water-source Heating and Cooling Systems* (Orlando, FL: WeatherKing Division of Addison Products Company), p. 3.

5. *WFI Industries Ltd. Annual Report, 1996* (Ft. Wayne, IN: Water Furnace International, 1996), p. 7.

6. "Micro-organisms and HVAC Equipment," Steril-Aire, Inc. Product Literature

7. The National Renewable Energy Laboratory.

8. *Geothermal Heating and Cooling Systems* (Columbia City, IN: Electric Institute of Indiana, 1996), p. 14.

9. *Geothermal Energy, Outlook Limited for Some Uses but Promising for Geothermal* (Geothermal Accounting Office, June, 1994).

10

Plumbing and Sprinkler Systems

INTRODUCTION

The evolution of modern plumbing can be traced back 4000 years to the Isle of Crete. It was around 1700 B.C. that the Minoan Palace of Knossos featured four separate drainage systems that emptied into great sewers constructed of stone. Water for fountains and faucets of marble, gold, and silver that jetted hot and cold running water were supplied by terra cotta pipe that was laid beneath the palace floor. Each section was about $2^1/_2$' long, slightly tapered at one end, and nearly 1" in diameter. The palace latrine featured the world's first flushing "water closet" (toilet) with a wooden seat and a small reservoir of water. The device, however, was lost for thousands of years amid the rubble of flood, decay, and literally, the "sands of time." (It would be another 3200 years before Sir John Harington would invent the "Ajax" water closet in 1596, built for his godmother, Queen Elizabeth I. Severely ridiculed, it would be another 200 years before another Englishman, Alexander Cumming in 1775, would patent the forerunner of the toilet used today.)[1]

Early American settlers knew nothing of lead or iron pipe —they knew only to build with wood, the country's bounty. Water pipes were made of bored-out logs, preferably felled from hemlock or elm trees. The trees would be cut into 7' to 9' lengths, their trunks around 9' to 10' thick. With a 5' steel auger between them, a handle at one end, they would fix the log by eye, size it up with a point of the ax, and drill or bore out the center. Ramming one end to make a conical shape, they would jam the logs together in a series, using a bituminous-like pitch or tar to caulk the joints. Sometimes they would split the log and hollow it out, put it together, connect the logs with iron hoops, or get the blacksmith to caulk the logs with lead.

They would set up a gravity water system, starting from a spring or stream on high ground, allowing water to flow downhill to the house or farm. It would cut a path back of the house, through the barn, and flow into a catch basin.[2]

Even in a nation as civilized as America, many rural dwellers and farms did not have in-house plumbing installed until the first half of this century. Water on demand is a convenience that most people in this hemisphere take for granted—until something goes wrong. The systems discussed in this chapter, the plumbing manifold, cross-linked polyethylene tubing, tankless water heaters, and fire sprinklers are designed to be more efficient, conserve resources, and even improve home safety. And when the inevitable malfunction occurs, the repair will be simpler and less costly.

MANIFOLD PLUMBING

The typical residential plumbing system runs in series throughout the home (Fig. 10-1). Simply, the water main (or private well) branches off to the house in which a cold water

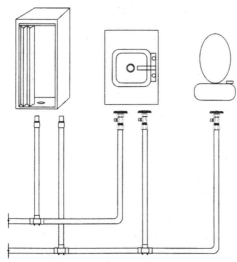

Figure 10-1 Branch method of residential plumbing. *(Wirsbo)*

supply line runs from fixture to fixture. One branch of this line goes to the water heater in which case the hot water supply line runs in series to each fixture in which hot water will be required.

Trouble occurs when the line develops a leak or other malfunction. Although a shutoff valve is typically installed at each fixture, there is no device available which will shut off the water in the line without turning off the entire water supply. This is because there are not adequate controls to shut off the water without shutting off the entire house.

The Manifold Principle

In a manifold plumbing system, all plumbing is run in a home run fashion. Each plumbing fixture is fed by its own distribution line which runs back "home" to a common manifold (Fig. 10-2). As mentioned in Chapter 2, the intent of this book is to discuss the means, methods, and materials in a nonproprietary manner. However, it is not possible with all construction products. The MANABLOC manifold water distribution system by Vanguard Industries is a patented water distribution system that has been in use in the United States for 10 years.

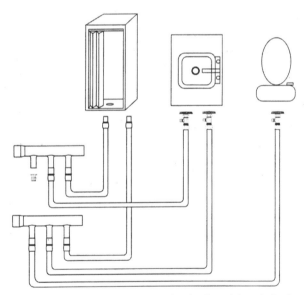

Figure 10-2   Home run method of residential plumbing. *(Wirsbo)*

The Manabloc Water Distribution System

The MANABLOC modular manifold control unit supplies water to individual plumbing fixtures through dedicated ports and distribution lines. Each port is equipped with a built-in shutoff valve which provides water control for each plumbing fixture. The ports are labeled, not unlike an electrical panel, so that fixture identification is simplified (Fig.10-3).

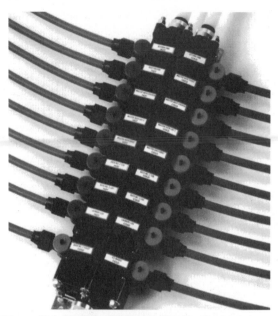

Figure 10-3 MANABLOC water distribution system. *(Vanguard)*

The modular manifold sections are made of polysulfone (PLS) plastic. According to the manufacturer, this engineered plastic material is used extensively in the medical industry and is highly resistant to hot water, chlorine, and other chemicals typically found in potable water systems.

Each manifold unit comes complete with necessary fitting hardware to connect cross-linked polyethylene (PEX) directly to the port (Fig. 10-4). PEX, a flexible tubing, which can be bent or curved around obstacles without the use of fittings, is discussed later in this chapter (Fig. 10-5).

Advantages

In a typical residential system, a common manifold control unit and properly sized distribution lines service individual termination points at each fixture. ($^3/_8$" lines can be used for all fixtures requiring up to a 2.5-gal/min demand. By providing each fixture with its own distribution line, smaller lines can be installed so water flows faster and hot water is delivered more rapidly.) For example, a bathroom faucet is fed by its own individual hot and cold distribution lines. The bathroom toilet is also fed by its own committed distribution line. By serving each fixture with individual distribution lines, manifold plumbing provides equalized flow and pressure throughout the system. Therefore, dedicated lines reduce the possibility of temperature changes in the shower caused when one or more fixtures are turned on in a conventional plumbing system. And, when the homeowner turns on the water to the faucet, the properly sized polyethylene line speeds the water to the faucet twice as fast as the conventional plumbing line.

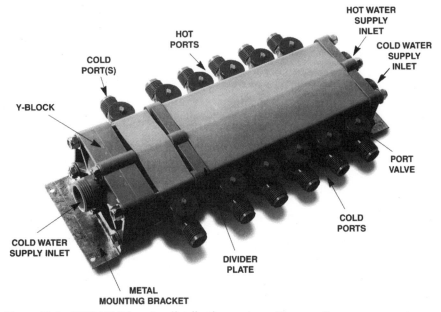

Figure 10-4   MANABLOC water distribution system. *(Vanguard)*

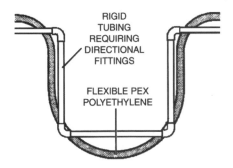

Figure 10-5   PEX tubing. *(Vanguard)*

The net result is that the homeowner wastes less water waiting for hot water to arrive for the intended use. In an average home, the amount of water wasted during incidental use in a 1-year period can easily be several thousand gallons.

In addition, when you consider that some homeowners in some areas are told to flush their copper plumbing with water for 2 to 3 minutes to clear lead solder leachates from the system, a manifold and PEX tubing system makes even more sense. Flushing a water system for 2 to 3 minutes could easily waste 4 to 5 gallons of water.

With a manifold system, nonleaded water is delivered faster and consequently wastes less. Since the plumbing lines are dedicated to a specific fixture, less cool water is purged from the line before the hot water is delivered.

Water conservation is not the only consumer benefit of a manifold plumbing system. By using less hot water, there is the potential to conserve energy at the water heater. When combined with the geothermal heating and cooling system discussed in Chapter 9, the results could be realized in extraordinary energy and cost savings. When hot water is utilized, cold water pours into the water heater to replenish what was removed during the use. If less water is removed from the water heater, less cold water is imported into the heating unit, thus lessening the chance that the heater, which utilizes a water temperature sensing unit, will cycle on.

It is generally stated that the weakest point in any plumbing system is where the fittings are located. The MANABLOC water distribution system reduces the number of connections needed in running the water lines. A fitting is placed at The MANABLOC unit and a transition fitting at the fixture. According to the manufacturer, this reduces the number of fittings to barely one-third of what is in a conventional flexible plumbing system. When compared to a rigid plumbing system, such as copper or CPVC (in which many fittings are used to create bends and turns in the supply lines), the number of fittings eliminated are even more. Fewer fittings reduce the chance of leaks or problems with connections concealed in walls.

As mentioned earlier, the dedicated lines have individual shut-off valves at the manifold, which make maintenance and repairs more convenient for the homeowner. The entire home's water system does not have to be shut off in the event of a leak or to repair or replace a fixture. The remainder of the home's plumbing fixtures can remain fully functional while repairs are being made.

Unlike many copper or other plumbing systems, the MANABLOC manifold is guaranteed for 10 years. This warranty covers the complete system including tubing, fittings and the control unit. The warranty also covers reasonable replacement costs for damage to personal property including furnishings and drywall. The 10-year warranty is fully transferable to subsequent owners of the home within the original 10-year period.

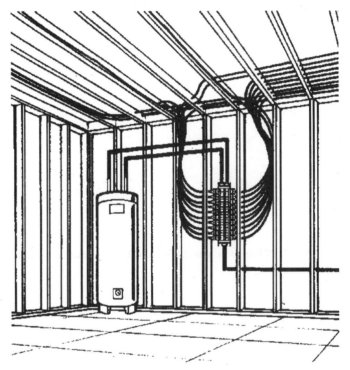

Figure 10-6   Accessible location. *(Vanguard)*

Disadvantages

Initial cost is going to be slightly higher due to the increase in material needed for a MANABLOC water distribution system.

Installation Guidelines

Upon delivery, the MANABLOC water distribution manifold system should be protected from impact and covered during the installation, sawing, sanding, or painting of finish materials. It is important that the MANABLOC not be disassembled or the tie rods adjusted. (They are factory preset.) Since the MANABLOC is made of an engineered plastic, the unit should not be exposed to open flame or excessive heat. Generally, the MANABLOC should be located in a permanently accessible location (Fig. 10-6). An interior wall with an access door or in the basement, laundry, or service closet are appropriate locations (Fig. 10-7). It is most efficient if the unit is located in an area that is centrally located among the largest number of fixtures in the home. For large homes, it may be desirable to use more than one MANABLOC. A large installation may benefit from manifolds located near concentrations of fixture groups.

Figure 10-7   Cabinet-mounted manifold. *(Vanguard)*

Generally, the MANABLOC should be located between 3' and 8' of the water heater (or as close as practical). The hot water service line, if PEX, should be at least 18" from the hot water heater. Metallic piping should be used between the water heater and the PEX tubing. The MANABLOC unit should also be located where it will not be exposed to freezing temperatures or ambient temperatures greater than 140°F.

The MANABLOC unit can be installed between two studs using Vanguard supplied metal straps (Fig. 10-8); 1 × 4 blocking can also be used for unit support. If the unit is not installed between studs, a $^1/_2"$ plywood board with appropriate tubing support as recommended by the manufacturer will suffice.

Figure 10-8   Manifold mounted between wall studs. *(Vanguard)*

The main service line should be installed with a shutoff valve. A check valve, pressure-reducing valve and backflow preventer or other devices may also be required per local plumbing codes. The service (or supply) lines should enter and the distribution lines should exit in a straight line perpendicular to the length of the MANABLOC. Hot and cold water lines can be bundled if allowed by the local building codes. The hot and cold water lines should be labeled at each end of the tubing or a color-coded PEX distribution tubing can be used to prevent cross connections.

The tubing connections at the supply inlet are a proprietary gasketed swivel type which require a MANABLOC transition fittings. (Water service connections to any type of plumbing supply materials are available from the manufacturer.) The connections for the distribution lines are mechanical-type compression fittings and will not work with standard pipe fittings. The PEX tubing is pulled from the unit to each fixture. It is recommended that some slack be left in the line for contraction when cold temperatures are encountered. (6" in 50' is a general rule.) When drilling through studs, the hole must be slightly larger to accommodate the tube's or bundle's need for free movement during expansion and contraction and to avoid binding.

It is not recommended that the MANABLOC system be installed where water contains free chlorine levels that consistently exceed recognized norms when measured at the fixture. All connections shall be approved for compatibility with the MANABLOC fittings. Standard pipe fittings, CPVC cements, or other agents could adversely affect the unit. It is important to follow all manufacturer's guidelines that are supplied with the unit and to verify installation with the appropriate local building codes.

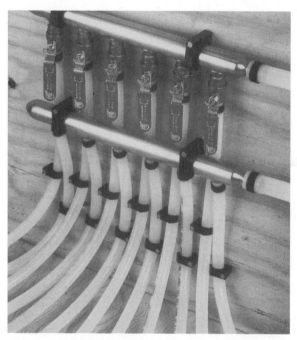

Figure 10-9   Copper manifold. *(Sioux Chief Manufacturing Company)*

Conclusion

Copper and brass manifolds are also available from various manufacturers (Fig. 10-9). When installed properly, these will provide some of the advantages as presented by the MANABLOC water distribution system. Unlike the MANABLOC, these manifolds do not have on/off valves as a standard option. However, the manufacturer stated these can be custom-fitted. In any event, the manifold distribution method for hot and cold potable water supply will make a difference in the quality and economy of service. One household might not make a significant overall contribution to water conservation. But, millions of homes each saving several thousand gallons of water each year though a properly designed plumbing system would translate into billions of gallons.

CROSS-LINKED POLYETHYLENE (PEX) PIPE

ABS, CPVC, PB (polybutylene), and copper have traditionally been the most common materials used for hot and cold potable water distribution systems in residential applications. Initial or life-cycle cost and ease of installation or expected material life are all factors in determining which tubing type to use. A "new" tubing material, cross-linked polyethylene (PEX), is quickly gaining popularity throughout the industry (Fig. 10-10). (The material is relatively new to North America. PEX systems have been widely used in the European market for hot water heating and plumbing applications for 25 years.)

Figure 10-10   PEX tubing. *(Vanguard)*

The "PE" refers to the raw material, a form of polyethylene, and the "X" refers to the cross-linking of the polyethylene across its molecular chains. Cross-linking is a permanent chemical change that transforms the material's molecular chains into a three-dimensional linked network. As a result, PEX is more durable within a wide range of temperatures and pressures as well as having increased flexibility. This makes PEX ideally suited for a variety of uses in addition to residential and commercial applications. These include such low-temperature heat transfer applications as radiant floor heating systems, snow-melt pipe systems and ice rinks or high-temperature distribution systems such as hot water baseboard heating, radiators, and convectors.[3]

PEX is not to be confused with thermoplastic polyethylene (PE). PE is used in a variety of applications throughout the construction industry but has a relatively low melting point of 110°C. This feature reduces its use to a maximum continuous temperature of 70°C. By converting the thermoplastic PE into PEX, the melting point is greatly increased and the weak points of PE are overcome by the improvement of thermal capabilities.

Advantages

The flexibility of PEX tubing allows for faster and easier installation since it has fewer fittings than rigid plumbing systems. PEX has a high- and low-temperature stability, is nontoxic, lead-free, resistant to corrosive water and soil, and has no odor or taste. The material is chemically resistant to most substances and does not require the use of solvent or chemical joining.

PEX tubing also provides resistance to damage from water expansion in freezing temperatures. The material will stretch to accommodate expansion of frozen water, then return to its original size when the ice thaws. (Although freeze-break resistant, no material is freeze-break proof under all circumstances and installation guidelines must be followed.) The piping's inherent flexibility also allows for a significant dampening of water hammer. Most PEX tubing products are available with a 25-year warranty and one manufacturer's accelerated testing methods indicate a minimum of 100 years of service can be expected.

Material Properties

As mentioned earlier, PEX is cross-linked polyethylene. PEX is formed by chemically joining individual polyethylene molecules to alter the performance of the base resin. Through one of several available processes, links between polyethylene macromolecules are formed to create essentially one large molecule of polyethylene. The resultant three-dimensional molecule is more resistant to temperature extremes, chemical attack, and creep deformation, which makes PEX ideal for use in hot water applications. Simply, the HDPE polymer material is changed from a thermoplastic to a thermoset. Thermosets have the unique ability to "remember" their structural shape.

There are three main categories of PEX, grouped according to the manufacturing method. These are commonly referred to as silane PEX, radiation PEX and Engel PEX. Each of the three processes have been manufacturing PEX for several decades. Regardless of the process, all pipe produced by any of the three methods must meet the same qualification requirements as specified in PEX referenced standards.[4]

The silane process was introduced in the 1950s. Silane PEX (also called moisture-cured vinylsilane) materials are often referred to as "moisture cure" materials because they cross-link or "cure" on exposure of the pipe to water. Silane PEX pipe is produced in a simple two-stage manufacturing process. The materials, typically a MDPE or HDPE (medium- or high-density polyethylene) resin, are extruded into pipe on standard pipe extrusion equipment. After the pipe has been extruded, cross-linking is achieved by exposing the pipe to moisture.[5] The chemical reaction stops when cross-linking reaches approximately 70 percent. Even with further exposure to hot water, no additional reaction will take place. (These chemical methods can be compared to the vulcanization of rubber.[6])

Another method, known as the radiation process, uses high-energy irradiation of the extruded pipe to form the molecular links. Radiation PEX pipe is also produced in a two-stage process. First, PE is extruded into pipe. Then, cross-linking is achieved by bombarding the extruded pipe with either electromagnetic radiation (gamma radiation) or high-energy electrons (beta radiation). These processes are also referred to as nuclear and electron beam, respectively.

The third method is commonly referred to as the Engel process. Also known as the peroxide process, this method was developed by Thomas Engel in the 1960s.[7] In the Engel process, peroxides are incorporated into the base PE resin during pipe extrusion. Cross-linking is achieved by heating the PE above the decomposition temperature of the peroxides to produce "free radicals" which initiate cross-linking of the PE.[8] This method, probably the most prevalent method of PEX cross-linking, has been undergoing testing at 203°F at 150 psi since 1973. According to one manufacturer, no degradation in quality has occurred.[9]

The aforementioned methods of producing PEX tubing have specific ratios expressed by the percentage of molecules available for cross-linking that are actually cross-linked. The higher the percentage of molecules that are cross-linked, the more durable and pressure and temperature resistant the tubing. This is not a specification that implies one pipe process is superior to another, it only shows the amount of cross-linking that is required by that specific process to meet the industry standards for PEX piping. Typical cross-linking levels in pipe range from 65 to 89 percent depending upon the manufacturer and the manufacturing process. For example, the Engel method PEX tubing usually has about 80 percent of its molecules cross linked. Radiation PEX is around 75 percent and silane PEX is usually below 70 percent.[10]

Standards and Specifications

In order for a PEX piping product to be available for public use, a number of industry standards must be met:

* ASTM F876, Standard Specification for Cross Linked Polyethylene Tubing
* ASTM F877, Standard Specification for Cross Linked Polyethylene Tubing Plastic Hot and Cold Water Distribution Systems
* ANSI/NSF (National Sanitation Foundation) Standard 61, Drinking Water Components- Health Effects.

The Hydrostatic Stress Board (HSB) of the Plastic Pipe Institute (PPI) has also developed a report, PPI TR3, outlining the policies and procedures to be used when estimating the long-term strength of thermoplastic materials.[11]

PEX tubing and fittings are available in a variety of sizes ranging from $1/4$" to 2" in diameter. The tubing is manufactured relative to copper tubing outside-diameter-controlled dimensions. The wall thickness is based upon SDR-9 (standard dimension ratio) values which yield pressure ratings of 160 psi at 73°F and 100 psi at 180°F. (Some manufacturers have produced tubing that is rated to 200°F at a pressure of 80 psi.)

PEX is listed in the BOCA National Plumbing Code, the BOCA National Mechanical Code, the Standard Plumbing Code (SBCCI), The CABO One and Two Family Dwelling Code, and the International Plumbing Code (IPC) for use in plumbing systems. As stated earlier, check with your plumbing official for state or local variances from these national codes before installing or specifying PEX.

Limitations

As discussed earlier, the three methods of cross-linking PE pipe produce subtle differences in the performance and subsequent limitations of each type. The manufacturer's literature must be consulted to verify proper application and installation. The following are general guidelines and may not apply to all products.

PEX should not be stored in direct sunlight since ultraviolet (UV) light may cause premature aging. (Although some manufacturers are experimenting with UV inhibitors that provide resistance of up to 2 years of continuous UV exposure, PEX should not be exposed to flame or excessive heat). Vanguard's VANEX PEX should not be installed downstream from a tankless or instantaneous water heater; however, Wirsbo's Engel-type PEX does not have this limitation. PEX should be no closer than 6" upstream. Diffuse light should not pose a problem. The water pressure should not exceed the pressure listed on the side of the tubing.

Thinners, pipe sealants, solvent cements, fluxes, lubricants, bleaches should not be used to seal or clean PEX. Adhesive tapes should not be used since this will restrict the movement necessary during expansion and contraction. Once again, Vanguard's VANEX PEX should not be used in continuously circulating hot water plumbing loops; however, Wirsbo's Engel-type PEX may be used. Since PEX tubing is softer than metals, the tubes could be damaged by abrasion or cutting. Tubing should be protected from possible damage or piercing by screws or nails. Installation requirements do vary. Depending on the type of PEX, bending radius, kink repair, and linear support required, strict guidelines as provided by the manufacturer must be followed carefully. Hangers made for use with plastic pipe are typically available from the tubing supplier. Metal hangers or supports with sharp edges should not be used.

The proper markings should be stamped or printed along the sheath of the tube. The tubing will have the manufacturer's name, the trade name and tubing type, the tube size, pressure rating, ASTM specification, the third-party specification, the standard dimension ratio (the outside diameter divided by the wall thickness) and the manufacturer's date code. Installation guidelines will provide specific information regarding procedures for fluid, hydrostatic or air pressure testing of the system.

It is important to note that all PEX tubing and fittings are not interchangeable. Proper compatibility of fittings and tubing type (or manufacturer) must be followed for proper performance of the water distribution system. Using fitting systems and tubing from different manufacturers may negate any warranty and, without specific recommendations from the pipe and fittings manufacturers, is done at the installer's risk. For example, Vanguard's VANEX Series PEX (silane method of chemical cross-linking) is a proprietary product designed to interface with Vanguard's MANABLOC water distribution system.

VANEX PEX piping is a copper tube size material, classified as SDR-9, with a 100-psi pressure rating at 180°F. VANEX PEX tubing is manufactured, sampled, tested, marked and third party listed in accordance with ASTM standards F-876 and F-877. All of the chemical additives used in making VANEX are depleted during the cross-linking process. After cross-linking, the tubing is thoroughly flushed with water and then purged with air. NSF International (formerly the National Sanitation Foundation) has tested VANEX tubing to Standard 61 (Health Effects) and found it safe for use in potable water systems.

TANKLESS HOT WATER HEATER

All too often, we miss things, possessions or even people, only after they are gone. This observation can be applied to household conveniences as well. A good supply of hot water is only truly appreciated once it stops. And if it stops while showering, this realization can arrive quite abruptly. This all too common occurrence can now be avoided altogether with the introduction of the tankless water heater. Although popular in Europe and Asia for a number of years, these units are now growing in popularity throughout North America.

Tank-Type Water Heaters

Most residences built or dwelled in during the 20th century probably rely on a tank-type water heater. A tank-type water heater stores water at a specific temperature and is able to provide a large volume of hot water for a limited period of time. As the water cools in the tank, the burners or element turn on to restore the desired temperature. The standard tank-type water heater is either electric or fuel-fired. In the latter, the fuel most commonly used is gas, either natural or propane, but oil-fired heaters and boilers are popular in many areas of the country.

The typical electric water heater unit heats water by sending electrical energy through electrical-resistance heating elements usually located at the middle of the tank and another one at the bottom. Gas-fired units have a burner that is fed gas through a control valve, thereby providing the heat energy. In an oil-fired heater, the burner is similar to that found on an oil-fired furnace. The burner is usually situated to throw a flame under the tank. The exhaust gases are vented either through a hollow core at the center of the tank or around the tank sides.

A thermostat regulates a switch that allows a current flow once the temperature in the tank drops and shuts off when the water temperature reaches its preset limit, generally between 120 and 140°F. When a hot-water tap is opened, cold water enters the tank and the drop in temperature triggers the thermostat, which activates the heating elements.

Tank systems require proper sizing to keep from running out of hot water too soon. Since the tank stores hot water, its capacity also affects the ongoing availability at the tap. Choosing a water heater that has an appropriate capacity and recovery rate depends on how much water the home demands as well as the rate at which the water is heated. The speed at which a tank-type unit heats water is called its recovery rate. This figure indicates the amount of water in gallons that can be heated to 100°F in 1 hour.

Typically, electric water heaters with low recovery rates have a high storage capacity of the tank. Although it takes longer to heat the water, there is more hot water available in storage for intermittent use. On the other hand, a fuel-fired heater with a high recovery rate can have a smaller tank since it can heat the water faster. In general, electric models have the lowest recovery rate, and oil-fired units have the highest.[12] The homeowner thus has two options in order to guarantee an ample supply of hot water: either set the water temperature very high or have a tank with a large capacity.

Tank-type water heaters are somewhat inefficient. The tank walls lose about 15 percent of the heat of the water.[13] These losses dramatically reduce the overall year-round efficiency of the units, particularly in cold climates. Tanks also waste energy in the cooling and reheating cycle, especially if oversized.[14]

The tank's cooling and reheating cycles cause expansion and contraction of the metal parts of the tank. This creates wear and tear, requiring the tank to be regularly replaced. Most tanks are made of steel, which is glass-lined on the inside to help prevent corrosion. In fact, corrosion is the primary reason that tanks fail.[15]

Statistics released by the department of energy indicate the average homeowner uses 20 gallons of hot water for the average bath or shower, 14 gallons of hot water when running the dishwasher, and 32 gallons of hot water for the washing machine. Even shaving uses approximately 2 gallons of hot water.[16] One can see that a 40-gallon tank-type hot water heater has difficulty in supplying the necessary amount of hot water when needed. The tankless water heater may be an alternative solution to the problem of limited hot water availability.

The tankless water heater has a variety of monikers depending upon the type or manufacturer. Instantaneous, on-demand or point-of-use are references to tankless water heaters. The most dramatic difference between a tank-type water heater and a tankless unit is that the tankless water heater does not store water. It only heats the water needed by the user as it passes through a heat exchanger. This allows the supply of hot water to continue as long as the supply of inlet water will continue. Tankless water heaters are lightweight and dramatically smaller than tank-type heaters since the bulky storage tank is eliminated. Many can be mounted under a sink or on a wall, depending upon the model selected. The tankless water heater has been popular in Europe for a number of years but is only now becoming available in the United States and Canada.

It is important to note that the tankless water heater discussed in this text is quite different from domestic hot water coils which are installed in central heating boilers. Gas-fired tankless water heaters utilize a coil and heat exchanger to heat water but are much smaller.

Principle of a Tankless Water Heater

The principles of a tankless water heater demonstrate its efficiency. When a hot water faucet is turned on, the heater senses the water pressure difference and immediately switches on the high-intensity heater. Water flows over the heating elements and out to the tap. Maximum temperatures are typically reached within 20 seconds and will be maintained for an infinite period of time (or until the flow of water is stopped.)

Types of Tankless Water Heaters

Although the nomenclature may vary between manufacturers, there are basically two types of tankless water heaters. The small units located at a sink or shower are typically referred to as point-of-use instantaneous water heaters (Fig. 10-11). These are also appropriate for individual fixtures that may require a continuous supply of hot water such as a spa or large bathtub given the demands required to fill a large tub with hot water. Renovation projects that place additional plumbing demands on an existing water heater can also benefit from a point-of use water heater.

Water heaters that supply an entire home's needs are referred to as tankless water heaters. Larger than the point-of-use type, tankless water heaters can be powered by natural gas, propane, or electricity (Fig. 10-12). If the capacity generated by

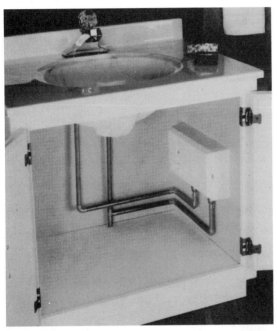

Figure 10-11   Point-of-use instantaneous water heater. *(Powerstream/CEC)*

one water heater is not sufficient, multiple tankless water heaters can be installed in series or parallel to meet the homeowner's hot water demands.

Depending upon the application, one energy type will be more appropriate. For example, an attached gazebo containing a hot tub, a manufactured home, or even a small cottage may benefit from a propane tankless water heater. If a renovation is in progress and natural gas is not already run to the house, electric tankless water heaters may be appropriate. Electric models are popular when point-of-use applications are required and/or gas venting is not possible or desired. If a homeowner is heating water for a large home or one under construction, natural gas may be the best choice.

Figure 10-12   Tankless water heater. *(Takagi Industrial Company)*

Advantages

The primary advantages of the tankless water heater over the tank-type are energy efficiency, a lower life-cycle cost, compact dimensions, and ease of use.

Energy Efficiency

The tankless water heater's superior energy efficiency is directly related to the elimination of any stand-by loss since the heater is activated by water flow only. Homeowners who have tankless water heaters save 30 percent or more of the cost of fuel used in heating water as compared to comparably fueled tank-type water heaters.   This is especially significant when one learns that heating water is the second largest demand for energy in the home, averaging 22 to 26 percent of annual fuel bills. Gas tankless water heaters are rated between 78 percent and 80 percent efficient by the American Gas Association as compared to tank-types at 46.7 percent AFUE (GAMA directory of water heaters). These energy savings are largely the result of not storing heated water and of modulation fuel use to match hot water demand.[17] (Modulation saves energy by consuming less gas during periods of lower hot water demand and increasing burner output only when increased demand requires it.) Stored water in vented tank-type heaters also loses heat as air thermosiphons through the vent when the burners are not on and as heat radiates through its outer walls.

Lower Life Cycle Cost

Cost savings are claimed by all tankless water heater manufacturers when appropriated over the life of the unit. Although actual savings will vary per the homeowner, the type of unit, and the efficiency of the system design, manufacturers claim anywhere from 35 to 60 percent savings in water heating bills. According to one manufacturer, the U.S. Department of Energy has calculated that the average family of four uses 64.3 gallons of hot water per day. Calculations show that with a standby heat loss of 3 percent and the cost of tank replacement yield an average total hot water cost of $549.00 per year. The manufacturer reports that two 9-kW units, run in parallel, will result in a cost savings of $210.00 per year as compared to the 50-gallon tank-type electric water heater.[18] Since the 9-kW units from this manufacturer are listed at $189.00 each, the tankless water heaters are paid for within 2 years of cost savings. Another manufacturer reports similar results with a single "twin module" 19-kW unit.[19] (The larger gas tankless water heaters cost about $600.00 each.)

Manufacturers claim that tankless water heaters last up to three times longer than tank types because they are less likely to corrode. Tankless units resist scale buildup because the internal heat exchanger swirls water through the pipes, actually scrubbing the inside. Heat exchanger elements of tankless units are usually of copper or brass construction. Manufacturers also claim that every part, including the heat exchanger, is easily replaced in the event of unit failure.

In areas with extreme hard water problems, the units may acquire a lime residue over a period of time, causing the unit to lose efficiency and heat output. Unlike tanks, which must be discarded when this occurs, tankless water heater parts are accessible and very simple to delime. Some manufacturers are providing units with optional coatings on all wetted surfaces of the heat exchanger to protect against corrosive environments and contamination of ultrapure water. These units are ideally suited for applications in the heating of deionized water, reverse osmosis water, and caustic alkalis.[20]

Less expense is also required for plumbing piping. The compact size will allow a tankless water heater to be located in a generally centralized location within the home, thereby reducing excessive runs of piping. Point-of-use units allow an additional savings to be realized since only one piping line, the cold water supply, is necessary to provide water to the individual unit.

Compact

Tankless water heaters are much more compact in size since a large storage tank is not required. Tankless water heaters are available in a wide variety of sizes depending upon the manufacturer. For example, a 77,500 Btu gas model measures 28" high × 12" wide × 10" deep, a 28-kW electric model measures $15^1/_4$" × $15^1/_4$" × $6^1/_4$', and a smaller, electric point-of-use model measures 11" × $5^1/_4$' × $2^1/_4$", and weigh only 3 lb (Fig. 10-13).

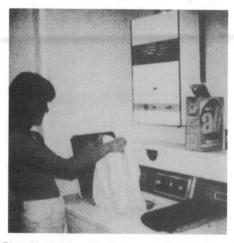

Figure 10-13   Wall mounted in a laundry room. *(AquaStar/CEC)*

Ease of Use

Many units are thermostatically controlled, which provides accurate automatic temperature control under varying water flow and inlet temperatures. This will allow the homeowner to regulate the power used to control the temperature of the water as opposed to the conventional method of blending cold and hot water. These are typically referred to as Thermostatic units, vary the water temperature by modulation, (i.e., reducing or increasing the amount of energy supplied to the heating element) and are usually dial controlled. Thermostats can even be remotely located from the water heater unit. Nonthermostatic models vary the temperature by adjusting the flow rate of the water.

Sizing

Correct sizing of a tankless water heater is essential to the homeowner's realizing the system's true benefits. The first step is to correctly assess the homeowner's needs and hot water demands. For example, supplying hot water to several sinks may require a 77,500-Btu gas tankless water heater. The increased water demands of a shower and washing machine may require a 165,000-Btu model. Although manufacturers will provide generalized tables to help determine the appropriate unit required, correct and accurate sizing of a tankless water heater involves two important factors: the temperature rise (°F) and the flow rate (gpm).

The flow rate is how fast the water comes through the supply over the heating elements. The temperature rise is the difference in the temperature of the cold water being supplied to the heat exchanger and the temperature desired at the output (faucet, shower head, etc.). The faster the water flows through the water heater, the lower the temperature rise. For example, if the inlet water supply temperature is 50°F, and the desired shower temperature is 105°F, the change in temperature is 55°F. The typical flow rate for a shower may be 2.5 gpm.

The following formula can then be applied to determine the proper sizing information for electrical units: $\{(gpm)(T)(500)\} / 3413 = kW$ required. Using this example, $\{(2.5)\,(55)\,(500)\} / 3413 = 20\ kW$. If an instantaneous unit is to be considered, a sink may require only .5-gpm flow rate and a desired temperature of 95°F. This results in the specific need for a 3.3-kW electric unit. (These examples are for illustration purposes only. Manufacturer's recommendations and specifications will vary.)

Limitations

Although the amount of hot water available in a tankless system is endless, the homeowner will need to vary his or her water usage habits. Since the tankless water heater unit is limited by the unit's flow rate and heating element capacity, the amount of hot water created at one time is also limited. A tank-type heater, due to its storage tank, will allow showers and the dishwasher to be run at the same time...at least until the hot water in the tank is used up.

The homeowner can accommodate this limitation by simple running only one shower at a time. This will mean that if three people want to take showers, the three showers must be taken in succession, not all at the same time. Many homeowners will consider this a minor adjustment to their daily rituals, and by doing so will have access to an unlimited amount of hot water. This also holds true for running certain appliances. The washing machine, the dishwasher, and the bathtub would need to be run in succession, not at the same time.

If a homeowner desires to run several large demand items at one time, other plumbing strategies are possible:

- A point-of-use water heater could be installed to supplement the supply at a specific location.
- Reduce the flow of water at the faucet.
- Place a restrictor valve in the line.

Finally, sufficient electrical power must be available to the electric tankless water heater for the unit to function properly. Many electric units for whole house use require approximately 75 to 80 A. If two heaters are to be installed, a minimum of 150 to 160 A will be required for service. This may be considered excessive by some homeowners. If natural gas is run to the home, a gas-fired unit may be more appropriate. Greater temperatures are possible for the heating elements, which allows the flow rate to be increased. The homes gas supply will require venting, which is not always convenient in retrofit applications.

Installation

Installation of tankless water heaters is somewhat similar to that of tank-type units. User-specific modifications are possible, including the implementation of a plumbing manifold as discussed earlier in this chapter. Manufacturer supplied literature should be followed in all actual installations. The following text is for general information only.

When installing a gas-fired tankless unit, black iron pipe should be used on natural gas hookups to insure proper gas pressure. All gas connections should be checked with liquid soap and water mixture. Proper ventilation is essential to assure safe operation, protect from carbon monoxide poisoning, prevent damage due to freeze-ups, and insure proper performance.[21] Proper clearance needs to be maintained as required by the unit's manufacturer. Most gas units can be installed in closets, but some, due to the amount of heat generated, may require location with one side of the room or space open for proper venting. For example, the 165,000-Btu unit referred to earlier in this section is 36" in height, 23" wide and 14" deep. This unit requires 6" clearance on each side, 12" from the ceiling and an open front. The 77,500-Btu model measures 28" × 12" × 10" and needs 6" clearance in front of the unit if installed in a closet.[22]

Electric tankless water heaters, although available in a wide variety of sizes, are typically smaller than gas units in physical dimensions. For example, one 28 kW model measures $15^1/4'$ × $15^1/4''$ × $6^1/4''$ and draws up to 91 A, resulting in a 78°F temperature rise at a flow rate of 2.5 gpm. Smaller point-of-use models measure 11" × $5^1/4'$ × $2^1/4''$, weighs 3 lb and draw between 23 and 40 A with a temperature rise of up to 32°F at a flow rate of 2 gpm or 65°F at 1 gpm.[23] As with large demand electrical appliances, specific-size breakers will be required for the tankless water heater unit. Since some models are powered by 220V, all applicable codes must be followed to guarantee a correct installation.

Summary

Popular in Europe and Asia for many years, tankless water heaters are poised to replace the tank-type water heater as a market leader in North America. Although sequencing is required when multiple-use demands are placed on the system, this small variation of daily rituals is a small price to pay for a system that will provide unlimited hot water in an energy-efficient, cost-effective and user-friendly manner.

FIRE SPRINKLERS

The Great Chicago Fire killed 300 people, left 100,000 homeless, and destroyed more than 17,000 structures on October 8–9, 1871. Although the origin of the fire has generated speculation since its occurrence, one popular legend has it that Mrs. Catherine O'Leary was milking her cow when the animal kicked over a lamp, setting the O'Leary's barn on fire and starting the spectacular blaze. The incident initiated a travesty that burned more than 2000 acres in only 27 hours. (It is important to note that the Chicago City Council's Committee of Fire and Police passed a resolution October 6, 1997, exonerating Catherine O'Leary and her scapegoat cow of any blame.)

Henry S. Parmalee invented the fire sprinkler system in 1874 to protect his piano factory.[24] Factories, warehouses, and other buildings soon saw the value in fire-suppression systems. Unfortunately, it took a series of fires involving dramatic losses of life to bring this issue into the public domain. Many historians attribute the tragic fires at The Coconut Grove Nightclub in Boston (1942 with 492 dead), the LaSalle Hotel in Chicago (1946 with 61 dead), and the Winecoff Hotel in Atlanta (1946 with 119 dead) for forcing fire and building officials to realize the need for automatic fire sprinklers in public buildings.

Statistics show that the United States had an average of 2.2 million reported fires over the 1985–1994 period, each year causing an average of 5300 civilian fire deaths, 29,000 injuries, and $9.4 billion dollars in losses.[25] Commercial construction (due in part to stricter building codes enforcing life safety measures that implement maximum travel distances), fire-resistant materials and wall assemblies, has embraced the need for greater fire protection within a building. Even with 3640 deaths by fire in 1995,[26] residential construction, by virtue of perceived increased cost or lack of public education, has been slow to realize the need for fire-suppression systems in the home, but the trend is starting to change.

How Sprinklers Work

The key to keeping a fire from reaching potentially dangerous and life-threatening proportions is early detection. Fire-suppression systems consist of individually heat-activated sprinkler heads connected to a network of piping containing water under pressure. Fire sprinklers operate automatically over the fire origin. When the heat of a fire raises the sprinkler to its operating temperature, usually between 155 to 175°F, a mechanism activates only the sprinkler that is over the fire, thereby releasing water directly over the source of heat. Additional sprinklers throughout the home will not be activated unless additional fires generate sufficient heat to do so. This means that less water is used to fight the fire, and subsequently less water damage is done to the property than if the fire department is fighting the fire.

Residential fire sprinkler systems activate five to seven times faster than standard commercial sprinklers and have a different spray pattern and droplet size. In most cases, fires are controlled with one or two sprinklers. The discharge rate varies depending upon the type and make of the sprinkler head but will typically range from a rate of 10 to 20 gpm. (The fire department will discharge up to 150 gpm.)

Sprinkler heads are activated in a variety of ways depending upon the manufacturer. Although some companies are manufacturing sprinklers with a fusible-link actuator, a growing number of companies are producing an operating mechanism that consists of a frangible glass bulb containing a liquid and a small air bubble. Also called "quick response," heat from the fire causes the liquid to expand, bursting the glass bulb, allowing the sprinkler to open (Fig. 10-14). Water is then discharged freely, striking the deflector. The water is then distributed in a pattern determined by the particular sprinkler's deflector. It is important to note that only heat will activate the sprinkler. A stubborn fireplace or a burnt piece of toast may sound a smoke detector but will not affect a residential sprinkler system.

Figure 10-14   Glass-bulb-activated fire sprinkler. *(Figgie Fire Protection Systems)*

More importantly, sprinklers prevent fire from growing to the flashover stage. This occurs when gases from burning materials accumulate and explode. Generally, flashover takes place when the temperature at ceiling level reaches between 1000 and 2000°F, occurring in a matter of minutes.

The Building and Fire Research Laboratory performed a controlled comparison of a residential fire. Two "living room" fires were set, one with and one without residential sprinklers. Both of the living rooms were furnished with a sofa, love seat, end table, lamp and carpeting. Room A had a smoke detector installed and Room B had both a smoke detector and a residential sprinkler system. A match was used to ignite the sofa. Within 40 seconds after ignition, the smoke detectors in each room activated. The fires in both rooms continued to grow. At 85 seconds the residential sprinkler activated in Room B. As a result of the water spray from the sprinkler in Room B, the fire was suppressed and safe conditions were maintained. The fire in Room A continued to grow until flashover occurred at 195 seconds after ignition, with temperatures exceeding 1100°F.[27]

Disadvantages

Accidental discharge by a sprinkler system is possible, but is rare. In fact, loss records maintained by Factory Mutual indicate that only 1 in 16,000,000 sprinklers per year will open accidentally due to a manufacturing defect. Accidental or unintentional operation can occur due to freezing, overheating, or mechanical damage but can be avoided with proper handling and installation.

Sprinkler Appearance

Sprinkler heads are available in a wide range of sizes and colors to coordinate or "disappear" into the background of almost any room (Fig. 10-15). These include brass, bronze, chrome, white, almond, and black. The typical sprinkler head stands out less than 1" from the ceiling and can accommodate escutcheons. Some sprinklers can be concealed in ceilings out of sight until needed to extinguish a fire. Ornamental cover plates are also available to coordinate with a particular décor.

Standards

NFPA 13D is the National Fire Protection Association's (NFPA) standard for the installation of fire sprinkler systems in one- and two- family dwellings and mobile homes. (NFPA 13 contains rules for the installation of sprinkler systems in most types of commercial occupancies while NFPA 13D was specifically written to cover the installation of listed residential sprinklers in one- and two-family dwellings and mobile homes.) The standard was adopted by the NFPA in 1975 with periodic reviews and updates to allow for new technological breakthroughs. NFPA 13R is a new standard, first available in 1989. Intended to bridge the gap between NFPA 13 and 13D systems, it provides life safety–

oriented economical sprinkler protection for low-rise (up to 4 stories) residential occupancies.[28]

Figure 10-15   Fire sprinkler types. *(Figgie Fire Protection Systems)*

NFPA 13D introduced the concept that the quick-response residential sprinkler, unlike its industrial counterparts, operates very quickly once the rated temperature is felt, thereby controlling a fire early in its growth. Residential sprinklers, as mandated by 13D, have a specifically designed spray pattern that delivers water to nearly the full height of the walls, based on typical residential room sizes.[29]

All sprinklers installed in conformance with NFPA standards must be listed. A listing means that the sprinkler manufacturer has successfully submitted the product to an independent laboratory for testing against an established standard of quality. Both Underwriters Laboratories and Factory Mutual research have established special listing categories for fire sprinklers.[30]

Underwriters Laboratories Inc. (UL) has been investigating and listing automatic sprinklers for fire protection for more than 90 years. Requirements in UL 199 (Standard for Automatic Sprinklers for Fire-Protection Service) and UL 1626 (Standard for Residential Sprinklers for Fire-Protection Service) cover testing of commercial and residential automatic sprinklers for fire-protection service. Automatic sprinkler manufacturers must meet all applicable test requirements described in the standards before receiving authorization to apply the UL mark to their products.[31]

A number of tests are performed on automatic sprinklers to determine their strength, durability, and ability to operate during a fire. For example, UL evaluates the strength of the elements that activate each individual sprinkler when exposed to heat from a fire. The heat-sensing elements must withstand up to 15 times the maximum design load, which includes water pressures up to 175 psi. Tests are also performed to determine the sprinkler's ability to withstand high water pressures when not in operation. During the test, sprinklers are subjected to water pressures up to 700 psi, which is four times the maximum allowable water pressure applied to sprinklers after installation. Requirements specify that the sprinkler must not rupture, operate, or release any operating parts during the test. UL also performs a 30-minute flow endurance test at 175 psi in which the sprinkler must uniformly disperse water without evidence of cracking, deformation or other damage to the sprinkler. Tests are also conducted to ensure that sprinklers will operate properly after sustaining possible rough usage that could occur during shipping or installation.[32]

Maintenance

According to the "Homeowners Guide to Fire Sprinkler Systems", published by the National Fire Sprinkler Association, a number of recommendations should be followed in assuring proper operation of a residential fire sprinkle system. First of all, sprinkler inspections should be made on a regular basis to detect possible damage or alteration. Many manufacturers recommend testing the system monthly. (If the system is monitored by a fire service agency, the monitoring agency must be notified prior to testing the system. This will prevent sending a false alarm.) All maintenance should be performed according to NFPA standards.

The homeowner and other adult occupants should be familiar with the system shutoff valve. The system control valve should be open at all times. Finally, the homeowner should contact the fire department when any activation occurs, even if the fire has apparently been extinguished.[33]

Although tested extensively, the sprinklers are not invulnerable to abuse or misuse. Sprinklers should never be painted, damaged, obstructed, or covered. Objects should never be hung from the sprinkler head. Once installed, the sprinklers should not be removed, or the system turned off or disconnected.

According to one manufacturer, residential sprinklers should be replaced after 20 years of service, or if they are painted, corroded or damaged. A sprinkler that has been actuated cannot be reassembled or reused.

Cost

The cost of a complete sprinkler system depends on many factors, such as the building type and construction, geographical area, availability of public water supply, and degree of hazard of the occupancy. The NFPA estimates that installation costs in new residential construction vary from approximately $1.00 to over $1.50 per square foot and approximately double that for retrofitting existing homes. The National Association of Home Builders determined that the average cost of a residential sprinkler system for new construction was $1.31 per square foot.[34]

Although fire is only a portion of typical homeowner's insurance, many insurance companies are offering premium discounts for homes with sprinkler systems. The discount recommended by the Insurance Services Office in most states is 13 percent for a 13D system covering all building areas, 15 percent if smoke detectors are also provided.[35] This discount is from the total homeowner's premium, not just the fire portion. Savings to the insurance industry are also irrefutable. A 1980 study by the Ad Hoc Insurance Committee on residential sprinklers concluded that residential sprinklers could reduce claim payments in single-family homes by up to 80 percent.[36] Although no specific data is available, a fire sprinkler system should also increase the resale value of a home.

Layout

Proper design and installation of sprinkler systems is standardized nationally in a consensus standard promulgated by NFPA 13D. The residential fire sprinkler system is a wet-pipe system. A wet-pipe system consists of a piping network that contains water under pressure at all times for immediate release through the sprinkler heads. The system typically consists of a gate valve, an alarm valve, a riser, a main pipe, branch pipe, and sprinkler heads.

Sprinkler heads are generally available in one of several types: pendent sprinkler, concealed sprinkler, recessed pendent, horizontal sidewall, recessed. Each one has its advantages (and disadvantages) as determined by the design of the head and the layout of the piping:

- A pendent sprinkler (Fig. 10-16). The pendent sprinkler head, hung overhead, is the most common design of all sprinkler head types.
- A recessed pendent (Fig. 10-17). The recessed pendent is similar to the pendent mount except that an escutcheon, available in a variety of finishes, allows the head to be partially recessed in the ceiling.
- A concealed sprinkler (Fig. 10-18). The concealed sprinkler has a cover, available in a variety of finishes that allows the sprinkler head to be completely concealed from view. The cover is attached by a fusible link that will melt at a lower temperature than the sprinkler head actuator.
- A horizontal sidewall sprinkler (Fig. 10-19). The horizontal sidewall type is wall-mounted and has a specially designed spray pattern for maximum wall and floor coverage.

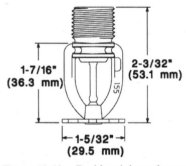

Figure 10-16 Residential pendent sprinkler. *(Star Sprinkler)*

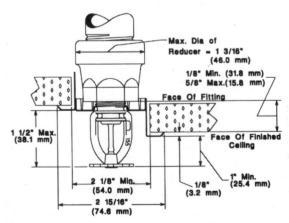

Figure 10-17 Recessed residential pendent sprinkler. *(Star Sprinkler)*

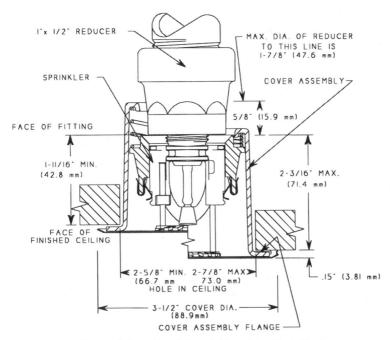

Figure 10-18   Concealed residential sprinkler. *(Star Sprinkler)*

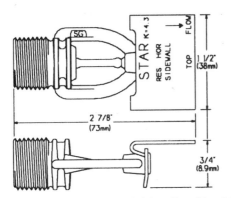

Figure 10-19   Horizontal sidewall residential sprinkler. *(Star Sprinkler)*

- A recessed horizontal sidewall sprinkler (Fig. 10-20). The recessed sidewall type is similar to the horizontal sidewall mount except that an escutcheon, available in a variety of finishes, allows the head to be partially recessed in the wall.

All of these sprinklers are covered by special listings, recognized within NFPA 13D, which permit their use at larger spacings if specified minimum flows and pressures are provided. Pendent sprinklers can provide coverage in spaces of 12' × 12', 14' × 14', 16' × 16', 18' × 18' or 20' × 20'. Currently available are sidewall sprinklers with coverage areas from 12' × 12' up to 16' × 20'.

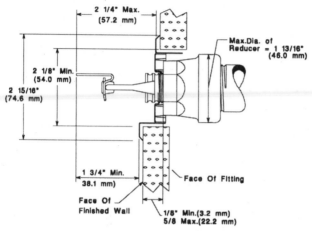

Figure 10-20   Recessed horizontal sidewall residential sprinkler. *(Star Sprinkler)*

The discharge capacity of each sprinkler is designated by a K-factor. This is the constant used in the equation $Q=K (\sqrt{P})$. Q is the flow in gallons per minute (gpm) and P is the pressure in pounds per square inch (psi). For example, if the K factor of a sprinkler head is 5, and the water pressure is 16 psi, the sprinkler head will deliver water at a rate of 20 gpm. Spray patterns and areas covered, K factors and the temperature of activation, are specifics provided by the particular manufacturer.

CPVC, copper, and even steel are piping materials that typically can be used for water distribution in a sprinkler system. Polyethylene, as discussed earlier in this chapter, can be used for fire sprinkler piping; however, compatibility should be verified with the sprinkler company. (As a result, the sprinklers can be tied into a manifold system so total control can be maintained from one location.)

As mentioned earlier, the design and installation of fire sprinkler systems must comply with the standards of the NFPA and/or meet the requirements of the local building codes. Installation and/or removal of sprinklers must be performed with the manufacturer-provided wrenches. Other wrenches may damage the sprinkler systems. Sprinkler cabinets are also available for the proper storage of spare sprinklers on site.

Freezing of sprinkler lines had been a concern in unheated attics but can easily be avoided. A leading fiberglass insulation manufacturing company states that this problem can be avoided if R-19 insulation is placed above sprinkler piping so as to seal off both sides of a joist space. This will protect a system for outdoor temperatures as low as 20°F. The piping must be directly above the gypsum sheathing ceiling and the space immediately below is maintained at a temperature of 40°F or above. It is important that insulation not be placed between the heated area and the sprinkler piping.[37]

Warranty

Most sprinkler manufacturers warrant their products to be free from defects in material and workmanship for a period of 1 year.

Summary

When President Calvin Coolidge proclaimed the first National Fire Prevention Week, October 4–10, 1925, he noted that in the previous year some 15,000 lives were lost to fire in the United States. More recent statistics show that a residential fire occurs every 70 seconds.[38] In 1995, residential property loss due to fire was more than $4.2 billion.[39] The awareness of the damage done by fire is prevalent; however, most homes rely only on a smoke detector and the fire department for alarm and control.

Fire sprinklers are an extremely reliable fire-protection system for the home. In Australia and New Zealand (where fires must be reported) from 1886 to 1986, 99.7 percent of all fires in sprinklered buildings were controlled by the sprinklers. Although fire records in this country are less dependable, mostly due to the lack of reporting small fires in which sprinklers were successful, the NFPA reports a 96.2 percent success record for the years 1925 through 1969.[40] (These figures include commercial structures since exclusive residential data was not available.)

Local ordinances are being passed from Scottsdale, Arizona, to Boca Raton, Florida, that require sprinkler systems in one- and two-family dwellings. Some industry personnel predict that most states will adopt fire sprinkler legislation in the coming years. Other communities such as Cobb County, Georgia, or Hilton Head, South Carolina, are providing incentive programs for sprinklers to be installed in one- and two-family dwellings.[41] In either event, it is clear that public awareness and improved technology show that the fire sprinkler system is not just for commercial use anymore.

CONCLUSION

At first glance, water is available for use everywhere...or is it? 97 percent of the earth's water is seawater, and another 2 percent is locked in glaciers or icecaps, leaving only 1 percent available for human consumption. In other words, if all of the earth's water could fit in a gallon jug, available fresh water would equal just over a teaspoon.[42] The anonymous nature of the things we take for granted is actually a curse. The devastating effect on us all will come when it is no longer available. Plumbing manifolds, PEX piping, tankless water heaters, and residential fire sprinkler systems are small steps homeowners can take to use water more efficiently, more enjoyably, and more safely.

APPENDIX

Aquastar
Controlled Energy Corporation
Fiddler's Green
Waitsfield, VT 05673
(800) 642-3111

"Automatic" Sprinkler Fire Protection
PO Box 400
Ransom, WV 25438
(800) 626-2682
Fax: (800) 858-6857

Eemax Inc.
472 Pepper Street
Monroe, CT 06468
(800) 966-0684

Plastics Pipe Institute
Division the Society of the Plastics Industry, Inc.
1801 K Street, NW
Washington, DC 20006
(202) 974-5351

Solvay Polymers Inc.
Technical Center
1230 Battleground Road
Deer Park, TX 77536
(800) 338-0489
Fax: (713) 307-3521

Star Sprinkler Corporation
7071 South 13th Street
Suite 103
Oak Creek, WI 53154
(800) 558-5236
Fax: (800) 877-1295

Tankless Hot Water Systems, Incorporated
IMI Santon
1676 Cordova Road
Germantown, TN 38138
(901) 756-7080

Vanguard Plastics, Inc.
831 N. Vanguard Street
McPherson, KS 67460
(800) 775-5039
Fax: (800) 775-4068

Wirsbo
5925 148th Street West
Apple Vallèy, MN 55124
(800) 321-4PEX

REFERENCES

1. *Plumbing and Mechanical Magazine* July 1986, July 1987.
2. *Plumbing and Mechanical Magazine*, July 1996.
3. Technical Note on Cross Linked Polyethylene, Plastics Pipe Institute, a Division of the Plastics Industry, Inc., Report #TN-17.
4. Ibid.
5. AT Plastics, Inc. website, December 16, 1997.
6. Vanguard Engineered Piping Systems Product Literature, QLTP26 396.
7. "Differences in Cross Linking Methods," Wirsbo Company Product Literature.

8. AT Plastics, op. cit.
9. "Differences in Cross Linking Methods," Wirsbo Company Product Literature.
10. Ibid.
11. Plastics Pipe Institute, op. cit.
12. Klenck, Thomas, How it Works: Water Heater.., Vol. 174, *Popular Mechanics*, 09-01-1997, pp. 90(2).
13. Ibid.
14. Ibid.
15. Ibid.
16. U.S. Department of Energy Codes and Standards (DOE/GO-10095-063 FS 204, January 1995)
17. AquaStar Tankless Water Heater Manual, Controlled Energy Corporation, November 1991, p. 3.
18. IMI Santon Instantaneous Tankless Water Heater Literature, Tankless Water Heater Systems, Inc., Product Literature.
19. Eemax "Series Two" Product Literature, 4/95-Ex-2.
20. Acutemp Product Literature, Keltech, Inc. website, 12/17/97
21. AquaStar Tankless Water Heater Manual, Controlled Energy Corporation, November 1991, p. 15.
22. Ibid.
23. Eemax, Inc., "Flow Controlled Electric Instantaneous Water Heaters"
24. "Fire Sprinkler Facts" National Fire Sprinkler Association website, 12/20/97
25. "A Profile of Fire in the United States 1985-1994," National Fire Data Center, United States Fire Administration
26. Herb Denenberg, "Residential Sprinklers: A Neglected Life Saver," NBC 10, WCAU-TV website, 12/20/97.
27. NIST Building and Fire Research Laboratory, Gaithersburg, MD.
28. "Homeowners Guide to Fire Sprinkler Systems," National Fire Sprinkler Association website, 11/18/97.
29. Ron Cote, PE, *Life Safety Code Handbook*, (Quincy, Massachusetts, National Fire Protection Association, 1994), p. 202.
30. "Residential and Quick Response Sprinklers" National Fire Sprinkler Association website, 11/18/97.
31. Underwriters Laboratories, Inc. (UL) website, 12/20/97
32. Ibid.
33. "Homeowners Guide to Fire Sprinkler Systems," National Fire Sprinkler Association website, 11/18/97.
34. Residential and Quick Response Sprinklers," National Fire Sprinkler Association website, 12/20/97.
35. Ibid.
36. Ibid.
37. Ibid.
38. National Center for Injury Prevention and Control, Division of Unintentional Injury Prevention, Center for Disease Control website, 12/20/97.
39. Ibid.
40. "Homeowners Guide to Fire Sprinkler Systems," National Fire Sprinkler Association website, 11/18/97.
41. National Fire Sprinkler Association website, 11/18/97
42. Michael Parfit, "Sharing the Wealth of Water," *National Geographic*, Vol. 184, No. 5A, p. 24.

Chapter

11

Electrical Systems and Accessories

INTRODUCTION

The first use of the word "electrica" was in 1600 in a book entitled *De Magnete* by Dr. William Gilbert, physician to Queen Elizabeth of England. However, it was 150 years before any significant progress was made in this field. Bishop Von Kleist, Dean of the Cathedral of Comin, Pomerania, was one of several men to be experimenting with the Leyden jar (the first such device that could store large amounts of electric charge). Von Kleist wrote: "When a nail, or a piece of thick brass wire is put into a small apothecary's phial [Leyden jar] and electrified, remarkable effects follow; the phial must be very dry or warm. I commonly rub it over beforehand with a finger, on which I have put some pounded chalk. If a little mercury, or a few drops of spirit of wine, be put into it, the experiment succeeds the better. As soon as this phial and nail are removed from the electrifying glass, or the prime conductor, to which it hath been exposed, is taken away, it throws out a pencil of flame so long, that with this burning machine in my hand, I have taken above sixty steps, in walking about my room. When it electrifies strongly, I can take it into another room, and there fire spirits of wine with it. If while it is electrifying, I put my finger, or a piece of gold, which I hold in my hand to the nail, I receive a shock which stuns my arm and shoulders."[1]

The Leyden jar can be viewed as the watershed event that excited and encouraged ensuing scientists for the next two centuries. For example, it was Benjamin Franklin, in the late 1740s, who discovered with his silken kite that lightning and the artificial discharge from it are identical to the electricity created in the Leyden jar. In 1796, Alessandro Volta, the Italian physicist, discovered the voltaic pile, or what is known today as the battery. The year 1844 witnessed Samuel F. B. Morse develop Morse code and improve communication with the telegraph. Thirty-two years later, United States Patent No. 174465 was issued on March 7 to Alexander Graham Bell. Three days later, March 10th, Bell speaks the first complete sentence transmitted by variable resistance transmitter ... "Mr. Watson, come here. I want you!" With that, the telephone was invented.

Thomas A. Edison, in his laboratory at Menlo Park, N.J., on October 21, 1879, revolutionized electric lighting methods by the introduction of the incandescent light. This resulted ultimately in a comprehensive system of generation and distribution of electricity. Einstein won the Nobel Prize for Physics due to his work on "photoelectrics" in 1921. Discoveries in radio transmissions were developed during the years prior to World War I and the first scheduled television programming in 1928. The late 1940s witnessed the invention of the transistor, for which Barden, Schockley and Brattain won the 1956 Nobel Prize for Physics. One year later, after the Soviet Union's 1957 launch of Sputnik, President Dwight D. Eisenhower saw the need for the Advanced Research Projects Agency (ARPA). In 1969, the ARPANET was commissioned by the Department of Defense for research into networking, renamed DARPA (Defense Advanced Research Projects Agency). This eventually became the Internet. In 1984, the total number of domain name server (DNS) hosts broke 1000. (Ten years later, in July of 1994, the number of hosts had exceeded 3 million.)[2] Finally, in 1988, the first transatlantic fiber-optic cable was completed along with the first "commercial" offering of ISDN service in the United States.

The evolution of technological innovation is a marvel of the human mind and spirit. These inventions, from the crude creation of the Leyden jar to the world wide communications of the Internet, combine to shape the way we live in our world today. Electricity generated by photvoltaic power systems, flexible and modular wiring and cabling systems, as well as whole-house automation will make the house more efficient, more convenient, more comfortable, and even safer in the years to come.

PHOTOVOLTAICS (PV)

The growing emphasis on renewable energy resources has seen the development of photovoltaic power systems as a method of harnessing the power of the sun. To demonstrate the enormous energy production by the Sun, some estimates show that the amount of sunlight striking the Earth in one second could meet the energy needs of the entire human race for 2000 years.[3] The obvious advantage to harnessing the sun's energy is that it is "free" and inexhaustible. Unlike coal, natural gas, or nuclear power, solar power technology is clean, emits no air pollutants or greenhouse gases, and does not leave behind dangerous radioactive waste. PV power systems are silent, virtually maintenance free, and require no fuel. Finally, PV power systems do not require the construction of massive, expensive central power-generating stations or a nation-spanning electrical grid.

The most common example of PV-powered devices can be seen in calculators and watches. However, it has been the commercial sector that has been quick to embrace PV systems for a number of applications. Some of these include:

- Water pumping for small-scale remote irrigation, stock watering, and marine sump pumps
- Communications by remote relay stations, emergency radios, orbiting satellites, and cellular telephones
- Lighting for streets and parking lots, pathways, billboards, security, highway signs

Only in the previous 10 years have PV systems acquired a growing acceptance among residential users. In fact, PV systems installed since 1988 provide enough electricity to power 150,000 homes in the United States (or 8 million homes in the developing countries where electrical needs are minimal).[4] This growth will continue to expand as an understanding of the technology and the benefits of this system become more widespread. The PV industry has grown from $2 million in sales in 1975 to $750 million in 1993.[5] In a few short years, it will be economically viable to create a hybrid system using the PV solar cells with a geothermal heat pump system (see Chapter 9).

History of PV

The awareness of the sun as an energy source has been with us since humans first walked on the earth. However, the ability to truly harness its power is a relatively recent development. The first solar collectors, used for heating water only, were patented by Clarence Kemp in 1891. The rooftop solar-powered water heaters continued to grow in popularity between World War I and II with over 60,000 units sold by 1941.

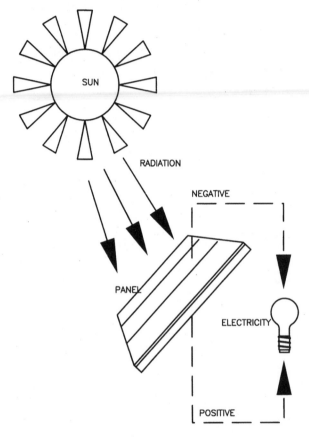

Figure 11-1 Photovoltaic principle.

The bulky, obtrusive solar panels graced many a roof, including the White House during the Carter Administration, after the oil embargos of the 1970s. Although still used in many residental applications, the solar collector will eventually succumb in popularity to the new advances found in PV technology.

Often referred to as solar electricity, the principle of PV power is the conversion of light energy (from the sun) directly into electricity (Fig. 11-1). Although first discovered in 1839 by French physicist Edmund Becquerel, it was popularized among the scientific elite when explained by a young Albert Einstein in 1905. What Einstein reasoned was that sunlight — all light, as a matter of fact — is made up of tiny packets of energy. When these packets, called photons, strike an object, some of that energy is handed over to electrons in the material, boosting their energy so high that they escape from the surface of the metal. Applied to PV cells today, the photons of sunlight boost the energy of electrons, so they are unbound from a particular atom and freed to move about in the material. Einstein won the 1921 Nobel Prize for Physics in part for this explanation.[6]

But it wasn't until 1954 that scientists at Bell Laboratories developed the first solar cell which was used to power satellites in space. It was an additional 27 years before the first solar electric house with an integrated PV system was built by MIT, the Department of Energy, and Solar Design Associates.

The PV Cell

In contrast to the solar collectors used for heating water, Photovoltaics is a revolutionary technology in which electricity is produced by solar cells. The solar cell (PV cell) is the basic unit of a PV system. The cell can range in size from ½" to 4" in width. The power output is directly related to the surface area of the cell; a ½" square cell will produce one-eighth as much power as a 4" square cell. For example, if a 4" cell produces 1.4 W of power, a similar ½" cell will produce .175 W.

In simplest terms, PV cells convert the light of the sun directly into electricity. PV cells are made of materials (usually silicon) that allow them to absorb photons from sunlight and release electrons. The free electrons are captured and an electric current is produced.

The technical composition of the cell is beyond the scope of this text. Generally speaking, PV cells are made not of metals, which are conductors, but typically of silicon, a semiconductor. (A semiconductor is a unique material with physical properties somewhere in between a conductor like aluminum and an insulator like glass. This means that it can conduct electricity only under certain circumstances.) Silicon is a gray, crystalline element. Although it is never found as a free element in nature, its compounds constitute nearly nine-tenths of the earth's crust. (Its most common form is sand or sandstone).

The cell is assembled as a system of layers. Below a layer of glass (the superstrate) is the N-Layer (negative) semiconductor (facing the sun), an interface layer, and a P-Layer (positive) semiconductor, thereby establishing an internal electrical field (Fig.11-2). The power generated is direct current (DC), not alternating current (AC), similar to a battery, so a DC/AC inverter will be necessary to supply AC power for all standard household appliances. (This is not necessary if recreational vehicle or marine industry appliances are used, since these devices run on DC power already.)

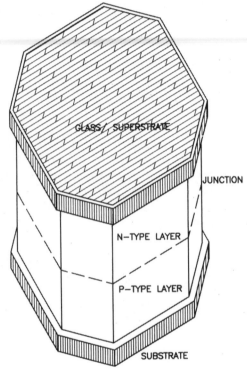

GLASS/ SUPERSTRATE

JUNCTION

N—TYPE LAYER

P—TYPE LAYER

SUBSTRATE

Figure 11-2 PV cell.

There are basically two main types of PV cells. The conventional PV cell is typically crystalline silicon. A second type of PV cell technology, referred to as thin film, has been emerging in recent years. Thin-film solar cells are made from inexpensive materials that can be deposited directly on a substrate, usually glass or metal. Easily mass-produced in sheets, thin-film PV cells are more durable since there is no glass to break. Although thin-film cells have an initial degradation, it is expected that this technology will make the PV systems more affordable for specific applications.

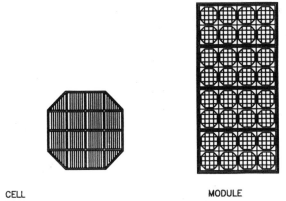

CELL   MODULE

ARRAY

Figure 11-3 PV cell, array and module.

The PV System

As previously mentioned, a single PV cell typically produces only 1 or 2 W of electricity. In order to produce enough electricity to power an object (a streetlight, for example), several cells must be ganged together to form a module. Modules, the "building blocks" of a PV system, are typically rectangular, ranging from 4 to 25 ft^2 in area. For large installations, several modules, when ganged together, form an array that can provide up to several megawatts of power (Fig. 11-3). In addition to the PV modules, the components needed to complete a PV system should include what is called a balance of system (BOS) equipment. A battery charge controller will regulate the flow of electricity from the PV modules to the battery and the load. These batteries should store electricity for use at night or day in the event the PV module is generating an insufficient amount of power. An inverter or power control unit which changes the DC power (generated by the PV module and stored in the batteries) into AC electricity. Additional components include safety disconnects and fuses, a grounding circuit, and, of course, wiring.

Advantages of a PV System

A number of benefits can be attributed to the use of PV power systems in addition to sunlight's being universally available. For example,

- Systems can be arranged in a variety of sizes and output. Since the components are lightweight, they can be transported to almost any installation.
- Modules can be added to existing systems when additional power needs are incurred.
- The components are solid-state. Maintenance is virtually eliminated since there are no moving parts. Most systems are guaranteed for a range of 10 to 20 years. (Power output monitoring and regular system inspections are recommended)
- PV systems are environment-friendly. Since the sun allows the PV system to produce power without fuel consumption, it is also noise-free and does not emit any pollutants.
- On a much larger scale, the lead time for the design, installation, and startup of new systems (or additions to existing ones) is a small fraction of the time compared to the time needed for nuclear and fossil-fuel power plants.
- Tax credits are available in some states.

Economics

If a home is already connected to a utility grid, or in close proximity to the grid, a PV system may not be cost effective. (One source has said that the cost of a power line extension is offset by the installation cost of a PV system if the residence is located over ¼ mile from the closest existing power pole.)[7] These are other instances where the cost of using PV is already comparable to using grid-connected power. It is reported that the average cost of extending power lines into non-urban areas ranges from $20,000 to $80,000 per mile, a cost usually borne by the consumer. At that price — and considering the average energy use of a remote, single-family residence or vacation home — "eliminating a power line extension of even one mile could well pay for the PV system."[8]

Applications

Historically, PV systems have been installed in a number of residences that are remote standalone applications.[9] Typical applications include vacation cabins, public campgrounds, and parks, highway signs and rest stops, public beach facilities, parking lots, cellular phone transmission towers, and navigation beacons. This lack of dependence on a power grid also makes PV systems an ideal choice for the millions of "households" in the remote locations of developing countries.

PV modules gather the most light when placed at an angle perpendicular to the sun. A southern orientation (for United States residents) is essential and should not be obstructed by trees, shade, or other structures (Fig. 11-4). Some assemblies can be mounted for a manual tilt depending on the sun's location. More sophisticated (and expensive) systems can have an active or passive tracking mechanism installed.

PV modules should at least have full exposure to the sun from 10 a.m. to 3 p.m. all year round.[10] Cold weather does not diminish the electrical output since it is the sun that generates the power and not heat. Power production is actually diminished as the cells heat up. It is important to note that if light is not available, the solar cell cannot produce electricity. Since cloudy weather also diminishes the electrical output, energy storage systems (or batteries) may be necessary.

The aesthetics of PV arrays have been changing as consumer demand increases. Recent installations are becoming more sophisticated in that the solar array is actually the integrated roof structure. At least one manufacturer has developed a flexible, thin film PV module roofing shingle. Available for shingles (Fig. 11-5) as well as standing seam roofing (Fig. 11-6), the PV shingle generates 5 W/ft^2 of power. Each shingle is 86.4" long, 12" in height with a 5" exposure. Each panel has two wires that penetrate the roof deck where the wiring is first routed to a DC disconnect switch, then to an inverter and finally into the home. The example demonstrated is a typical home that uses 400 kWh per month or about 13 kWh per day. An 800 ft^2 roof producing 20 W/hr per square foot generates 16 kWh per day. The disadvantage at the current pricing is that the shingle roof array, battery backups, inverters, and appropriate safety disconnects amounts to approximately $40,000.[11] The standing seam panels are typically 16" in width and available in 9'-6" or 18"-4" lengths.

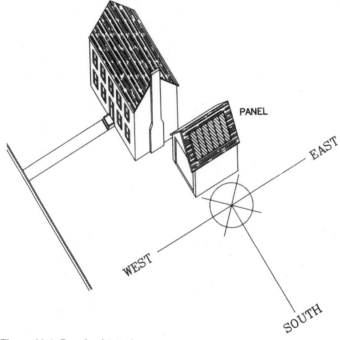

PANEL

EAST

WEST

SOUTH

Figure 11-4 Panel orientation.

Utility Connected Systems

Due to its growing popularity, some residential PV systems are connected to an electric utility's power transmission grid. The system owners can sell their excess electricity to the utility company, and buy electricity when their PV system cannot meet their electricity demand. In effect, they use the utility grid for storage. Inverters are available that produce electricity of the quality acceptable to electric utilities. They incorporate safety features to automatically disconnect the PV system from the grid in case of a power outage on the grid. Some intertied systems have a small-capacity battery for emergency power supply if the grid goes down.

Figure 11-5 PV roofing shingle. *(United Solar Systems Corp.)*

Figure 11-6 PV standing seam roofing panel. *(United Solar Systems Corp.)*

Cost

It is difficult to predict the cost of a PV system because of the site and owner-specific variables involved in system sizing and installation. The first solar modules used on spacecraft of the 1950s cost thousands of dollars per watt of generating capacity. By the early 1970s, PV modules were down to about $30 per watt at the factory. Likewise, by 1980 the cost was down to $10 per watt. Solar modules in 1997 price out between $4 and $5 per watt at the factory, according to Ken Zweibel, manager of thin-film solar cell research at the National Renewable Energy Laboratory (NREL) in Golden, Colorado.[12] Depending on the size and sophistication of the system, other component prices and installation costs may add $3 to 5/Wp for a total system cost of $7 to $10/Wp. Advances in cell and module technologies continue to increase output, and extend operating life. At the same time, component prices decrease due to increased competition and larger economy-of-scale productions.

The publicity generated by high-profile projects, such as the rooftop array located on the 1996 Summer Olympic swimming facility in Atlanta, will bolster the public's awareness of PV systems. The $17 million swimming and diving facility houses two pools, seats 15,000 spectators, and contains 40,000 ft^2 (3716 m^2) of PV modules on its roof. Each PV module has its own DC-to-AC microinverter. Being the single largest installation of its kind in the world, the modules provide nearly 350 kW of electric power, offsetting the electricity consumed by the building. It is estimated to save 25 to 30 percent of the building's total electric bill, or about $33,000 per year.[13]

Installation

An analysis by an experienced PV system designer will be performed on the home site to determine the amount of sunlight levels available. The designer will also determine how much electricity is needed. Calculations based on the daily watt-hours consumed will determine the number of PV modules necessary to produce the power and the number of batteries needed to store the power. All components should be UL (Underwriters Laboratories) or FM (Factory Mutual) listed to ensure safety and insurability. Installation of a PV system should be performed in compliance with the NEC (National Electric Code) or other applicable codes.

It is important to note that PV modules have varying efficiency ratings and warranties. The consumer should consult as many PV equipment dealers as possible to obtain the most favorable system and component prices.

WIRING AND CABLING

"Structured wiring systems" is a generic term used to describe the newest approach to home wiring and cabling. (Fig. 11-7) The materials and techniques discussed herein will allow the homeowner to utilize and/or adapt to the ongoing evolution of electronic technology in the home. Put simply, structured wiring systems collect and distribute electronic signals within a home. The "centralized" panel, or "hub", allows a trained technician to access and/or modify systems that can control security, energy and lighting. These will be discussed further under the Home Automation section of this chapter.

Communications

Telephone wiring has historically consisted of category 1 or 2 wire, which was designed for low-bandwidth voice communications only. This system, referred to in the technical world as POTS (plain old telephone service), was quite sufficient for its original purpose. Category 1 wire was usually run in parallel from one source to another in sequence. This topology uses quad wire, consisting of four color-coded twisted pairs (8 wires) capable of carrying four phone or fax lines. This cable has been adequate for standard analog telephone service, but is incapable of meeting the 21st century demands of fax/modem and other forms of data (i.e., computer) transmission.

Upgrading to category 5 cable will help meet these ever-increasing data transmission demands by offering a higher bandwidth. (Bandwidth is the measurement of the information carrying capacity of the cable and is measured in hertz (Hz), or cycles per second. The higher the bandwidth, the higher the capacity for transmitting information.) Like category 1 and 2, category 5 still uses four color-coded twisted pairs but the difference is the number of twists per foot in each pair and the way they are arranged within the insulated sheath. This configuration is used to minimize interference between pairs, commonly referred to as NEXT (near-end cross talk). This occurs when the stronger transmitted signal "couples" or interferes with a signal on an adjacent receiving pair.

WIRE TYPE	QUANITY	LOOKS LIKE	DESCRIPTION
Standard telephone cable		STOP (Don't use!)	A pair of twisted wires per telephone line
High capacity telephone/data wire (Category 5)	1	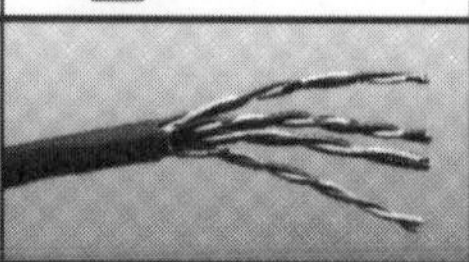	4 twisted pairs of high-capacity wire enclosed in an insulated sheath
Coaxial cable (RG 6)	2		Heavily shielded and insulated copper core carries signal
High capacity telephone/data wire (Category 5)	2	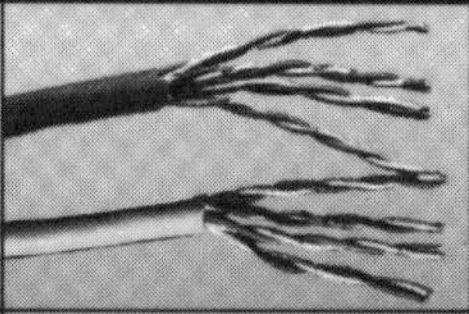	4 twisted pairs of high-capacity wire enclosed in an insulated sheath
Coaxial cable (RG 6)	2	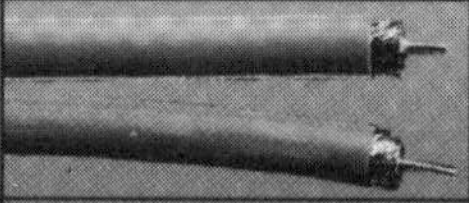	Heavily shielded and insulated copper core carries signal
Fiber-optic cable	2	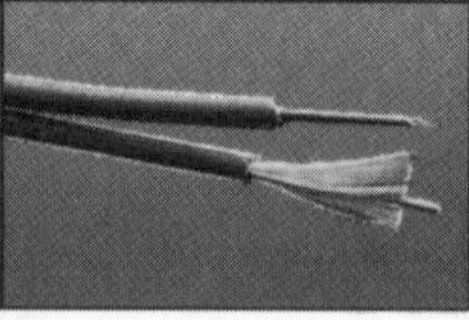	Glass-lined cable passing laser light pulses which transmit voice, data, and image signals at the speed of light

Figure 11-7 Wiring and cabling types. *(Home Intelligence)*

The current category 5 cables available can handle more telecommunications possibilities, such as all-digital phone service. Originally recommended for home offices, tomorrow's homeowners will more than likely have computers in almost every room of the house and will need to be able to meet these demands. Many experts recommend running a separate feed of category 5 cable from a central patch point to each telephone wall jack, TV jack, computer locations, and doorbell.

The cost of category 5 wire, at $100.00/1000 feet is a little higher than category 1, at $60.00/1000 feet but the tradeoffs are well worth the investment. The speed of data transmission is increased from 4 megabits/second (Mb/s) for category 1 to 100 Mb/s for category 5.[14]

When installing, it is important to follow a few simple guidelines. Cables should be "home" run in a "star" configuration. This means that all cable runs are concentrated at a central distribution point and terminated on a utility panel. Each location has its own port, which allows greater flexibility if there is a need to make moves or changes. The older "daisy chain" method would prevent this because, if all elements are connected together and there is a break in the chain, any locations downstream are affected.

All cable runs should be a maximum length of 295'. The installer should avoid kinks in the cable and maintain a minimum bend radius of no more than 2" at any location. The installer should be at least 8" away from electrical power lines or any object that emits electromagnetic interference or radiofrequency interference (EMI/RFI) such as fluorescent light ballasts, electric motors, and generators. These types of interference can affect the signal being transmitted. Category 5 cable should never share the same conduit or run parallel with electrical wiring. If electrical wiring is unavoidable, the cables should cross perpendicular to each other to avoid interference.

It is also recommended to run a 2"-diameter PVC pipe from the basement to the attic. This will allow the opportunity to pull future new wires between floors without cutting into the walls, ceiling or floors.

Television/Video

Coaxial cable (or "coax") includes a shield of foil and braided wire that surrounds the core. The signal is conducted through the core, and the surrounding foil and wire braid is connected to ground and used to shield the core from outside interference. The "new kid on the block" is RG-6 coaxial cable, an 18-gauge, solid-center conductor with dual or quad shielding. RG-6 is superior in its ability to send video, analog, and digital signals to multiple sources such as televisions and computers, and should be used in lieu of the standard R-59 coaxial cable. The price for RG-6 is about the same as RG-59 but the signal loss is reduced from 7.1 decibels (dB) per 100' to 5.9 dB per 100'.[15]

As mentioned earlier, the home run method should be used for flexibility, future adaptability, and possibly centralized controls. Two cables should be run to each cable television junction box. (Installers recommend using different colors of each of the dual runs of RG-6 to make installation easier.) This allows even the most prudent planner to have dual jacks of coax installed in all rooms in which a computer, television, or video camera may eventually be installed. Dual runs allow a signal to be received by a monitor as well as other signals (or the same) to be sent to other rooms. This is essential if networking between rooms (LAN or local area network) or closed circuit television (for example, remote video monitoring for security) is to be installed.

ISDN

As mentioned earlier, the analog-based telephone system, typical in most homes, is referred to in the technical world as POTS (plain old telephone service). POTS was quite sufficient for its original purpose, to transmit a voice over a phone line. The growing popularity of the Internet and home (or home office) fax modems have turned the POTS into a massive data communication link. ISDN, which stands for Integrated Services Digital Network, will serve as the next generation of communication services to be provided by telephone companies. First conceived in the 1970s, this high-speed technology uses digital phone connections instead of analog. This new technology permits voice conversations and data transmission, such as a fax, to travel at the same time on existing category 1 or category 5 home wiring.

One of the biggest advantages of the digital system over an analog setup is the tremendous increase in communication speed. ISDN maximizes the transmission capability of existing copper wires, allowing for the simultaneous transmission of voice and data transmissions. The homeowner's capabilities are virtually endless, ranging from telecommuting, desk-top video conferencing, large file transfer, and Internet access. Transferring a file to someone while talking on the phone or seeing their live picture on a video screen will be possible without adding additional phone lines. Since the line is digital, it is also easier to keep the noise and interference out while combining these signals.

The modem was a big breakthrough in computer communications. It allowed computers to communicate by converting their digital information into an analog signal to travel through the public phone network. There is an upper limit to the amount of information that an analog telephone line can hold.

Currently, it is about 56 kilobits per second (kbps). ISDN can support modem transmission up to 128 kbps. The change comes about when the telephone company's switches can support digital connections. At the present, most of the phone company's transmissions and switching are already digital. However, the phone line to the house (and subsequently inside the home) is still analog. Therefore, the same physical wiring can be used, but a digital signal instead of an analog signal is transmitted across the line. Digital phone equipment is needed and typical analog phones will not work. The wiring from the phone company to the house is the same, but a digital connection will need to be added at the house. This scheme permits a much higher data transfer rate than analog lines. Customers will also need special equipment to communicate with the phone company switch and with other ISDN devices.

The biggest barrier to universal installation of ISDN is cost. The homeowner's digital phone equipment is more expensive than the common analog equipment in use today. The economic trend of price reduction for new technology as it matures will ensure that ISDN service will be affordable to all in the very near future.

Fiber Optics

Fiber optic technology is based on the transmission of light through transparent fibers of glass or plastic. The medical field was one of the first industries to embrace this new technology. Its benefits can readily be seen in the now routine procedures of arthroscopic surgery. Fiber optics are used in high-speed computer networks but are also capable of handling all digital uses in the home.

Many cable and telephone companies are now installing fiber optic cables from their service center to "the curb." (The homeowner or builder will need to verify availability with the local phone service company.) Fiber optics are lighter, immune to electrical interference, and carry information faster than standard network cables made of copper wire. Using the traditional copper wire to carry information, it would take 33 tons to transmit the same amount of information that $1/4$ lb of optical fiber would. Two optical fibers can transmit what would be equal to 24,000 phone calls at the same time[16].

The main barrier to widespread use is material and installation costs. Although a number of communities are promising "to-curb" installations, the minimum bending radius of fiber optic cable makes installation a little more tricky. Splicing fiber optic cable is also expensive. Many office networks are using fiber optic cable to communicate between buildings or departments, but category 5 wire is used to run the last leg of the LAN to each office or workstation. This strategy may prove to be the most feasible for home use as well.

Fiber optics are also being used in architectural lighting applications. These bundles of fiber are used to carry light from a remote light source to provide illumination in a variety of applications (Fig. 11-8). Difficult-to-access ceilings in a house, and niche, step, and alcove lighting are appropriate applications. A feature lighting design such as fiber optic lighting is often used to illuminate corridors, allowing running cost and replacement bulb savings. Landscape lighting systems are also popular.

Figure 11-8 Fiber optic lighting. *(SuperVision International, Inc.)*

The components are fairly simple. A remote light source, the necessary runs of fiber optic cable, and the corresponding number of fixtures or lenses are all that is required for installation. Recessed fixtures, decorative downlights, and spots are among a wide range of fixtures available. Color wheels are also available for the remote light source to change the light colors automatically without changing the fixtures.

Surge Protection

Surges are commonly caused by nearby lightning activity and motor load switching created in air conditioners, refrigerator, etc. Computers and other electronics are designed to receive power within a certain voltage range. Anything outside of these levels will stress delicate components and even cause premature failure. Telephones are also susceptible. Surge suppressors provide protection from spikes and other overvoltages.[17] A variety of surge protectors are available as standalone multireceptacle units at all computer stores but should always be UL 1449–listed. A growing number of receptacle and switch manufacturers are now providing the same UL 1449–rated protection against transient voltage surges such as lightning, brownouts, and surges. Surge suppressors typically start around $20.00.

A study by Bell Labs concluded that 87 percent of all power irregularities were caused by power sags, or "brownouts."[18] Home office computers are especially susceptible to data loss in the event of a voltage irregularity. Uninterrupted power supplies (UPSs) are recommended for additional electronic protection against surges, swells, brownouts, and blackouts. The UPS is actually a recharging battery that allows the computer user to save any data or even work for a period of time in the event all power is lost. Home UPSs can range in price from $100 to $500, provide surge suppression, and include jacks for power plugs, coax, fax, and phone lines.

SURFACE-MOUNTED RACEWAYS

Standard 120/240 service to dwellings has led a simple, unassuming life...until now. Typically, nonmetallic sheathed cable, "romex" cable, or armored cable (BX cable) have been the standard for running power throughout a residence. These cables are snaked, fished, twisted, and ultimately concealed, however haphazardly or covertly, in a wall for the remainder of their existence. Telephone lines, coaxial cable, and other low-voltage wiring such as security or even computer lines are woven in and out of this confusing net of metal and plastic. Receptacle and other junction boxes are located around the room, many times without regard to actual homeowner needs. The end is near for the traditional installation methods with the introduction of the surface mounted raceway (Fig. 11-9).

Raceways are an enclosed channel of metallic or nonmetallic materials designed expressly for holding wires and cables. Long used in commercial applications and prefabricated panelized office partitions, raceways are now growing in popularity for residential installations of branch circuit wiring and other electronic needs such as phone, data, video, or other television/video coax jacks as well as security and automation cabling.

Figure 11-9 Surface-mounted raceway. *(Wiremold)*

Surface-mounted raceways will simplify initial electrical installations and also allow easy reconfiguration possibilities as needs or lifestyles change. Given the fast-paced development of new and emerging technologies (power or communications), rewiring, adding additional cable, or relocating jacks and outlets is a very real probability in the life of a home. Systems that can be adapted or updated without major construction also reduce overall life-cycle costs.

The use of raceways is also more energy efficient. Typically, receptacle and junction box placement compromise the integrity of the home's energy envelope. Boxes and wires compress or even inhibit the correct placement and thickness of wall insulation. Since raceways are attached on the finished surface of the drywall or other interior sheathing, the walls, vapor barriers, and insulation remain intact.

Material Properties

Nonmetallic raceways are typically constructed of extruded PVC. Depending upon the manufacturer, raceways may have one, two, or three channels. These channels are linear compartments which are separated by an integral barrier. The barrier provides the necessary separation of high voltage (>120 V) and low voltage (<120 V) wiring as required by the NEC. A variety of finishes are available, including white or other standard colors, vinyl laminates, or a variety of wood veneers such as cherry, mahogany, maple, and oak. Surface-mounted raceways are to be installed in dry, interior use locations.

Made of durable PVC material, nonmetallic raceways are lightweight and easy to cut. Supplied in standard 5' or 8' lengths, raceways can be installed by one person. (Custom lengths may be available by some manufacturers). All products should be UL listed.

Installation

Installation of surface mounted raceways is relatively simple. Designed to serve as a baseboard or chair-rail trim, actual mounting heights can vary as needed by the homeowner. For example, if ADA requirements are to be met, the raceway can be raised to a chair-rail height to allow proper accessibility within the required reach range. (See Chapter 1.)

The raceways are typically a three-piece design with a base, snap-on cover, and snap-on trim cover. Once the finished wall is completed, the base is attached to the wall and all of the necessary wiring is run. (If a two-channel raceway is used, one channel will contain the power service and the other raceway will contain all low-voltage wiring.) Specific jacks and other devices will be selected as the homeowner's needs warrant. Covers and trim plates are then attached.

HOME APPLIANCE CONTROLS

The remote control that never leaves the hand of a television addict or the rotary dial light timers used to "fool" passersby that someone is actually home are the simplest examples of appliance control devices. More sophisticated systems have been growing in popularity over the previous 20 years. These technologies, known as power line carriers and low voltage wiring, are the basic components of home automation technology.

One of the oldest (all of 20± years) and most common is known as X-10. X-10 is an industry standard and a proprietary product manufacturing system for compatible products by other manufacturers. X-10 components can be found in various makes of light switches, security systems, remote controls, computer interfaces, and telephone responders (Fig. 11-10). It is important to note that a number of systems are in existence such as CEBus (consumer electronic bus), a newer and slightly more sophisticated system was first released in 1992. Similar in principle to X-10, CEBus defines protocols for communication by products via electrical wires, low-voltage twisted pairs, coax, infrared, and fiber optics. X-10 will be discussed in this text, but the general principles are the same among all systems. The consumer-driven market, by way of competition, may eventually determine which system is most advantageous to use.

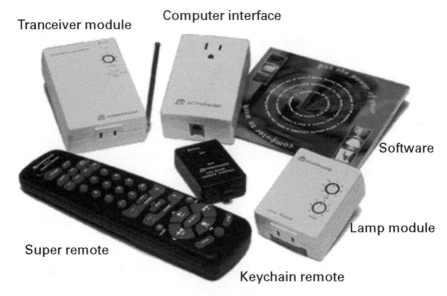

Tranceiver module   Computer interface

Software

Lamp module

Super remote

Keychain remote

Figure 11-10   X-10 devices. *(X-10/ActiveHome)*

As previously mentioned, X-10 is a powerline carrier communications protocol, or "language," that allows compatible devices throughout the home to communicate with each other via the existing 110-V standard wiring in the house (Fig. 11-11). Power line carrier technology makes it possible to control lights and virtually any other electrical device from anywhere in the house with no additional wiring. Transmitters and receivers generally plug into standard electrical outlets. There are also clock timer transmitters or special purpose transmitters that send certain X-10 commands at sunup or sundown, upon detecting movement, or as commanded by tones over a telephone.

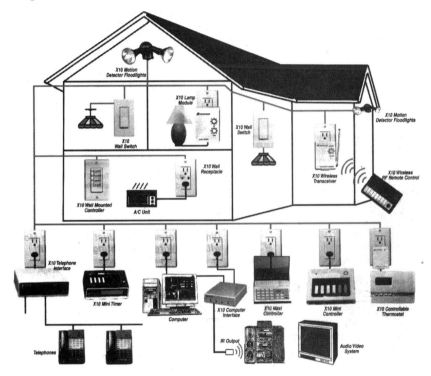

Figure 11-11   X-10 and power line carrier technology.
(Home Automation Systems, Inc.)

X-10 light switches are available starting at $10 each and remote controls start around $15 each.[19]   Not only is this the most inexpensive method for retrofitting an existing house, it is the easiest method of installation. Additional units can be added as needs or the number of devices in the home change.

The operating principles are fairly simple. An X-10 receiver is any device that is to be controlled, e.g., lamps or radios. Each device has its own "address."   An X-10 transmitter, such as a wall switch, is the device that controls the receiver. After each device is plugged into standard electrical outlets, the transmitter communicates with the receiver by sending a coded low-voltage signal that is superimposed over the 110-VAC current (Fig. 11-12). Any X-10 receiver plugged into the household 110-V power supply will see this signal but will only respond when it sees a signal that has its address. Set the devices to the same address if more than one device is to respond to the same signal. Any combination of modules, switches, controllers, and timers can be arranged in the home as long as standard switches, outlets, etc., have been replaced with corresponding X-10 devices.

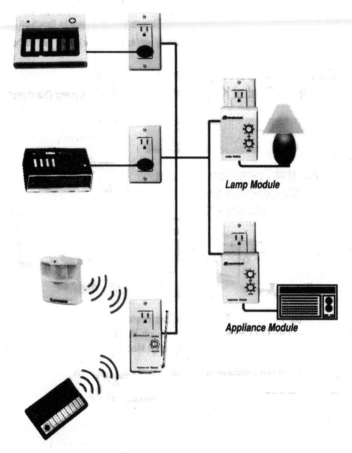

Figure 11-12   X-10 transmitters and receivers. *(Home Automation Systems, Inc.)*

There are some limitations to power-line carrier technology and specifically the X-10. X-10 does not control equipment located on twisted-pair, coax, infrared, RF, and fiber optics lines. The 256 addresses and six functions (On, Off, Dim, Bright, All lights on, All lights off) are the limits for standard consumer products. The technology is also more vulnerable to undesirable conditions such as "noise," surges or spikes along the powerline. Some physical limitations of distance may exist with X-10 receivers in larger homes. Moving the transmitters or installing signal amplifiers in the electrical breaker box can usually solve this problem.

Low-voltage wiring is the other type of home appliance control technology and is best used in new construction applications. Although first introduced into home applications as a carrier for telephone communications, it is now used for all Internet, fax, modem, or other networking applications. This concept involves special low-voltage wiring that attaches between the wall switches/receptacles and control modules which attach to the lighting/appliance circuits. Although more expensive than power line carrier technology, low voltage is growing in popularity because of the capabilities provided by more sophisticated automation systems and software. Additional commands and controls can be implemented with low-voltage wiring from the computer to the user interface.

Programmable thermostats are readily available. These allow an HVAC system to be programmed to reduce energy consumption during the daytime when the homeowner is away or at work and return the climate control systems to the appropriate temperatures by the end of the work day. This eliminates the needless running of the HVAC when no one is home. The energy savings realized pay for the thermostat within a year of use.

HOME AUTOMATION

Microwave ovens, answering machines, VCRs, compact discs, personal computers, and even audiocassettes are examples of technology's contributions to the households of the last 20 years. It may be hard to believe, but each of these items was greeted with resistance by many consumers when first available, but are now almost as commonplace as the toothbrush or washing machine. Home automation systems may also be an example of the old adage, "One generation's luxuries is the next generation's necessities." Also referred to as Smart Home, Smart House, Intelligent Homes, Whole House Control, or Home

Control, the concept of home automation refers to a network within the home that has the ability to understand current conditions and provide appropriate system responses as well as to exercise a series of scenarios based on pre-programmed instructions. In the simplest of definitions, home automation systems are intended make life easier and more comfortable for the inhabitants.

Home automation is basically an extension of what the homeowner already uses throughout the day to manage the home, such as changing the television channel with a remote control or turning off the light at the wall switch. The remote control or operating mechanism is taken one step further with home automation, in which the microprocessor is the artificial intelligence that integrates or controls the electronic products in the home. Home automation typically uses a central processor unit (computer) and several user interfaces to control security systems, HVAC systems, lighting control systems, home theater systems, irrigation systems, and just about any other appliance required.

Benefits

Home automation systems are interlinked with home security systems, which is why an overlap occurs between the two industries. The biggest difference is that home security systems generally monitor the perimeter and interior, the exterior is usually avoided due to the possibility of false alarms. When a security system sensor trips, the system goes into full alarm without any warning. The home automation system adds another layer of protection around the home by its capabilities to provide warnings to potential intruders via lights and/or sirens without notifying the security monitoring service.

There are a number of other reasons as to what homeowners expect from a home automation system in addition to security. Convenience, 31 percent; ease of use, 18 percent; central control, 11 percent; reliability, 8 percent; fun/entertainment, 8 percent; comfort, 8 percent; increased value/quality, 6 percent; appearance, 5 percent; savings, 4 percent; security, 3 percent; and service, 1 percent.

Features

Integrated systems can include a wide range of features, options, and controls (Fig. 11-13). The activation of these components and/or by preset life-style modes can be by remote control, keypads, telephone, motion, light, moisture, or timed events.

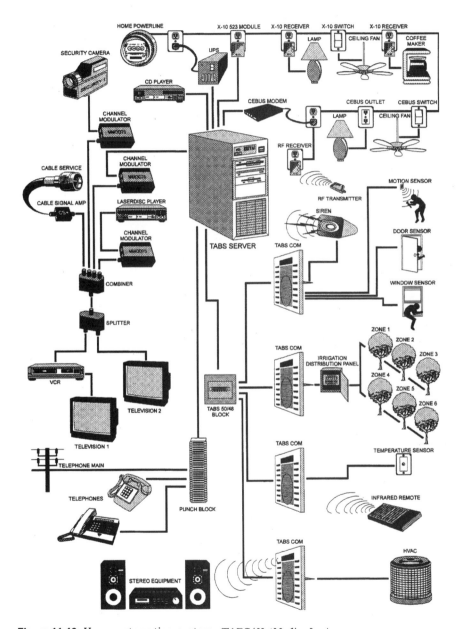

Figure 11-13 Home automation system. *(TABS/NetMedia, Inc.)*

Telephone
- Voice mail (Each family member can have his or her own "mailbox" for incoming messages)
- Paging and message forwarding
- "Hold calls" feature upon going to bed
- Intercom throughout the home
- Daily scheduling reminders
- Dictation
- Announcing the caller's name on an external speaker prior to answering
- Interactive communities—A LAN in the neighborhood that can disperse information to all residents relating to weather, community events, babysitters, contacting the local school, etc.

Security
- Closed-circuit television (Monitoring children in other rooms, reviewing babysitters on tape, viewing who is at the front door, or other security strategies)
- Window, door, motion, and glass breakage sensors
- Monitor radon and carbon monoxide levels
- Check for frozen pipes
- Close automatic drapes when leaving the home or at sunset
- Outdoor motion sensors can activate or flash exterior lights
- Operate security gates

Safety
- Personal medical emergency notification
- Illumination of appropriate exit lights or path in the event of a fire

Lighting and Appliances
- Light fixtures that turn on upon entering a room
- Fans
- Coffee maker activation

Plumbing
- Irrigation systems
- Decorative landscape features such as fountains, waterfalls
- Bathtubs or whirlpools can be filled prior to arrival
- Hot water heaters can be used more efficiently

Home Entertainment

- All entertainment components (CD player, tape, television, VCR, laserdisc player, satellite) can be listened to or viewed in any room throughout the home
- Whole-house audio can be activated when moving from room to room

HVAC

- Zones (By segregating a home into two or more zones, HVAC controls can be configured by a variety of methods to reduce energy consumption while enhancing the home's comfort levels.) This can be accomplished by the following types of zone control including: damper zoning; equipment zoning; combinations of damper, valve, and equipment zoning, and priority zone designation
- HVAC equipment controls can activate gas/oil furnaces, heat pumps, air conditioners, radiant or electric heating, hydronic floor heating
- Temperature profiles or presets based on time, date, or user patterns such as "Sleep," "Holiday," or "Good-bye."
- Indoor temperature sensor
- Outdoor temperature sensor
- Water temperature sensor

Scenes

Also known as lifestyle profiles or scenarios, scenes can be pre-programmed to deliver the appropriate instructions to a variety of systems when directed to do so. For example, home automation can perform an infinite number of scenarios but the following are a few examples:

- The Morning. The rising sun activates a sensor that opens the automatic drapes in the bedroom while gentle music plays to awaken the homeowner. The lights and heat are then activated in the bathroom while the automatic coffee percolator starts on a pot of coffee in the kitchen. The television turns on 5 minutes after this scenario has begun, tuned to the homeowner's favorite sports or news channel and the bedside radio turns off. The sprinkler system has already completed all lawn watering cycles by this time unless the moisture sensor determined it had rained during the night, in which case the cycles were not activated.

- The Day. After leaving for work, the home automation systems are checking all appliances to insure they were not left on. The security systems were activated when the doors were locked and the HVAC systems are programmed to reduce cooling (or heating) during the day to save energy while the homeowner is away. (Of course, if the homeowner is staying home, the doorbell has been configured to send a signal to the vacuum cleaner to turn off in the event it is rung.)

- The Evening. Returning home from dinner (or work), an instruction, based on the time, a telephone-entered code, or a keypad direction will have the temperature and humidity levels set in the appropriate rooms, subdued lighting will illuminate the home while classical music plays throughout the intercom system. The intercom tells the homeowner, in a pleasant voice (of course), that they have four voice messages, a fax, and two e-mails. The whirlpool bath will have been filled at a preset temperature and the towel warming racks for preheating will have been activated. The electric blanket has been turned on to prewarm the bed and all security systems activated and doors locked. The day is done.

Granted, these examples of home automation may seem extreme to many, but are all well within the realm of possibilities to be implemented and are predominantly limited only by the homeowner's imagination and budget. One can also see the accessibility benefits inherent in the installation of such a system.

Components

Whether the home automation system is of the power line carrier type (PLC such as the X-10) or uses low-voltage wiring, a variety of components will be used in the residence. Nomenclature varies among manufacturers, which makes a specific proprietary discussion difficult within the scope of this text. Generally speaking, the home automation system uses: (1) actuators (switches), (2) user interfaces such as a keypad or TV screens (remote or touch), (3) sensors to detect motion, humidity, light, etc., and (4) an automation controller (computer). The system accessories should include a UPS, a surge suppressor, and lightning protection.

Installation

There are many types of wiring and control systems available. Many home automation systems can be installed by "do-it-yourselfers," especially PLC types. (Many PLC systems can be added incrementally, based on user needs or budget.) If selecting a professional home automation installer, it is recommended that he or she have intermediate knowledge of hardware, software, communications wiring and systems configurations, NEC and local building codes, and any other licenses as required.

Most of the systems are designed so that the automation signals and controls flow over the existing power lines in the home (For more information on power line carrier technology, see Home Appliance Controls in this chapter.) Also known as "soft wiring," this method is especially effective for renovation projects, since additional wiring is not needed. Systems using low-voltage wiring are typically installed only in new construction, and are referred to as "hard wiring." The hard-wiring method has one advantage over soft wiring. In many installations, "noise" may be present when multiple devices share the same power line. This is avoided since the controls are sent via the low-voltage wiring.

When installing in new construction, the core wiring systems are placed first. Standard electrical wiring is the medium for all power line carrier technology. Low-voltage wiring and coax cables will be necessary for more sophisticated systems. Actuators are installed in lieu of wall switches and receptacles. Although actuators have the same manual switching capabilities as the typical light switch, these devices will enable the home automation systems to function. The user interfaces, generally the remote control devices that allow the homeowner to communicate with the electronic devices, are then installed (Fig. 11-14). Interface types include wall-mounted transmitters, plug-in remote controls, handheld infrared remote controls, telephone remote controls, and computers. Temperature, light, water, and motion sensors are also installed at this time.

Finally, a central closet or small room is ideal for the location of the computer or automation controller. It is best to allow a generous distance of at least 5' from the breaker panel to avoid unnecessary electrical interference. If a computer is to serve as the automation controller, it should be connected by category 5 wiring to the various user interfaces located strategically and conveniently throughout the house.[20] Humidity, dust, excessive temperature swings, and poor ventilation can adversely affect or damage sensitive electronic components. Once the automation software is installed, customized, and tested, the system should be ready for operation.

Figure 11-14 User interface. *(Honeywell, Inc.)*

Cost

Due to the wide variety of systems and options, the average cost is difficult to quantify. As mentioned earlier, PLC systems can start with just one receiver and one transmitter and an RF remote for under $30.00. Fully automated systems are equally as varied based on the sophistication and types of controls desired. Many units can range in the $1500 to $5000 range, but a good rule of thumb is 2 percent of the cost of construction.[21]

Savings

Home automation systems are capable of saving expenses typically incurred by nonautomated homes. The reduction of energy-consuming devices such as HVAC or water heaters during non-occupied times can result in a total savings of up to 40 percent, depending on project location and typical use patterns.[22] One source presented documentation that a 10°F setback of the HVAC system twice a day can cut 18 to 30 percent off of the energy bill. Controlling zoned systems can add additional savings of 7.5 percent. The average total of all HVAC savings is 31.5 percent. The simple task of lights being turned off when the room is unoccupied adds up to additional energy bill savings. Lighting controls proved to save an additional 6 percent and water heater controls saved an additional 4 percent. The total average savings of 41.5 percent on a typical $200 per month utility bill equals a savings of $996 per year.[23]

Limitations

The best home automation system will not brew coffee in the morning if the homeowner forgets to put coffee in the percolator the night before. In other words, like the cruise-control feature in a car, some human interaction is still required. The user should select a system that is user friendly, easy to program, and convenient to operate. Anything less will be wasted money. Similarly, an improperly installed or configured system will also cause unexpected problems. In the worst-case scenario, if the automation controller fails, many, if not all, of the systems may not operate properly if at all.

"Knowing when to jump" may be another complication with home automation systems. Like VCRs, calculators, and computers, electronic appliances and technologies will inevitably reduce in price with time. The market leaders today may not be the market leaders tomorrow while automation software continues to improve. All of these factors make it difficult to predict the best time to purchase the "very best" system. If making the decision is unresolved at the time of construction, the homeowner should at least try to "future-proof" the home.

Wiring chases, surface-mounted raceways and "home-run" topology will allow the homeowner to be as flexible as possible when changes, upgrades, or a new system purchase is made.

The lack of a universal standard specification has also compromised the automation industry. X-10 technology, continually being improved and updated, is still the oldest standard being used today and typically the least expensive. Newer protocols, such as CEBus and LonWorks (developed by the Echelon Corporation) are being implemented as a response to the limited functionality of X-10 standards (although industry sources claim that since the X-10 patent recently expired, new X-10–type products are being introduced that have higher transmission speed, greater reliability, and backward compatibility).

CEBus is a communications standard for in-home networks developed by the Electronics Industry Association (EIA) and the Consumer Electronics Manufacturers Association. Development of this communications protocol first began in 1984. CEBus is an open standard, which means anyone can develop products using this communications protocol. CEBus allows any node (i.e., appliance, light, or TV) to communicate easily with any other node irrespective of the medium through which the communication is sent. In other words, CEBus products will be able to use whichever medium might be most appropriate. For example, power line carrier (PLC) will be used for light switches and appliances, coax for video equipment, twisted pair for thermostats and infrared (IR) and radiofrequency (RF) for remote controls, are some examples of the versatility of CEBus. The primary advantage of CEBus over X-10 is the data transmission speed. The disadvantages of CEBus are the relatively few products currently available and the very high cost of those products.[24] Similar to CEBus, LonWorks also communicates over virtually any type of cabling, with a variety of media, and with more sophistication than X-10.[25]

The industry anticipates that once a particular communications protocol becomes standard, appliance manufacturers will be more at ease incorporating these components. This should also simplify the retail purchase, installation, and management of home LAN (networked) products as well as allow incremental installation by homeowners and professional installers without compatibility problems.

Finally, it is not clear as to how the insurance industry will affect the implementation of home automation systems. A computer virus or malfunction could disable or damage the components or contents of the home. Whether homeowners insurance or supplemental riders would cover such damage remains to be seen.

Summary

To say that technology is gaining popularity is an extreme understatement. Installations of home automation systems in the United States grew 457 percent from 1992 to 1994, from 4000 to 20,200.[26] Industry analysts estimate that the total automation revenue will increase from $200 million in 1996 to $10 billion by the year 2005.[27] It is quite possible that the home automation industry will have advanced in such a way that the systems discussed herein will be outdated by the time the book goes to press. (Such is the curse of attempting to stay current with the pace of quick change inherent with electronic technologies.)

CONCLUSION

It has been reported that in 1899, the head of the U.S. Patent Office said "Everything possible has been invented." This observation may have been attributed to ignorance, a lack of imagination, or little faith in the human spirit of invention. In either case, this gentleman could not have been more mistaken. If the technologies discussed in this chapter, photovoltaics, wiring and cabling, as well as home automation, appear outdated within a few years of publication of this book, it will not be due to the authors' lack of sound research. Rather, it will be a testament to the fast pace of change inherent in technology's quest for better, faster, and more efficient electronic systems.

APPENDIX

The Energy Efficiency and Renewable Energy Clearinghouse (EREC)
PO Box 3048
Merrifield, VA 22116
(800) 363-3732
Fax: (703) 893-0400

Hubbell Premise Wiring
14 Lord's Hill Road
Stonington, CT 06378-0901
(800) 626-0005
Fax: (860) 535-8328

Supervision International, Inc.
8210 Presidents Drive
Orlando, FL 32809
(407) 857-9900
Fax: (407) 857-0050

Wiremold
Access 5000
60 Woodlawn Street
West Hartford, CT 06110-2500
(800) 741-7957

REFERENCES

1. T. Commerford Martin and Stephen Leidy Coles, eds., *The Story of Electricity* (University of Rochester website)
2. Internet Timeline Copyright (c) 1993-4 by Robert H. Zakon.
3. Randy Quinn, "Finally Catching the Sun," Vol. 12, *The World and* I, 03-01-1997, pp. 156.
4. The National Renewable Energy Laboratory (NREL website)
5. Ibid.
6. Randy Quinn, op. cit.
7. The Energy Service Company, Eugene, Oregon.
8. Randy Quinn, op. cit.
9. "An Architect's Guide to Photovoltaics," *AIARCHITECT*, October 1996, p. 13.
10. Energy Efficiency and Renewable Energy Clearninghouse.
11. Steve Culpepper, "New Solar Roofing Actually Looks Like Real Roofing," *Fine Homebuilding*, 110, p. 38.
12. Randy Quinn, op. cit.
13. Ibid.
14. Julie Jacobson and Scott Lohraff, "Futureproofing Your Home," *Electronic House*, October 1995.
15. Ibid.
16. Kristina Cullen, Fiber Optics Presentation, Syracuse University.
17. Solutions '95, American Power Conversion Catalog.
18. Back-UPS Pro, American Power Conversion Catalog.
19. Home Team Network Reference website, 11/23/97.
20. Ibid.

21. "Homes Get Smart with Automation Services," *USA Today*, 9/2/97.
22. Home Team Network Reference, op. cit.
23. Ibid.
24. 1995–1997 Home Automation Systems, Inc. website, 12/1/97
25. Margo Bell, "Protocol Roundup," *Electronic House Magazine*, December 1997.
26. "Homes Get Smart with Automation Systems," op. cit.
27. TABS, NetMedia, Inc. Information Package

Residence Comparison, Example, and Cost Estimate

HOUSING COMPARISON

The following narrative compares conventional and alternative building systems as applied to the residence example illustrated within this section.

1. The house illustrated in this example is approximately 1600 ft² of finished space on the main floor.
2. Full basement (approximately 1600 ft²).
3. Spaces include three bedrooms, two full bathrooms, a living room, a dining room, and a kitchen.
4. Not included are interior finishes, land cost, appliances, cabinets, light fixtures, plumbing fixtures, site preparation, and excavation.

ACCESSIBILITY

Conventional – Nonaccessible
Alternative - Accessible

FOUNDATION

Conventional – 8' concrete masonry unit with waterproofing, insulation
Alternative – 8'-2" superior wall

FLOOR SYSTEM

Conventional – 2 × 8 at 16" o/c w/ $^3/_4$" T&G plywood
Alternative – $11^7/_8$" Wood-I-beams at 24" o/c w/ $^{23}/_{32}$" T&G OSB and $^3/_8$" FiberBond underlayment.

EXTERIOR WALLS

Conventional – 2 × 4 at 16" o/c w/ $^1/_2$" OSB sheathing, R-13 insulation/vapor barrier and $^1/_2$" gypsum wallboard.
Alternative – Structural insulated panels, R-15, TimberStrand for the sill and head plates, w/$^1/_2$" FiberBond.

INTERIOR WALLS

Conventional – 2 × 4 at 16" o/c w/ $^1/_2$" gypsum wallboard on each face.
Alternative – $3^1/_2$" metal Carpenter's Studs at 24" o/c w/TimberStrand for the sill and head plate, and $^1/_2$" FiberBond wallboard.

ROOF SYSTEM

Conventional – Trusses at 24" o/c w/ $^1/_2$" CDX sheathing, R-30 insulation and $^1/_2$" gypsum wallboard.
Alternative – Structural insulated panels laying flat, R-36 w/ $^1/_2$" FiberBond, Wood-I-beam to form the roof slope at 24" o/c w/ $^1/_2$" OSB.

ROOFING

Conventional – 25-year asphalt shingles over 30# felt.
Alternative – 50-year cement shingles over 30# felt.

SIDING

Conventional – Vinyl siding with brick accent
Alternative – Werzalit siding with cultured stone brick accent

WINDOWS

Conventional – Aluminum-cladded wood w/wood interior.
Alternative – Fiberglass w/wood interior.

DOORS

Conventional – 3068 exterior wood, 2868 interior molded, knobs
Alternative – 3068 fiberglass, 3068 interior molded, levers

HVAC

Conventional – Air-to-air heat pump
Alternative – Geothermal heat pump

PLUMBING

Conventional – Copper tubing for water, PVC for drainage,
electric hot water heater
Alternative – Vanguard MANABLOC plumbing distribution
system, PVC for drainage, geothermal hot water, fire sprinklers

ELECTRICAL

Conventional – Standard system
Alternative – Wiremold surface applied electrical system

COST ESTIMATE

This cost estimate is based on a 1600 ft² house with a 1600 ft² unfinished basement. These estimates are related only to the items listed and do not include finishes in the home including cabinets, finish floors, painting, carpeting, and plumbing and electrical fixtures. These estimates are provided by manufacturers and subcontractors, and will vary in different parts of the country.

Housing Estimate	Conventional	Duration	Alternative	Duration
Foundation	$9,660	5 days	$9,118	2 hours
Floor System	$5,000	2 days	$3,500	8 hours
Exterior Walls	$5,500	3 days	$4,445	8 hours
Interior Walls	$3,623	3 days	$2,175	12 hours
Roof Structure	$6,050	3 days	$7,000	2 days
Roofing	$1,200	8 hours	$2,000	8 hours
Siding	$4,332	5 days	$5,776	5 days
Windows	$2.500	8 hours	$2,300	8 hours
Doors	$2,500	8 hours	$3,200	8 hours
HVAC	$3,750	2 days	$4,500	3 days
Plumbing	$3,500	4 days	$3,500	2 days
Electrical	$3,000	4 days	$3,500	2 days
TOTAL	$50,615	34 days	$51,014	20.75 days

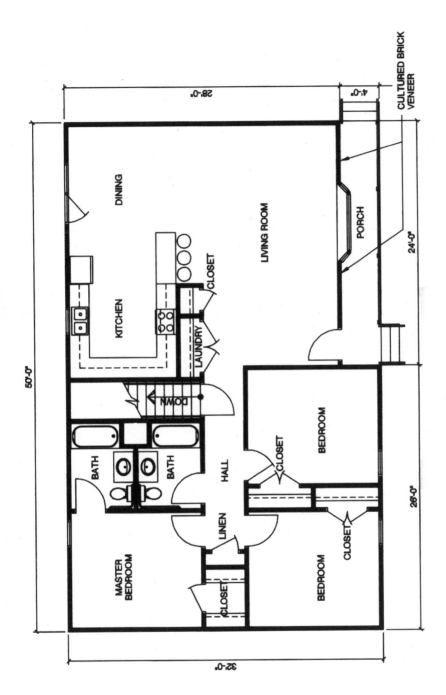

Figure A-1 Floor plan.

A-5

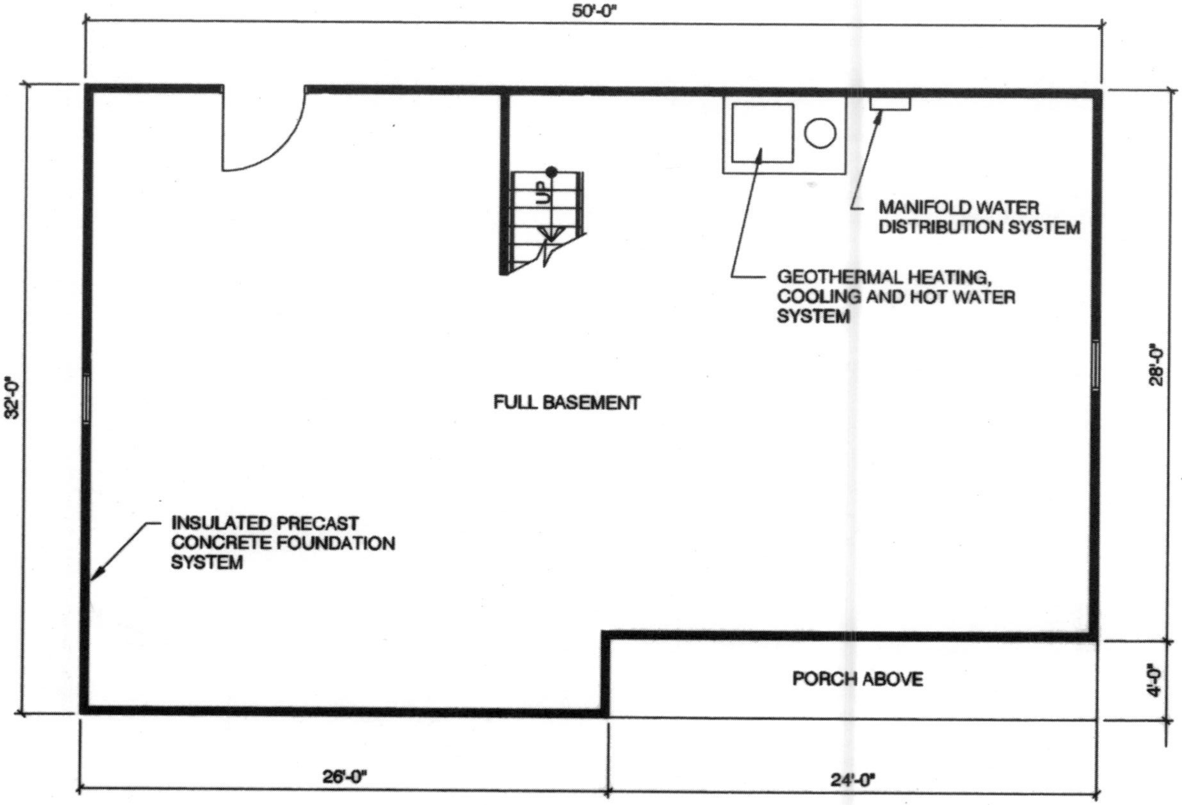

Figure A-2 Basement plan.

50'-0"

28'-0"

4'-0"

MANIFOLD WATER
DISTRIBUTION SYSTEM

GEOTHERMAL HEATING,
COOLING AND HOT WATER
SYSTEM

PORCH ABOVE

24'-0"

FULL BASEMENT

UP

INSULATED PRECAST
CONCRETE FOUNDATION
SYSTEM

26'-0"

32'-0"

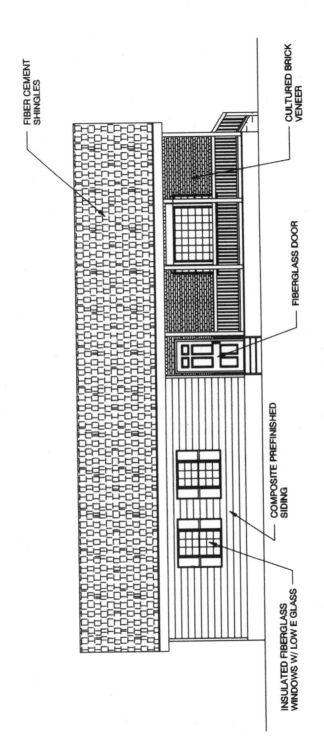

Figure A-3 Front elevation.

FIBER CEMENT SHINGLES

CULTURED BRICK VENEER

FIBERGLASS DOOR

COMPOSITE PREFINISHED SIDING

INSULATED FIBERGLASS WINDOWS W/ LOW E GLASS

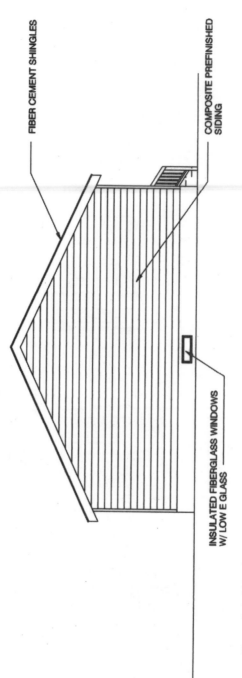

FIBER CEMENT SHINGLES

COMPOSITE PREFINISHED SIDING

INSULATED FIBERGLASS WINDOWS W/ LOW E GLASS

Figure A-4 Side elevation.

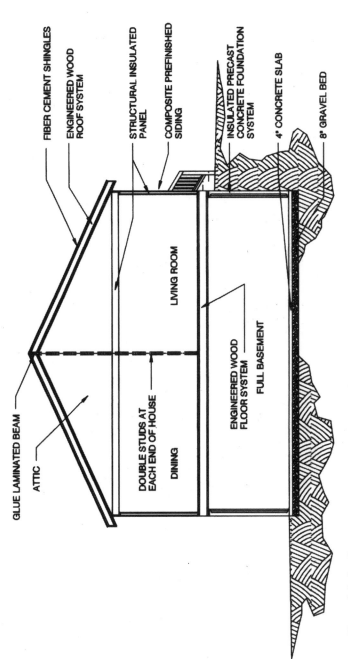

GLUE LAMINATED BEAM

ATTIC

FIBER CEMENT SHINGLES

ENGINEERED WOOD ROOF SYSTEM

STRUCTURAL INSULATED PANEL

COMPOSITE PREFINISHED SIDING

INSULATED PRECAST CONCRETE FOUNDATION SYSTEM

4" CONCRETE SLAB

8" GRAVEL BED

DOUBLE STUDS AT EACH END OF HOUSE

LIVING ROOM

DINING

ENGINEERED WOOD FLOOR SYSTEM

FULL BASEMENT

Figure A-5 Section.

B

Directory of Manufacturers, Suppliers, and Associations

The information contained within this directory has been obtained from an extensive list of sources during the research for this book. This directory is not intended to be all-inclusive; however, the information is presented as a service to the reader and to facilitate further research or education. Every effort has been made to insure the accuracy of the material. The authors and the publisher will not accept any liability for omissions or errors.

CHAPTER 1

Universal Design Sources

Architectural and Transportation Barriers Compliance Board
1111 18th Street NW, 5th Floor
Washington, DC 20036
(202) 653-7834

ADA Information
PO Box 66118
Washington, DC 20035
(202) 307-2222

Center for Accessible Housing
North Carolina State University
School of Design
Box 8613
Raleigh, NC 27695
(800) 647-6777

National Council on Disability
800 Independence Avenue SW
Room 814
Washington, DC 20591
(202) 267-3235

Grab Bars

Franklin Brass
PO Box 4887
Carson, CA 90749-4887
(800) 421-3375

Hafele America Co.
3901 Cheyenne Drive
PO Box 4000
Archdale, NC 27263
(910) 889-2322

HEWI, Inc.
2851 Old Tree Drive
Lancaster, PA 17603
(717) 293-1313
Fax: (717) 293-3270

Millwork

KraftMaid
16052 Industrial Parkway
Middlefield, OH 44062

Auto-Drapes

Makita U.S.A., Inc.
14930 Northam Street
La Mirada, CA 90638-5753
(714) 522-8088

Ramps

Infinite Access Corporation
PO Box 942
Mt. Vernon, IL 62864
(800) 656-2314

Universal Ramp Systems
6587 S.R. 21N
PO Box 658
Keystone Heights, FL 32656
(800) 648-3696

Fixtures

American Standard Inc.
PO Box 639
Hanover, MD 21076
(800) 752-6292
Fax: (800) 948-1185

AquaBath
921 B Cherokee Avenue
Nashville, TN 37207
(800) 232-2284

Aqua Glass Corporation
PO Box 412
Industrial Park
Adamsville, TN 38310
(800) 238-3940

Bobrick Washroom Equipment, Inc.
225 Bobrick Drive
Jackson, TN 38301-5635
(901) 424-7000
Fax: (901) 424-7800

Crane
1235 Hartrey Avenue
Evanston, IL 60202
(847) 864-9777

Delta Faucet Company
55 East 111th Street
Indianapolis, IN 46280
(317) 848-1812

Grohe
241 Covington Drive
Bloomingdale, IL 60108
(630) 582-7711

Moen Incorporated
25300 Al Moen Drive
North Olmsted, OH 44070-8022
(800) 321-8809, ext. 2829

Doors

Karona
PO Box 888410
Grand Rapids, MI 49588-8410
(800) 829-9233

National Guard Products, Inc.
540 North Parkway
PO Box 70343
Memphis, TN 38107
(800) 647-7874

Elevators

Concord Elevator Inc.
107 Alfred Kuehne Blvd.
Brampton, ON, Canada L6T 4K3
(800) 661-5112

Equipment

Leviton Manufacturing Co., Inc.
59-25 Little Neck Pkwy
Little Neck, NY 11362-2591
(800) 323-8920
Fax: (800) 832-9538

Whirlpool Corporation
Benton Harbor, MI 49022
(800) 253-1301

CHAPTER 2

ICF

AAB Building System
840 Division Street
Cobourg, ON K9A4J9
(905) 373-0004

AFM Corporation
PO Box 246
Excelsior, MN 55331
(800) 255-0176
Diamond Snap-Form

American ConForm Industries
1820 South Santa Fe Street
Santa Ana, CA 92705
(800) CONFORM
SmartBlock

American Polysteel Forms
5150-F Edith NE
Albuquerque, NM 87101
(800) 9PS-FORM
Fax: (505) 345-8154

Superior Walls of America, Ltd.
PO Box 427
Ephrata, PA 17522-0427
(800) 452-9255

CHAPTER 3

APA/ The Engineered Wood Association
PO Box 11700
Tacoma, WA 98411-0700
(206) 565-6600
Fax: (206) 565-7265

Engineered Wood Products

Alpine Structures
317 Providence Road
Oxford, NC 27565
(800) 672-2326

Boise Cascade
PO Box 2400
White City, OR 97503-0400
(800) 232-0788

Georgia Pacific
133 Peachtree Street, NE
Atlanta, GA 30303
(800) BUILD-GP

Louisiana Pacific
111 SW Fifth Avenue
Portland, OR 97204-3601
(800) 999-9105

Trus Joist MacMillan
200 E. Mallard Drive
PO Box 60
Boise, ID 83707
(800) 628-3997

Open-Web Trusses

Trus Joist MacMillan
200 E. Mallard Drive
PO Box 60
Boise, ID 83707
(800) 628-3997

Joist Hangers and Connectors

Alpine Construction Hardware
1950 Marley Drive
Haines City, FL 33844
(941) 421-4707
Fax: (941) 422-6573

Hughes Manufacturing, Inc.
11910 62nd Street, North
Largo, FL 33773
(800) 443-6442

Simpson Strong Tie
4637 Chabot drive, Suite 200
Pleasanton, CA 94588
(800) 999-5099

United Steel Products Company, Inc.
PO Box 80, 703 Rogers Drive
Montgomery, MN 56069
(800) 328-5934
Fax: (507) 364-8762

Fire-Retardant-Treated Lumber and Plywood Products

Dricon Fire Retardant Treated Wood
Hickson Corporation
1955 Lake Park Drive, Suite 250
Smyrna, GA 30080
(404) 362-3970

Hoover Treated Wood Products
PO Box 746
Thomson, GA 30824
(800) 832-9663

CHAPTER 4

Structural Insulated Panels

Structural Insulated Panel Association
1511 K Street NW
Washington, DC 20005
(202) 347-7800

AFM Corporation
Box 246
24000 W. Highway 7
Excelsior, MN 55331
(800) 255-0176

Apache Products Company
Industrial Park
PO Box 160
Union, MS 39365
(800) 530-7762

FischerSIPS Incorporated
1843 Northwestern Parkway
Louisville, KY 40203
(502) 778-5577

"Insulspan" SIPS
Supplier is Perma "R" Products Inc.
Johnson City, TN
(800) 251-7532

Winter Panel Corporation
RR 5, Box 168B
Glen Orne Drive
Brattleboro, VT 05301
(802) 254-3435

Residential Steel Framing

American Iron and Steel Institute
1101 17th Street, NW
Suite 1300
Washington, DC 20036-4700
(800) 79-STEEL

Advanced Framing Systems, Inc.
215 W. Hickory, Suite 200
Denton, TX 76201
(800) 252-0069

Allied American Studco
2525 N. 27th Ave.
Phoenix, AZ 85009
(602) 272-6606

Clark Steel Framing Systems
101 Clark Boulevard
Middleton, OH 45044
(800) 543-7140
Fax: (888) 874-1949

Classic Steel Frame Homes
7301 Fairview
Houston, TX 77041
(713) 896-7425

Grace Building Systems, Inc.
23 Jayar Rd.
PO Box 351
Medway, MA 02053
(508) 520-1818

Tri-Steel Structures, Inc.
5400 S. Stemmons Frwy.
Denton, TX 76205
(800) TRI-STEEL
Fax: (940) 497-7497

Unimast Inc.
4825 North Scott Street, Suite 300
Schillar Park, IL 60176
(708) 928-3400

Autoclaved Aerated Concrete (AAC)

Hebel Southeast
3340 Peachtree Road
Suite 150
Atlanta, GA 30326
(800) 99-HEBEL

Hebel South Central
4550 Sunbelt Drive
Dallas, TX 75248
(888) 88-HEBEL
Fax: (972) 735-8473

YTONG Florida Ltd.
3701 C.R. (County Rd) 544
Haines City, FL 33844
(800) 986-6435
Fax: (941) 421-7602

CHAPTER 5

Fiber Cement Products

James Hardie Building Products
26300 La Alameda
Suite 250
Mission Viejo, CA 92691
(800) 348-1811

MaxiTile, Inc.
17141 S. Kingsview Avenue
Carson, CA 90746
(800) 338-8453
(310) 217-0316
Fax: (310) 515-6851

Eternit Inc.
210 Corporation Drive
Reading, PA 19605
(800) 233-3155

FCP
Excelsior Industrial Park
PO Box 99
Blandon, PA 19510
(888) 327-0723

GAF Fiber Cement Roofing
1361 Alps Road
Wayne, NJ 07470
(800) ROOF-411

Re-Con Building Products Inc.
PO Box 1094
Sumas, WA 98295
(800) 347-3373
Fax: (800) 700-7121

Werzalit Cladding

Werzalit of America, Inc.
PO Box 373
40 Holley Avenue
Bradford, PA 16701
(800) 999-3730

Manufactured Stone Veneer

Stone Products Corporation
PO Box 270
Napa, CA 94559-0270
(800) 225-7462
Fax: (707) 255-5572

L&S Stone Inc.
PO Box 69
Greencastle, Pa 17225

Coronado Stone Products
11191 Calabash Avenue
Fontana, CA 92237
(800) 847-8663
Fax: (909) 357-7362

CHAPTER 6

Fiberglass Doors & Windows

Accurate Dorwin Industries
660 Nairn Avenue
Winnipeg, Manitoba, Canada R2L0X5
(204) 982-4640
Fax: (204) 663-0020

Andersen Windows
100 4th Avenue North
Bayport, MN 55003
(612) 439-5150
Fax: (612) 430-7364

Atlantic Pre-Hung Doors
PO Box 1258, 143 Conant St.
West Concord, MA 01742
(508) 369-5600

Beveled Glass Designs
3185 N. Shadeland
Indianapolis, IN 46226
(317) 353-0472
(800) 428-5746
Fax: (317) 547-1926

Blomberg Window Systems
PO Box 22485
1453 Blair Ave.
Sacramento, CA 95822
(916) 428-8060
Fax: (916) 422-1967

Castlegate Entry Systems
911 E Jefferson
Pittsburgh, KS 66762
(316) 231-8200
(800) 835-0364
Fax: (316) 231-8239

Ceco Entry Systems
One Ceco Pl
PO Box 699
Dickson, TN 37055
(615) 446-6220
Fax: (615) 441-4226

Columbia Aluminum Windows and Doors
1600 N. Jackson
Kansas City, MO 64120
(800) 892-8703
Fax: (816) 241-5809

Comfort Line
5500 Enterprise Blvd.
PO Box 6998
Toledo, OH 43612-0998
(419) 729-8520
(800) 522-4999
Fax: (419) 729-8525

Crestline/SNE Enterprises
1 Wausau Ctr.
PO Box 8007
Wausau, WI 54401
(715) 845-1161
(800) 552-4111
Fax: (715) 847-6520

Entries
PO Box 39153
Redford, MI 48239
(313) 532-8022
(800) 735-4671
Fax: (800) 927-2814

Escon Corp.
2437 S. Eastern Ave.
Commerce, CA 90040
(213) 721-2211
(800) 368-7850
Fax: (213) 721-4104

Fibertec Window Manufacturing
157 Rivermede Rd., No. 2
Concord, ON L4K 3M4
905-660-7102
Fax: 905-660-6581

Fibertec Window Mfg
361 Rowntree Dairy Rd #4
Canada, Woodbridge, ON L4L 8H1
(905) 856-1600
(800) 551-4429
Fax: (905) 856-1654

H Window Co.
1324 E. Oakwood Dr.
Monticello, MN 55362
(612) 295-5305
(800) 843-4929
Fax: (612) 295-4656

The Hess Manufacturing Company
PO Box 127
Quincy, PA 17247-0127
(717) 749-3141
(800) 541-6666
Fax: (717) 749-3712

Inline Fiberglass
30 Constellation Ct.
Etobicoke, ON M4W 1K1
(416) 679-1171

Inline Fiberglass
141 Snidercroft
Concord, ON L4K 2J8
(905) 738-1052
Fax: (905) 738-6392

Insulated Steel Door Institute
30200 Detroit Rd
Cleveland, OH 44145
(216) 899-0010
Fax: (216) 892-1404

Kaylien
PO Box 711599
Santee, CA 92072
(619) 448-0544
(800) 748-5627
Fax: (619) 448-5196

Masco Corp
21001 Van Born Rd
Taylor, MI 48180
(313) 274-7400
Fax: (313) 374-6666

Milgard Windows
1010 54th Ave. E.
Tacoma, WA 98424
(800) MILGARD

Omniglass
1205 Sherwin Rd.
Winnipeg, MB R3H 0V1
(204) 987-8522
Fax: (204) 694-9336

Oldach Wood Windows & Doors
813 N Union Blvd
Colorado Spring, CO 80909
(719) 636-5181
Fax: (719) 636-9006

Outlook Window Partnership
PO Box 4468
Lincoln, NE 68504
(402) 464-0202
(800) 669-3696

Peachtree Doors
PO Box 5700
Norcross, GA 30091
(404) 497-2000
(800) 477-6544
Fax: (404) 497-2437

Pease Industries
7100 Dixie Hwy
Fairfield, OH 45014
(513) 870-3600
(800) 88-DOORS
Fax: (513) 870-3670

Philips Products
3221 Magnum Dr
Elkhart, IN 46516
(219) 296-0000
Fax: (219) 296-0147

Pollard Windows
338 Harris Hill Rd
Williamsville, NY 14221
(716) 626-0969
(800) 846-4746
Fax: (716) 632-8587

Premdor Corp
5110 Clifton St., PO Box 152
Tampa, FL 33684
(800) 663-DOOR (3667)
Fax: (813) 882-0914

R & D Equipment
1150 Tri-View Ave.
Sioux City, IA 51102
(712) 255-5205
(800) 798-5678
Fax: (712) 255-8292

Stanley Door Systems
1225 E Maple Rd
Troy, MI 48083
(810) 528-1400
(800) 521-2752
Fax: (810) 528-1424

Therma-Tru Corp
1687 Woodlands Dr
Maumee, OH 43537
(419) 891-7400
(800) 537-8827
Fax: (419) 891-7411

Wenco of Iowa
PO Box 741
Grinnell, IA 50112
(800) 877-9482

Wenco of Mississippi
540 E. Industrial Park
Holly Springs, MS 38635
(800) 877-9482

Wenco of North Carolina
5427 N. Sharon Amity Rd.
Charlotte, NC 28215
(800) 877-9482

Wenco of Ohio
335 Commerce Dr.
Mt. Vernon, OH 43050-4643
(614) 397-3403
(800) 877-9482
Fax: (614) 397-7442

Wenco of Pennsylvania
PO Box 259
Ringtown, PA 17967
(800) 877-9482

Windsor Window Co.
900 S. 19th St.
West Des Moines, IA 50265
(515) 223-6660
(800) 887-0111

Low-E Glazing

3M Construction Markets Division
3M Center Building 225-4S-08
St Paul, MN 55144-1000
(800) 328-1684, ext. 228
(612) 736-2388
Fax: (612) 736-0611

AFG Industries, Inc.
PO Box 929
Kingsport, TN 37662
(423) 229-7200
Fax: (423) 229-7319

Eagle Windows and Doors
375 E. Ninth Street
PO Box 1072
Dubuqe, IA 52004-1072
(319) 556-2270
Fax: (319) 556-4408

Guardian Industries
14600 Romine Road
Carleton, MI 48117
(800) 521-9040
(313) 962-2252
Fax: (800) 521-0211

Libbey-Owens-Ford Co.
PO Box 799
Toledo, OH 43697
(419) 247-4721
(419) 247-3731
Fax: (419) 247-4517

Marvin Windows
PO Box 100
Warroad, MN 56763
(800) 346-5128
Fax: (218) 386-3832

Peachtree Doors and Windows
PO Box 5700
Norcross, GA 30091
(800) 477-6544
Fax: (770) 497-2437

Pella Windows
102 Main Street
Pella, IA 50219

PPG Industries, Inc.
One PPG Place
Pittsburg, PA 15272
(412) 434-3131
(412) 434-2858
Fax: (412) 434-3991

Weather Shield Windows
One Weather Shield Plaza
PO Box 309
Medford, WI 54451
(800) 477-6808
Fax: (715) 748-6999

Fiberglass Pultrusions

OMEGA Pultrusions Incorporated
1331 S. Chillicothe Road
Aurora, OH 44202
(330) 562-5201
Fax: (330) 562-4908

Thermoplastic Pultrusions, Inc.
121 North Adeline Avenue
Bartlesville, OK 74003
(918) 337-0591
Fax: (918) 337-0539

National Fenestration Rating Council
1300 Spring St Suite 120
Silver Spring, MD 20910
(301) 589-6372
Fax: (301) 588-0854

National Wood Window and Door Association
1400 E. Touhy Ave.
Suite 470
Des Plaines, IL 60018-3305
(847) 299-5200
(800) 223-2301
Fax: (847) 299-1286

Northeast Window and Door Association
PO Box 15822
Philadelphia, PA 19103-0822
(215) 546-8480
Fax: (215) 546-7289

CHAPTER 7

Solid Core Molded Interior Doors

Atlantic Pre-Hung Doors
PO Box 1258
143 Conant St.
West Concord, MA 01742
(508) 369-5600

Doorcraft of Alabama
1101 Young Dr.
Hartselle, AL 35640-0757
(800) 877-9482

Doorcraft of California
3901 Cincinnati Ave.
Rocklin, CA 95765-1303
(800) 877-9482

Doorcraft of Indiana
2526 N. Western Ave.
Plymouth, IN 46563-1000
(800) 877-9482

Doorcraft of Iowa
820 Industrial Ave.
Grinnel, IA 50112
(800) 877-9482

Doorcraft of North Carolina
647 Hargrave
Lexington, NC 27292
(800) 877-9482

Doorcraft of Oregon
Williamson Business Park, Suite A
31725 Hwy. 97 N.
Chiloquin, OR 97624-9702
(800) 877-9482

Doorcraft of Pennsylvania
215 Packer St.
Sunbury, PA 17801-0746
(800) 877-9482

Doorcraft of Texas
2201 Baker Blvd.
PO Box 1021
Temple, TX 76503-1021
(800) 877-9482

Doorcraft of Vermont
146 Pleasant St. Extension
Dean R Brown, Jr Industrial Park, PO Box 465
Ludlow, VT 05149-0465
(800) 877-9482

Jeld-Wen, Inc.
PO Box 1329
Klamath Falls, OR 97601
(800) 877-9482

Ledco
801 Commerce Cir.
Shelbyville, KY 40065
(800) 626-6367
Fax: (502) 633-6461

Masonite Corp.
1 S. Wacker Dr., Suite 3600
Chicago, IL 60606
(800) 255-0785
Fax: (312) 263-5808

National Wood Window and Door Assn.
1400 E. Touhy Ave.
Suite 470
Des Plaines, IL 60018-3305
(800) 223-2301
Fax: (847) 299-1286

Northeast Window and Door Assn.
PO Box 15822
Philadelphia, PA 19103-0822
(215) 546-8480
Fax: (215) 546-7289

Premdor
1 N. Dale Mabry Highway #950
Tampa, FL 33609
(813) 876-2726
Fax: (813) 876-1435

Smith Millwork
920 Robbins St.
Lexington, NC 27292
(910) 243-2688
(800) 222-8498
Fax: (910) 243-2688

The Marwin Co.
PO Box 9126
Columbia, SC 29290
(803) 776-2396
Fax: (803) 776-5852

Woodwork Institute of California
PO Box 980247
Sacramento, CA 95798-0247
(916) 372-9943
Fax: (916) 372-9950

Dunbarton Corporation
Slimfold Products Division
P.O. Box 6416
Dothan, AL 36302
(800) 633-7553
(334) 794-0661
Fax: (334) 793-7022

Plastic Laminate Clad Doors

VT Industries
1000 Industrial Park
Holstein IA 51025
(800) 827-1615
(712) 368-4381
Fax: (712) 368-4320

Formica Corp.
10155 Reading Road
Cincinnati, OH 45241
(513) 786-3400
Fax: (513) 786-3024

Wilsonart International
2400 Wilson Place
PO Box 6110
Temple, TX 76503-6110
(800) 433-3222

Hardware

American Hardware Manufacturers Assn.
801 N. Plaza Dr.
Schaumburg, IL 60173-4977
(847) 605-1025
Fax: (847) 605-1093

Baldwin Hardware Corp.
841 E. Wyomissing Blvd.
PO Box 15048
Reading, PA 19612
(610) 777-7811
(800) 959-3568 (West)
Fax: (610) 775-5564

Corbin Russwin Architectural Hardware
225 Episcopal Rd.
Berlin, CT 06037-1524
(203) 225-7411
Fax: (203) 828-7266

Kwikset Corp.
1 Park Plaza, Suite 1000
Irvine, CA 92714
(714) 474-8800
(800) 327-LOCK
Fax: (714) 474-8862

Master Lock Co.
2600 N. 32nd St.
Milwaukee, WI 53210
(414) 444-2800
Fax: (414) 449-3162

Schlage Lock Co.
2401 Bayshore Blvd.
San Francisco, CA 94134
(415) 467-1100
Fax: (415) 330-5626

Nylon Hardware

HEWI, Inc.
2851 Old Tree Drive
Lancaster, PA 17603
(717) 293-1313
Fax: (717) 293-3270

CHAPTER 8

Fiber Reinforced Gypsum Panels

United States Gypsum Company
125 South Franklin Street
PO Box 806278
Chicago, IL 60680-4124
(800) 874-4968

Laminated Strand Lumber

TimberStrand LSL
Trus Joist MacMillan
200 E. Mallard Drive
PO Box 60
Boise, ID 83707
(800) 628-3997

Metal Stud Framing for Wood Plates

HL Stud Corp The Carpenter's Steel Stud
4726 Arlington Centre Blvd
Columbus, OH 43220
(614) 451-8100
(800) HLSTUDS

Drywall Steel Framing

American Iron and Steel Institute
1101 17th Street, NW, Suite 1300
Washington, DC 20036-4700
(800) 79-STEEL

American Institute of Steel Construction
One East Wacker Drive, Suite 3100
Chicago, IL 60601-2001
(312) 670-2400
Fax: (312) 670-5403

Light Gauge Steel Engineers Association
2400 Crestmoor Road, Suite 309
Nashville, TN 37215
(615) 386-7139
Fax: (615) 386-7056

Advanced Building
PO Box 131
Brawley, CA 92227
(800) 504-1230
Fax: (909) 694-7145

Alabama Metal Industries Corp.
PO Box 3928
Birmingham, AL 35208
(205) 787-2611
Fax: (205) 786-6527

Alternative Construction Systems
1713A 23rd Street
Sacramento, CA 95816
(800) 633-9889

American Studco, Inc.
PO Box 6633
Phoenix, AZ 85005
(602) 272-6606
Fax: (602) 269-1324

Angeles Metal Systems
4817 East Sheila Street
Los Angeles, CA 90091
(213) 268-1777
Fax: (213) 268-8996

Angeles Metal Systems
4841 83rd Street
Sacramento, CA 95826
(916) 383-4192
Fax: (916) 383-1842

C&G Construction Company, Inc.
965 North Second Avenue
Upland, CA 91786
(909) 982-9965
Fax: (909) 920-1169

C&S Builders
1761B McCoba Drive
Smyrna, GA 30080
(404) 432-2793
Fax: (404) 431-9373

CEMCO
263 Covina Lane
City of Industry, CA 91744
(818) 369-3564
Fax: (818) 330-7598

Classic Metal Homes
6800 Northwinds
Houston, TX 77041
(713) 466-5549
Fax: (713) 466-0388

Consolidated Systems, Inc
605 Rosewood Drive
Columbia, SC 29201
(800) 654-1912
Fax: (803) 540-2256

Crown Building Systems
6390 Philips Highway
Jacksonville, FL 32216
(904) 737-7144
Fax: (904) 737-3533

Curoco Corporation
1200 Hansley Street
Richmond, CA 94801
(510) 233-3221

Dale/Incor
1001 NW 58th Court
Ft. Lauderdale, FL 33309
(305) 772-6300
Fax: (410) 772-7124

Dale/Incor
4601 N. Point Blvd.
Baltimore, MD 21219
(410) 477-4000
Fax: (410) 477-1550

Delta Metal Products, Inc.
10340 Denton Drive
Dallas, TX 75220
(214) 350-1716
Fax: (214) 350-7252

Design Shapes In Steel
10315 East Rush Street
S El Monte, CA 91733
(818) 579-2032
Fax: (818) 579-0513

Dietrich Industries, Inc.
500 Grant Street, Ste 2226
Pittsburgh, PA 15219
(412) 281-2805
Fax: (412) 281-2965

Environmental Framing Concepts Inc.
PO Box 1859
Kitty Hawk, NC 27949
(800) 398-8889
Fax: (919) 453-9325

Excalibur Steel Structures of TN
4930 Adams Road
Hixson, TN 37343
(423) 842-2821
Fax: (423) 842-8926

FMP Residential Steel/Formed Metal Prod. Corp.
1118 W Spring Street
PO Box 1007
Monroe, GA 30655
(770) 267-2551
Fax: (770) 267-4396

Force 10 Engineered Building Systems
314 East Randolph Street
Glendale, CA 91207
(818) 247-8805
Fax: (818) 956-5641

Hanson Steel Inc.
242 West Alley Ave, Ste. 310
Birmingham, AL 35209
(205) 942-2629
Fax: (205) 942-2240

Harrison Manufacturing Company
415 East Brooks Road
PO Box 13186
Memphis, TN 38113-0186
(901) 332-4030
Fax: (901) 332-9302

Kent Builders
970 Huff Road
Atlanta, GA 30318
(404) 350-0888
Fax: (404) 355-8129

Knorr Steel Framing Systems
PO Box 5267
Salem, OR 97304
(503) 371-8033
Fax: (503) 363-6671

Knudson Manufacturing, Inc.
10401 W 120th Avenue
Broomfield, CO 80021
(800) 435-4356
Fax: (800) 548-2622

LNJ Steel Framing Systems, Inc.
209 Pheasant Cove
Canonsburg, PA 15317
(412) 873-1801
Fax: (412) 854-0427

Lite Steel & Truss
8989 N. Pima Road
Scottsdale, AZ 85258
(602) 451-6975
Fax: (602) 451-6903

Marino Ware Industries
400 Metuchen Road
S Plainfield, NJ 07080
(908) 757-9000
Fax: (908) 753-8786

Metro Metals
760 Braddock Ave
E. Pittsburgh, PA 15112
(412) 825-0800
Fax: (412) 829-2466

Novatek International
1340 Neptune Drive
Boyton Beach, FL 33426
(407) 736-6659
Fax: (407) 736-1919

O'Leary Construction Co.
12630 Timbermeadow Drive
Houston, TX 77070
Fax: (713) 955-9565

Omni-Frame by Curoco Corp.
1200 Hensley Street
Richmond, CA 94801
(510) 233-3221
Fax: (510) 233-3385

Pacific Metal Export
1753 Valley Park Ave.
Hermosa Beach, CA 90254
(310) 374-2394
Fax: (310) 318-0195

Perfection Metal & Supply Co.
PO Box 8010
Birmingham, AL 35218
(800) 354-8634
Fax: (205) 787-9666

PRD Company, Inc.
1321 West Winton Ave.
Hayward, CA 94545
(510) 782-7242
Fax: (510) 887-5639

Pioneer Residential Steel Corp.
PO Box 14546
Austin, TX 78761
(800) 637-5414
Fax: (512) 467-2857

Joseph Porretta Builders, Inc.
551 Anderson Avenue
Hammonton, NJ 08037
(609) 561-6391
Fax: (609) 567-9398

Pride Industries, Inc.
14432 State Route 141 S
Clay, KY 42404
(502) 333-9552
Fax: (502) 333-9702

San Diego Steel Frame Co.
9840 Carmel Mount Road
San Diego, CA 92129
(619) 484-1111
Fax: (619) 484-1406

Sheldon Metals, Inc.
8917 Sheldon Road
Houston, TX 77049
(713) 456-7960
Fax: (713) 456-7960

Shelter International
1 Evergreen Place
Morristown, NJ 06962-1927
(201) 292-0111
Fax: (201) 292-0225

Shenango Steel Buildings Inc.
33 Carbaugh Street, POB 268
West Middlesex, PA 16159
(412) 528-9925
Fax: (412) 528-2452

SJV Building Systems
6645 N Remington Avenue
Fresno, CA 93704
(209) 447-0340
Fax: (209) 435-2558

Southeasten Metals Manufacturer Co., Inc
11801 Industry Drive
PO Box 26347
Jacksonville, FL 32218
(800) 737-7327
Fax: (904) 751-0431

Steel Building Components
2921 N. Alexander Drive
Baytown, TX 77520
(713) 422-2922
Fax: (713) 427-3362

Steel Starts
325 West Hwy 20
Upper Lake, CA 95485
(707) 275-2285
Fax: (707) 275-2287

Steel Technology by Madray
PO Box 712
Okeechobee, FL 34973
(813) 763-8856
Fax: (813) 783-0005

Steel Tite Inc.
700 Chase Street
Gary, IN 46404
(219) 949-7500
Fax: (219) 949-7575

Steel Visions
145 Cedar Brook Lane
Kingston, TN 37763
(423) 376-7989
Fax: (423) 376-8799

Steel Construction
1711 West Culver Street, Ste. 8
Phoenix, AZ 85007
(602) 257-4110
Fax: (602) 257-8851

Steel Frame Construction Inc.
PO Box 507
Dona Ana, NM 88032
(505) 525-9108
Fax: (505) 525-9108

Steel Frame Construction Inc.
3220 W. Ina Road, #20204
Tucson, AZ 85741
(520) 797-8335
Fax: (520) 797-8335

Studco of Hawaii (Kirii)
224 Baker Way
Honolulu, HI 96819
(808) 845-9311
Fax: (808) 842-1698

Super Stud Building Products, Inc.
8-01 26th Avenue
Astoria, NY 11102
(718) 545-5700
Fax: (718) 726-0293

Swirnow Corp.
112 25th Street, East
Baltimore, MD 21218
(410) 338-1122
Fax: (410) 338-1105

Tecorp International, Inc.
2803 East 208th Street
Carson, CA 90810
(310) 886-1366
Fax: (310) 764-0033

The House Factory/Belen
906 Lee Trevion Bld.
Belen, NM 87002
(505) 861-1277
Fax: (505) 861-2357

The House Factory/Farmington
810 W. Arrington
Farmington, NM 87401
(505) 327-0249

The House Factory/Glenwood Springs
3762 Hwy 82, Ste. 1
Glenwood Springs, CO 81601
(970) 945-0429
Fax: (970) 945-6309

The House Factory/Los Cruces
PO Box 6025
Los Cruces, NM 88006
(505) 382-6012
Fax: (505) 526-4741

Thompson Stud & Track
2105 East 2nd Avenue
Tampa, FL 33605
(813) 247-3443
Fax: (813) 247-4616

Tri-Chord Systems
344 Coogan Way
El Cajon, CA 92020
(619) 588-2591
Fax: (619) 588-8127

Unimast
4825 N. Scott Street
Suite 300
Schiller Park, IL 60176
Southeast: (800) 631-6287
Northeast: (800) 524-0712
Midwest: (800) 241-7085
Southwest: (800) 241-7085

Unisteel Industries, Inc.
2500 S Main Street
Kennesaw, GA 30144
(404) 419-0500
Fax: (404) 419-8555

United Construction Supply
9800 East Rush
South El Monte, CA 91733
(818) 443-9323
Fax: (818) 443-2660

United Shelter Systems
970 Huff Road, NW
Atlanta, GA 30318
(404) 350-0767
Fax: (404) 350-8129

VicWest Steel
9000 Wessex Place - 201
Louisville, KY 40222
(800) 842-9378
Fax: (502) 339-8980

Western Metal Lath
6510 General Drive
Riverside, CA 92509
(714) 360-3500
Fax: (714) 360-3131

CHAPTER 9

Geoexchange Heating and Cooling

WaterFurnace International, Inc
9000 Conservation Way
Fort Wayne, IN 46809
(219) 478-5667

United States Department of Energy
Geothermal Division
1000 Independence Ave., S.W.
Washington, DC 20585
(202) 586-5340

Geothermal Heat Pump Consortium, Inc.
701 Pennsylvania Ave. NW, 5th Floor
Washington, DC 20004-2696
(202) 508-5512

The IGSHPA
(International Ground Source Heat Pump Association)
Oklahoma State University
482 Cordell South
Stillwater, OK 74078

UVC

Steril-Aire, Inc.
11100 E. Artesia Blvd.
Suite D
Cerritos, CA   90703
(562) 467-8484
Fax: (562) 467-8481

CHAPTER 10

Plumbing Manifold

Sioux Chief Manufacturing Company
24110 South Peculiar Drive
PO Box 397
Peculiar, MO 64078
(800) 821-3944
Fax: (800) 758-5950

Vanguard Plastics, Inc.
MANABLOC
831 N. Vanguard Street
McPherson, KS 67460
(800) 775-5039
Fax: (800) 775-4068

Cross-linked Polyethylene (PEX) Pipe

Plastics Pipe Institute
Division the Society of the Plastics Industry, Inc.
1801 K Street, NW
Washington, DC 20006
(202) 974-5351

Solvay Polymers Inc.
Technical Center
1230 Battleground Road
Deer Park, TX 77536
(800) 338-0489
Fax: (713) 307-3521

Vanguard Plastics, Inc.
Vanex PEX
831 N. Vanguard Street
McPherson, KS 67460
(800) 775-5039
Fax: (800) 775-4068

Wirsbo
5925 148th Street West
Apple Valley, MN 55124
(800) 321-4PEX

Tankless Water Heaters

Aquastar
Controlled Energy Corporation
Fiddler's Green
Waitsfield, VT 05673
(800) 642-3111

Bosch
Distributed by:
Astravan Distributors Ltd.
123 Charles Street
North Vancouver, BC, Canada V7H1S1
(604) 929-5488
Fax: (604) 929-4883

Eemax Inc.
472 Pepper Street
Monroe, CT 06468
(800) 966-0684

Takagi Industrial Co. USA, Inc.
14191 Myford Road
Tustin, CA 92680
(714) 505-9039
Fax: (714) 505-9042

Tankless Hot Water Systems, Incorporated
IMI Santon
1676 Cordova Road
Germantown, TN 38138
(901) 756-7080

Fire Sprinklers

"Automatic" Sprinkler Fire Protection
PO Box 400
Ransom, WV 25438
(800) 626-2682
Fax: (800) 858-6857

Badger Fire Protection Systems
Charlottesville, VA
(804) 973-4361

Globe Fire Sprinkler
Home Sprinkler
4077 Air Park Drive
Standish, MI 48658
(800) 248-0278

Star Sprinkler Corporation
7071 South 13th Street
Suite 103
Oak Creek, WI 53154
(800) 558-5236
Fax: (800) 877-1295

National Fire Sprinkler Association, Inc.
Robin Hill Corporate Park
Route 22 PO Box 1000
Patterson, NY 12563
(914) 878-4200
Fax: (914) 878-4215

United States Fire Administration
16825 South Seton Avenue
Emmitsburg, MD 21727
(301) 447-1000
Fax: (301) 447-1052

National Fire Protection Association
1 Batterymarch Park
PO Box 9101
Quincy, MA 02269-9101
(800) 344-3555
Fax: (800) 593-NFPA

CHAPTER 11

Photovoltaics

Electric Power Research Institute
3412 Hillview Ave.
PO Box 10412
Palo Alto, CA 94303
(415) 855-2411

Solar Technical Information Program
Solar Energy Research Institute
A Division of Midwest Research Institute
1617 Cole Boulevard
Golden, CO 80401-3393
(303) 231-7303

The Energy Efficiency and Renewable Energy Clearinghouse
(EREC)
PO Box 3048
Merrifield, VA 22116
(800) 363-3732
Fax: (703) 893-0400

Renewable Energy & Efficiency Training Institute (RETI)
1800 M Street, NW
Suite 300
Washington, DC 20036
(202) 496-1417
Fax: (202) 496-1494

Solar Energy Industries Association (SEIA)
122 C Street, NW
4th Floor
Washington, DC 20001
(202) 383-2600

PV Shingles
United Solar Systems, Inc.
1100 West Maple Road
Troy, MI 48084
(800) 397-2083
(248) 362-4170
Fax: (248) 362-4442

Wiring

Carlon Electrical Products
25701 Science Park Drive
Cleveland, OH 44122
(800) 321-1970

Hubbell Premise Wiring
14 Lord's Hill Road
Stonington, CT 06378-0901
(800) 626-0005
Fax: (860) 535-8328

Wiremold
Access 5000
60 Woodlawn Street
West Hartford, CT 06110-2500
(800) 741-7957

Surge Suppression

American Power Conversion
132 Fairgrounds Road
West Kingston, RI 02892
(800) 800-4APC

Fiber Optic Lighting

Supervision International, Inc.
8210 Presidents Drive
Orlando, FL 32809
(407) 857-9900
Fax: (407) 857-0050

Home Automation

Aiphone Intercom Systems
Home Security
1700 130th Ave. N.E.
Bellevue, WA 98005
(206) 455-0510

AMX Corp.
Home Automation
11995 Forestgate Drive
Dallas, TX 75243
(800) 222-0193

Carrier Corp.
Home Automation
Carrier Pkwy.
Syracuse, NY 13221
(800) 227-7437

CEBus Industry Council
4405 Massachusetts Ave.
Indianapolis, IN 46218
(317) 545-6243
Fax: (317) 545-6237

Cumberland Woodcraft
Home electronics
PO Drawer 609
Carlisle, PA 17013
(800) 367-1884

Draper Shade & Screen
Rear Projection System
411 South Pearl
Spiceland, IN 47385-0425
(317) 987-7999

EH Publishing, Inc.
Electronic House Magazine
526 Boston Post Road, Suite 150
PO Box 340
Wayland, MA 01778

Home Automated Living
An affiliate of Shriver Communications
14311 Old Columbia Pike
Burtonsville, MD 20866
Fax: (301) 384-8275

Home Automation Association
808 17th St., NW, Suite 200
Washington, DC 20006
(202) 223-9669
Charlie McGrath, Executive Director

Home Automation, Inc.
2709 Ridgelake Drive
Metairie, LA 70002
(504) 833-7256
Fax: (504) 833-7258

Home Automation Systems, Inc.
151 Kalmus Drive, Suite L4
Costa Mesa, CA 92626
(800) SMART-HOME

Home Intelligence Journal
PO Box 409
Uxbridge, Ontario Canada L9P1M8
(800) 810-0159
Fax: (905) 985-8980

Honeywell
PO Box 524
Minneapolis, MN 55440
(800) 328-5111

Imaginetics Co.
7000 Terminal Sq.
Upper Darby, PA 19082
(215) 734-1245

Interactive Technologies, Inc. (ITI)
2266 North 2nd Street
North St. Paul, MN 55109
(612) 777-2690
Fax: (612) 779-4879

Intellihome
8350 N. Central, Suite M-2076
Dallas, TX 75206
(214) 361-4044

IntelliNet
2640 Golden Gate Pkwy.
Suite 101
Naples, FL 33942
(813) 434-5888

LiteTouch
3550 S. 700 W.
Salt Lake City, UT 84119
(801) 268-8668

Lutron Electronics Co.
7200 Suter Road
Coopersburg, PA 18036
(610) 282-3800

Simply Smart Home
536 S. Decatur Blvd
Las Vegas, NV 89107
(800) 273-0085
(702) 258-5161

Smart Homes Technologies
15111 Freeman Avenue
Suite #31
Lawndale, CA 90260-2100
(800) 679-5509
Fax: (800) 679-5510

Sony Corporation of America
1 Sony Drive
Park Ridge, NJ 07650
(800) 222-7669

TABS (Total Automated Building System)
NetMedia, Inc.
10940 N. Stallard Place
Tucson, AZ 85737
(520) 544-4567
Fax: (520) 544-0800

Unity Systems
2606 Spring Street
Redwood City, CA 94063
(650) 369-3233
Fax: (650) 369-3142

UNITY Systems
2606 Spring Street
Redwood City, CA 94063
(650) 369-3233
Fax: (650) 369-3142

X-10 (USA)
91 Ruckman Rd
Closter, NJ 07624-0420
(201) 784-9700
Fax: (201) 784-9676

Index

ABOUT THE AUTHORS

RICHARD T. BYNUM, JR., is an innovative architect who owns his own firm in Greenville, South Carolina. He has been a feature writer for a number of architectural publications and is an active member in the American Institute of Architects. Mr. Bynum earned his Master of Architecture degree from Clemson University and a Bachelor of Environmental Design in Architecture from North Carolina State University. He formerly was a project architect with Thompson, Ventulett Stainback & Associates in Atlanta, Georgia.

DANIEL L. RUBINO is Director of Operations of the Bi-Lo Center in Greenville, South Carolina, a 16,000 seat sports arena. Previously he was a construction administrator for Odell Associates, Inc., a prestigious architectural firm in Greenville. He also worked for Kevin Roche John Dinkeloo Associates and operated his own residential construction firm to experiment with many of the materials indicated in this book. He is a graduate of Porter and Chester Institute in Connecticut, where he majored in architectural design and construction.